Heaven Is Here

*An Incredible Story
of Hope, Triumph,
and Everyday Joy*

Heaven Is Here

Stephanie Nielson

with Amy Ferguson Hackworth

voice

HYPERION • NEW YORK

Library of Congress Cataloging-in-Publication Data

Nielson, Stephanie, 1981-
    Heaven is here : an incredible story of hope, triumph, and everyday joy / Stephanie Nielson ; with Amy Hackworth. — 1st ed.
        p. cm.
    ISBN 978-1-4013-4179-4
    1. Nielson, Stephanie, 1981- 2. Burns and scalds—Patients—United States—Biography. 3. Burns and scalds—Patients—Family relationships—United States. 4. Aircraft accident victims—United States—Biography. 5. Mormon women—United States—Biography. 6. Mothers—United States—Biography. I. Hackworth, Amy. II. Title.
    RD96.4..N54 2012
    617.1'1092—dc23

                                                    2011043550

Hyperion books are available for special promotions and premiums. For details contact the HarperCollins Special Markets Department in the New York office at 212-207-7528, fax 212-207-7222, or email spsales@harpercollins.com.

Book design by Susan Walsh

FIRST EDITION

10 9 8 7 6 5 4 3 2 1

THIS LABEL APPLIES TO TEXT STOCK

We try to produce the most beautiful books possible, and we are also extremely concerned about the impact of our manufacturing process on the forests of the world and the environment as a whole. Accordingly, we've made sure that all of the paper we use has been certified as coming from forests that are managed, to ensure the protection of the people and wildlife dependent upon them.

For Claire, who never gave up.

For Jane, who looked at me, and changed my recovery.

For Ollie, who never cared.

For Nicholas, who was my baby then and always will be.

For Little Peanut, who showed me how amazing my body is.

Heaven
Is Here

Prologue

....

A voice whispered, "Roll."

I fell to the ground and crushed the brilliant flames that licked at my clothes, my skin, my hair. The mangled wreck of our airplane blazed nearby.

I lay on my back at the base of a tree, looking at the clouds moving across the sky. Through my tears, I noticed a leaf that fluttered in the breeze, bright green against the blue sky, far above the chaos.

A stranger rushed toward me and knelt at my side. He cradled my head in both of his hands and put it in his lap. "It's going to be all right," he said, a hint of doubt in his eyes.

The fire roared in my ears. An oppressive wall of heat pulsed against me. The air was sour—a sickening mixture of fuel, singed hair, and burning flesh. *That smell is me. I am burning. How did this happen?*

Where is my husband? Just minutes ago, I was in the backseat of the Cessna, admiring how capable he looked staring out the window of the cockpit as we taxied down the runway. *Where is he now?*

I had pizza dough rising on the counter at home and four young children to feed. Christian and I had planned to pick them up from my in-laws in an hour and a half. I felt an irrational desire for someone to just pick *me* up, brush me off, and send me on my way. If I didn't get home, who would make Claire's butter and honey sandwiches for her first-grade lunch box next week? Who would know to get Jane off the kindergarten bus in the middle of the day? I pictured her little red head climbing off the bus to an empty porch—no mother to hug her home from school, no little brothers playing in the yard. I imagined the bus pulling away, Jane locked out of the house.

People rushed in and out of my line of vision with a sense of urgency. Some of them wore work clothes, as if they'd been mowing their lawns or working in the garden until the moment our airplane crashed on their street and they'd been called to duty. I felt guilty for interrupting their Saturday. Like me, they all had other things to do.

"Thank you for being here," I said to the man who held my head. "You don't have to stay."

"I'm going to stay," he said. "I'm going to be right here."

Other people hovered around me a few minutes at a time. They tried to reassure me, but it seemed they needed convincing as much as I did. Their lips mouthed words of comfort, but their faces betrayed them.

They are scared, I realized. *When they look at me, they are scared.*

Until then, some miraculous dam of adrenaline or heavenly help had held back the agony of my injuries. But the faces around me were crowded with worry, and the dam buckled. Suddenly, pain spilled over, crashing relentlessly against me, wave after stinging wave. Every inch of my body throbbed, overloaded with agony.

"It's going to blow!" someone yelled. "Get the hose!" The burning airplane popped and crackled dangerously near a propane tank, and neighbors-turned-rescue-workers yelled back and forth above the noise. I braced myself for another explosion, but the roar of the fire held steady.

My jeans kept the heat tight against my legs. I rubbed my hands against them, trying to pull them off, but my hands didn't seem to be working. I lifted them to see why. Flaps of skin hung from my wrists. My hands themselves were gray and bloody. I saw my bones. I dropped my arms to the ground and willed away the image.

"Hey, you're going to be OK," the stranger said with believable conviction. The doubt in his eyes was gone. "You're going to be all right."

Above him, the leaf fluttered, alive and healthy. A feeling swept over me and took root in my heart.

I am going to be all right.

The dark smoke billowed around us, and blackened the sky, the tree, and my leaf.

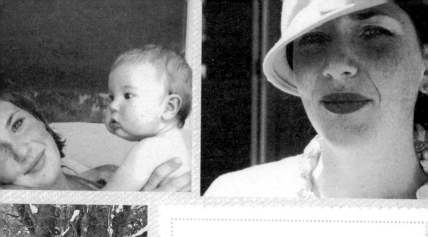

PART ONE

. . . .

The power of finding beauty in the humblest things makes home happy and life lovely.

—Louisa May Alcott

One

....

The summer Christian learned to fly was the happiest summer of my life. After eight years of marriage, I was more in love with Christian than I'd ever been. We had four beautiful children, and mothering them was an inexpressible joy. We lived in a lovely home in Mesa, Arizona, and had put our hearts and souls into making it our own. We were blessed with great friends and a civic and church community we loved. Christian had a great job as a facility manager, doing work he enjoyed, and he was just weeks away from getting his pilot's license. Life was undeniably good.

One Saturday afternoon in June he called to say he and his instructor, Doug, would be flying over the house soon. A few minutes later, I heard the buzz of the engine overhead, and I hustled everyone out to the driveway.

"Hey, guys! Come look! It's Daddy!" Six-year-old Claire, five-year-old Jane, and three-year-old Oliver ran outside, with twenty-month-old Nicholas toddling out after them, wearing only a diaper, as usual.

The airplane circled high over our heads. The kids looked up and waved while I jumped up and down in the driveway, shouting and waving both arms. "That's your dad, guys! Flying an airplane!" I waved and jumped some more while my children and a few kids from the neighborhood stared at me. "Hellloooo, Christian!" I shouted into the clouds. The older kids ran off to play in the backyard, but I scooped Nicholas into my arms and smiled at that airplane for as long as I could see it in the sky.

A year and a half earlier, as a surprise for his twenty-eighth birthday, I had given Christian a helicopter flight over Scottsdale. He had always dreamed of flying, so it was a gift I knew he would love. Near the end of the flight, the pilot gave Christian the stick. He came out of the helicopter a new man. For the rest of the night, Christian couldn't stop talking about the exhilarating freedom of flying and how alive he'd felt in the air. But he didn't need to tell me about it; I could see it all over his face. His mother tells the story of her little boy swallowing a handful of birdseed in hopes that he would sprout wings. I had awakened that sleeping giant, and when Christian told me he wanted to enroll in flight lessons, I didn't think twice about supporting him. A year later, Christian was interviewing flight instructors and found the perfect fit in Doug Kinneard, a retired air force major and trained fighter pilot, and Christian's coworker at Boeing. Christian had finished ground school a few weeks earlier and had just begun in-flight training.

Even after the Cessna two-seater flew out of sight that warm Saturday evening, my smile didn't fade. Christian's dreams were coming true, and I was so happy for him.

I nuzzled kisses on Nicholas's chubby cheeks. "Did you see Daddy in his airplane, Gigs?" His big brown eyes fixed on mine as he nodded. Nicholas had earned the family nickname Gigs when he was a brand-new baby and two-year-old Oliver could only manage "Gigolas."

"Let's go inside and finish dinner," I said.

In the kitchen, I put Gigs in his wooden high chair and tied an apron around my waist. Raising nine children, my mother had practically lived in her apron, and I thought of her every time I put one on. I added the finishing touches to the homemade veggie pizza we had for dinner every Saturday. So many of my favorite memories from childhood were anchored in family traditions. I wanted my kids to have the same kind of memories, and Saturday night pizza was just one way I was hoping to create that for them. I made whole wheat pizza dough and smothered it with fresh mozzarella, basil, corn, and squash. I expected Christian in just a few minutes, and the pizza would be ready soon. I had just enough time to quickly check my e-mail and respond to a message about the yoga class I was teaching the following week, before I heard the familiar rumble of Christian's motorcycle drive into the neighborhood. I shut my laptop, took off my apron, and did a quick mirror check before I went outside to greet him.

In seconds, the children joined me. They raced to the driveway, swarming their father and pleading for a ride. When Christian pulled in, we kissed a quick hello, and then he took each child around the block on the motorcycle. They sat safely between their father's arms, and their squeals of delight carried through the neighborhood. It reminded me of when I was in diapers, and my brother Matt would pile us kids on his Honda dirt bike and drive us around the neighborhood.

When he finally parked his motorcycle in the garage, Christian wrapped his arms around me and kissed my neck, still exhilarated from flying. "Stephanie, I love you," he said, pulling me closer. "And I *love* flying." And then he kissed my neck again, and my cheeks, and my lips, long and hard before we went inside the house and gathered our family for dinner.

This was one of my favorite times of the day, when we sat down together at the kitchen table every evening to eat the meal I'd prepared. Even on the busiest or messiest of days, when Nicholas had eaten dog food or Claire and Jane had fought over their favorite dress-up outfit, there was always a quiet moment, however brief, when we all sat down for dinner. Hands and faces all clean—for now—the children waited for Christian to call on someone to ask a blessing on our food. In that brief moment before our prayer, I could look at each darling child—Claire, a miniature version of me, with dark hair, green eyes, and freckles; Jane with red hair and freckles and clear blue eyes; Oliver, a dark-haired, tiny Christian with freckles; and our baby Nicholas, who looked just like my dad—minus the freckles—with big brown eyes and round-like-peaches cheeks. Throughout the day, I might be too busy and distracted to focus on how blessed I was, but in that moment I soaked it all in—my happy, healthy family, my incredible good fortune.

Shortly, Nicholas would smear food everywhere, and the table would erupt in noisy conversation, but those few seconds before the prayer fueled me. I had learned that doses of quiet joy like that can be brief, but their effects are long lasting and often carried me through the busy and challenging times of running our household.

During dinner, Christian told us how tiny we'd looked from the airplane, like little ants on the ground. The children loved it when he told them how the cars looked like toys and the houses on our street looked tiny enough to be dollhouses. We'd all been swept up in Christian's passion for flying, and conversations about aviation had become common around our house. Christian often pulled out navigation charts after dinner, and the kids would crowd around as he plotted the route for his solo flight. Oliver was especially interested, and for his third birthday Christian had made him a plywood runway for Matchbox airplanes. I painted it black and then painted the white lines and numbers. Christian had used a strand of red Christmas lights to mimic the runway lights. The children often asked when Daddy would be able to fly us all together to Utah to visit my parents, Umi and Grandpa, or to the Nielson family ranch in Bluewater, New

Mexico. Christian enthusiastically explained that it wouldn't be long—by Thanksgiving for sure.

"I'm going outside. Who's coming with me?" Christian asked as the kids finished their meals. The kids raced outside after him, their clothes stained with pizza sauce, and soon I could hear them all in the backyard, climbing up the tree house Christian had built for them in our mulberry tree, which I'd named Mulberry Bungalow. Christian usually played with the children while I cleaned the kitchen. It was a perfect arrangement. He had the chance to connect with our kids after being at work, and I enjoyed cleaning the kitchen all by myself. Uninterrupted, I could turn my music up loud. Those few minutes with Adele or Ryan Adams recharged me, and I was ready for the rest of the evening.

When I joined them in the backyard Christian and the children were playing "crack the egg" on the trampoline. The children held themselves in tight little balls, and Christian tried to bounce them loose. I sat on the wooden porch swing and watched. Christian's father, Russ, had built the swing for us as a wedding gift, and we had carried it around the country with us. We thought it might have a permanent home here in Mesa. Christian bounced the children one last time on the trampoline, and then they all ran over.

"Mommy," Claire said with her typical matter-of-fact spunk, "did you know that a lizard loses its tail and then it grows back again?"

I looked over Claire's head at Christian, and we smiled, the smile of parents who know their children must be the most darling in the world.

"I want one!" Ollie cried.

"Let's go find lizards!" Jane shouted, and the children scattered through the yard.

I leaned against Christian's shoulder, and he wrapped his arm around me.

"Tell me about your day," Christian said.

"Well, let me tell you about what happened at Trader Joe's today," I began. "Ollie really had to go to the bathroom, but I told him to just wait a minute and we'd go home. So I was loading the groceries into the back of the car and I had no idea what he was up to, but when I came around to the front he was *peeing* in the parking lot." I shook my head. "I'm sure people were appalled."

Christian laughed. "The girls probably told him to do it. Can't you just hear Jane saying, 'You're a boy, Ollie. Just go outside'?" Christian's impression of Jane was so dead-on that we both burst out laughing.

The most entertaining stories of the day were always about the children, but our conversation also drifted to Christian's day at work, the relay race I was training for, and our upcoming Fourth of July trip to Utah. Then we sat swinging in comfortable silence—contentment our easy companion.

"OK, let's go in and give these babies a bath," I said, reluctantly leaving Christian's cuddle, one of my favorite places on earth to be. Four baths, two tantrums, and one missing (and then found!) binky later, and I sat in the rocking chair reading *Goodnight Moon* to Nicholas. After we'd said good night to "noises everywhere," I cradled him in my arms for our favorite bedtime ritual, a game called "Chickie" I'd learned from my Nana Aurora. I can still feel her fingers on my five-year-old cheeks. She'd softly pinch little bits of my chubby cheeks and then pretend to nibble on the bites she'd taken. It was a miraculous sleep inducer, and Nicholas was a sucker for it. His eyes got heavier with each delicious "bite" I took of his cheeks, and I stood to walk him slowly around the bedroom he shared with Oliver. His head dropped against my shoulder and I felt his body relax, one step closer to sleep. The room was full of touches of my work as a mother: a shelf that I had reclaimed and restored from our days in New Jersey was lined with favorite toys and books. Animal artwork I had made hung on the walls. Ollie's runway was tucked safely under the crib, and I had hung an old flight navigation chart on the wall above it. I made a point of lining up their little shoes in the closet, and I loved to look at them while I walked Gigs around the room. Finally, when his breathing was slow and regular, I carefully laid him in his crib and tucked the blanket around him. His long eyelashes brushed his sweet round cheeks, flushed pink with sleep. I stared at my baby, whose once-chubby fingers were getting longer and thinner. I couldn't imagine his cheeks would ever lose their roundness, but I could see this boy was growing up. I felt that familiar yearning for another baby and smiled to think that Christian and I had already planned to try to get pregnant in the fall or winter. I couldn't wait to have another baby. I wanted nothing more than a house full of children. Christian had grown up in a family of eleven and I grew up in a family of nine. We were joking—but not completely—when we agreed to compromise on ten.

Once Nicholas was asleep, it was time for prayers and a story for Claire, Jane, and Oliver. Christian joined us for the prayer, and we all knelt to thank God for our day. That summer we were reading *Little House in the Big Woods*. I had loved the stories of Laura Ingalls Wilder as a girl, and I wanted my children to learn the lessons of hard work and simplicity that her books teach. Her pioneer life reminded us of our own Mormon pioneer heritage—the Jones family on my mother's side, and Christian's Nielson ancestors, who had crossed the plains in covered wagons to settle in Salt Lake City. It was six generations ago that his great-great-great-grandfather Peter Nielson came. His son, Frihoff Nielson, settled the family ranch in New Mexico.

As the children drifted off, their little bodies were so relaxed and still, they seemed to radiate an almost tangible peace. I imagined the wonderful dreams that awaited them. Claire would be creating her own little book of stories and pictures that only her brilliant imagination could dream up, Jane would dream of organizing some sort of neighborhood trampoline extravaganza, Ollie's dreams would find him flying a fighter jet that turned into a motorcycle that turned into a boat that turned into a spaceship, and Nicholas, baby Nicholas, would be dreaming of a delicious meal of big, milky boobs.

*S*oon, *I was in bed, too, snuggled up to Christian. We had* an industrial-size box fan and a ceiling fan to combat the stifling Arizona heat, and they hummed a cocoon of white noise around us. I loved that cozy, intimate feeling of being separate from the world. Essentially, that's what had always mattered most to me, creating my own little universe with Christian. We lay in bed that night quoting movies to each other. It was a little game we'd started when we first got married.

"'If there is any honor in you, promise me you'll never do that again.'" I started with one of our favorite lines from *First Knight*.

"'I don't know about honor. But I promise you. I won't kiss you again till you ask me to,'" Christian answered.

"Hmmm," I teased. "Will you kiss me . . . now?"

He pulled me close and kissed my forehead.

"OK, how about this one?" I said. "'Where . . . is . . . my . . . super . . . suit?'"

"Too easy," Christian laughed. "*The Incredibles*. Here's one." He spoke in a sugary falsetto. "'What makes you different is what makes you special.'"

I rolled my eyes. "Baaaar-bie."

We went back and forth through our favorite lines from classics like *The Man from Snowy River* and the movies our children watched over and over: *The Incredibles*, *Monsters, Inc.*, and Barbie's animated masterpieces.

After the last silly movie quote, our bedtime conversation ended the same way it had for the past several weeks. We talked about how blessed we felt, how grateful we were for our life—it was so comfortable and secure, so happy. We shared this sense of wonder, which we never could seem to get over, at our good fortune. It was a time in our life when everything just fell into place, when we felt a sense of serenity that our world was just how it should be.

Of course, everything wasn't *perfect*. Christian left for work at dawn and then went flying after work, making long days for me. Four children make a mess and a mountain of laundry. The girls battled over who got the prettiest doll, and Ollie and Nicholas fought over the Superman cape—a family treasure that Christian's mother had made for him when he was little. At times, all four children wanted something from me at the exact same moment. Sometimes when it got to be too much, I'd shoo them all out to the backyard and then close the sliding glass door and lock it, just for a moment's peace and quiet. And often the grocery budget was spent before the end of the month—that was stressful. I wanted a long list of things we couldn't afford, from the beach cruiser I'd seen online to a new wardrobe of beautiful clothes, not to mention the antique furniture I'd regularly covet at estate sales. But as we lay in bed and talked on those summer nights, any feelings of discontent were chased away by the realization of our blessings.

The fans whirred around us and I closed my eyes. Life wasn't perfect, but even with its flaws, it was wonderful.

Two

....

I had dreamed of the man I would marry since I was a little girl. My mom had a set of ornate paper dolls from Hallmark that her mother had bought her when she was a little girl in the 1950s. Those were saved for very special occasions, but when I was eight, my mom bought me a set of Madame Alexander paper dolls of my own. I adored those dolls, and began collecting more. I received them as gifts and would save up to buy them whenever I could. I had a set from the musical *Oklahoma!* that I especially cherished. They were actually my sister Page's, but I loved them like they were mine. When I played with them, Curly and Laurey always got married and happily raised a houseful of Madame Alexander dolls.

Oklahoma! wasn't my only reenactment. There was also *Pirates of Penzance, Seven Brides for Seven Brothers,* and any Esther Williams movie. My mother had an entire VHS collection of MGM classics that inspired my paper doll world. Those tapes were also my construction materials when building houses for the dolls. Whether the movies influenced my idea of happily ever after, or simply confirmed some innate sense of romance I had been born with, I can't say, but I loved everything about them—the dashing heroes and beautiful lead actresses, the unforeseen obstacles, the hoped-for resolution, and my favorite part, the smooch right before the credits rolled.

I played on the two-tiered end table in our living room, setting up a house for the girls on one level and a house for the boys on the shelf below. The boys would come calling, *Seven Brides for Seven Brothers*–style, and the whole affair ended in, you guessed it, a happy marriage. There were always more girls than boys in my paper doll collection, though, so out of necessity some hearts were broken and certain tragic events led to untimely deaths.

I followed the storyline of my favorite movies with my paper dolls, and then always took the story past that final movie kiss. My dolls went on to get married, have children, build houses, hold church, and plan birthday parties. I had no end of activities for my happy paper doll families.

In a way, my paper dolls lived my fantasy life. Even from that very young age, I knew that the life I wanted for myself centered around romance, a loving husband, and a houseful of children. Of course, I am sure the happy family I was born into also influenced these desires. I come from a long line of champion romantics, or at least that's how I saw it. My grandparents were an example of the kind of love I looked forward to. I often saw my grandfather, Layton Jones, or Papa as we called him, hold his wife Aurora's hand. Always a gentleman, he stood until she was seated and opened every door for her. Together, they loved their children and grandchildren with such attention, in a love affair that lasted for more than fifty-seven years.

I'd always felt close to my nana Aurora because I was her namesake, Stephanie Aurora, and at her funeral when I was thirteen, Papa Jones had held my hand as we walked down the chapel aisle. As a teenager, my mother had always told me how much I reminded her of her mother, Aurora, not just in the way I looked, although there was a strong resemblance, but also in my mannerisms and tastes. I could only hope I'd have a marriage as genuinely loving as my grandparents' had been.

And my parents' marriage was also happy and loving. They had a very traditional arrangement where my father worked and provided for the family and my mother was the homemaker. I saw firsthand how happy they were in their roles. Most of my cousins, neighbors, and friends had similar family situations, and I grew up with the belief that being a mother who stayed home to raise children was nothing less than an honor. My parents' relationship and commitment provided an innate foundation of security and love under which their children thrived. Growing up as number eight of nine meant I was never alone, and the greatest gift of those five brothers and three sisters was how safe I felt, always. With Stevie, Matt, Page, Christopher, Andrew, Courtney, Jesse, and Lucy around, I always had someone to talk to, play with, or borrow clothes from. They were devoted brothers and sisters—my best friends, greatest role models, and fiercest protectors.

When we were little, Lucy and I played dolls or roller-skated across the kitchen linoleum. Often we huddled together in our closet well after bedtime, giggling because Mom was coming upstairs, this time with the broom in her hand to scare us, to put us back to bed—again. Sometimes, instead of sleeping in my own bed in the room I shared with Lucy, I'd sneak into my older brothers' beds. I'd get in and usually be asleep by the time they came to bed. Sometimes they'd carry me back to my room, but often they let me sleep with them. I especially loved sleeping next to Christopher—the five Swatch watches on his wrist glowed in the dark. I also loved to tag along with my older brothers and sisters. Once Page, a nurse, took me to work with her at the hospital, and I fell asleep under her desk, perfectly content. When I was just five, my brother Stevie was a grown-up college student, but somehow he always had time to sit down and watch our favorite show, *Family Ties*, together, and he'd tickle the long dark fuzz that had covered my back since I was a baby. Matt, in honor of those hairs, had started calling me Baboon, a nickname that stuck all my life. Maybe that's why I never felt bad about raiding the drawer in his bedroom that always had spare change for a treat or a handful of Jolly Ranchers. Andrew drove me to horse-riding lessons every Thursday for years. He complained about it, but always told me he loved me when I got out of the car. As a teenager, I looked up to Courtney and was sometimes allowed to tag along with her. I often played an essential role as a prop when she carried out the elaborate plans to ask boys to high school dances. In high school, Jesse told me his friends thought I was cute, but that he wouldn't let them touch me.

On summer mornings, all of us living at home woke up to Mom's Bisquick pancakes and then spent entire days at my grandma Marion's backyard pool or on the lake. We'd make movies with a cast of cousins and neighborhood kids, Christopher always the genius behind the camera. We went to Lake Powell, jumped off cliffs, laughed and talked in the boat, and let Christopher scare us with his creepy stories. We took family trips to Washington state to see my auntie Karen, and gathered seashells on the beach. In the winter, Mom baked cookies for us when we got home from school, and after big snowstorms, we rode behind the station wagon in a sled. It all sounds very Partridge family and it was—minus the singing voices.

I grew up in Provo, Utah, a member of the Church of Jesus Christ of Latter-day Saints—a Mormon. Every Sunday we went to church with most of our neighborhood at the chapel a block away from our house. It was chock-full of young mothers whom I envied and admired. Many of them were only in our congregation for a year or two while they or their husbands finished degrees at Brigham Young University. I loved to watch them with their children and their husbands. Even as a teenager, I saw something in them that drew me in, and I looked forward to the life I saw them living.

While other thirteen-year-olds might have been preoccupied with trying on makeup, or strolling through the mall, you could often find me cleaning our living room, then vacuuming and fluffing the pillows. My final touch was a healthy dose of Glade air freshener.

Then I'd walk outside and look in our windows from the sidewalk, trying to see our house the way a stranger might. *A nice family must live there,* I'd think to myself approvingly.

For some, the dream of a fairy-tale life fades away, but for me, it never did. When my friends started talking about college, I became even more certain that what I wanted most was to be a wife and a mother. I knew there was a meaning and purpose to my life that I wouldn't really experience until then.

Although I would not have publicly admitted it at the time, I played with my paper dolls until I was a freshman in high school. As the world around me changed and I became surrounded by the complexities of adolescence—teenage crushes, dramatic friendships, hurt feelings, and insecurity—I was comforted by the beautiful paper dolls and their reliably happy endings. Ironically, the childish game was an antidote to the immaturity I was steeped in at school. When I played paper dolls, I was reinforcing the reality I believed in, and what mattered most to me.

Don't get me wrong, I liked the idea of having a boyfriend, someone to hold hands with, someone to take me to prom, someone to really love me. But it never made sense to me to flirt with a boy I didn't really like, and there were so few boys who showed the kind of maturity and responsibility that interested me. Of course, there were boys I thought were cute and wanted to impress, but I also wasn't willing to change for anyone else. If a boy was interested in me, they would have to be interested in *me*, not in someone I was pretending to be. I wore my hair short, and loved my pixie haircut, but I remember realizing that boys don't like girls with short hair. Well, then boys in high school wouldn't like me, because I loved my short hair. While I dreamed of a loving and romantic relationship, I was never the least bit interested in something that wasn't authentic. I was always sure of that, even then. I knew what I was waiting for, and I saw it in almost no one in high school.

No one except Graham. Graham and I met when we were fifteen, the summer before our sophomore year, and we dated all through high school. Graham was kind, honest, fun, creative, and very attentive. He seemed to understand me and could see life beyond high school. We often drove to a small cemetery on the east bench of Provo's foothills and looked out over the valley. We talked about the future, about things that were really important to me, about life and faith and family. Graham was the only person outside my family who I could really talk to about the things that mattered most to me, and I appreciated that about our relationship. Graham and I talked about getting married when he returned home from his mission.

At age nineteen, young men in the Mormon Church are asked to spend two years in full-time missionary service. If young women choose to serve, they go at age twenty-one. Serving a mission shows faith and commitment, as missionaries sacrifice much to serve. They say good-bye to their homes and families for two years. They write and receive letters and e-mails from home, but never visit and only call on Mother's Day and Christmas. They devote themselves to studying and teaching about God and Jesus Christ, hopeful that they can bless the people where they serve.

My brothers and sisters had served missions all around the world. Stevie in Peru, Matt in Chile, Christopher in Finland, Andrew in Spain, Courtney in Montreal, and Jesse in Puerto Rico. And after I was married, Lucy served in London. I missed them all horribly while they were away, and each of their absences left a hole in our family. As a child, I didn't completely understand what their service meant, but I believed it was work that really mattered, and I felt proud that they were missionaries.

When my brother Andrew left on his mission the summer before I went to junior high, he wrote on the bathroom mirror in my brand-new purple Lip Smacker, "Have a great year at nerd school, Baboon. I love you—Love your favorite brother Andrew." I left Andrew's message on the mirror the entire time he was away.

So I missed Graham like crazy when he left on his mission to Cordoba, Argentina, and I cried for days and moped for months, but I wouldn't have wanted him anywhere else. Even when Graham's letters became a little distant or lacked the connection I hoped for, I still looked forward to the life we would begin when he got home from his mission. In fact, I was so focused on the future that, at first, I couldn't see what was right in front of me.

Three

That spring, *a few months before my nineteenth birthday,* I was filling in for the receptionist at my dad's office, Clark Mechanical Contractors. The office was usually pretty quiet, and if we did have visitors, they were construction types decades older than me. So when a handsome stranger showed up one day selling cell phones, it was impossible not to notice him. But I didn't give it too much thought. My heart was in Argentina.

"You're cutting your thingy wrong," he said. I was slicing a grapefruit.

"What?" I asked.

"Your grapefruit, you're cutting it wrong." I had sliced the grapefruit in half lengthwise, instead of crosswise.

"I like it that way," I claimed, embarrassed and defensive. He was tall and had wavy strawberry blond hair, dark brown eyes, and a huge, easy smile with a gap between his two front teeth. He was unquestionably handsome, but then again, I wasn't really looking. However, he kept coming by and my brothers Stevie, Matt, and Andrew, who worked in the office with my dad, began to tease me about getting a date with "Cell Phone Boy."

A few weeks later when he came to meet with my dad he only stayed for a minute, but he did flirt, and I surprised myself by flirting back. Soon enough, he was back again, this time in a suit, and this time, in spite of myself, my heart dropped when he walked in the door. I could barely admit that I might be interested in someone besides Graham. My dad was out but I set up an appointment for a few days later. I wrote "Cell Phone Boy" on the appointment calendar.

I still didn't know his name, but as I watched him leave, something completely unexpected happened. A feeling came over me like electric waves pulsing through my body. It was like trumpets sounding and angels singing, as if a real-live cupid arrow had struck my heart. I'd never felt anything as powerful and specific. *That's the boy I'm going to marry*, I thought. In a total daze, but without a doubt, I knew it.

I had been taught, and believed, that heavenly help would guide my life. I often prayed for answers or assistance and trusted God to deliver the guidance I needed, especially for something as important as marriage. So while I was surprised by the content of the message, I wasn't surprised to receive it.

When Cell Phone Boy came back for his appointment, my dad was gone again. This time, in light of my recent revelation, my heart raced as he walked through the door.

"Hi," I said, and then stumbled through an explanation. "Uh, my dad's still at lunch. In fact, everyone's out. Um, you could maybe sit down, or whatever? I'm sure they'll be back soon."

Cell Phone Boy didn't sit down. Instead, he walked over to me. "That's okay," he said. "I can wait." He draped his arm across the counter and leaned against it.

"I'm so sorry," I said. "I know you're on the schedule. Of course you are, I put you there." I laughed nervously. "Let me just call him and see where he is." My dad's cell phone went straight to voice mail. I hung up and avoided looking directly at Cell Phone Boy. "I think they're still at lunch."

I dialed my three brothers, who had all gone to lunch with my dad, but none of them picked up. *Where could they be? And why weren't they back yet?*

"I am sorry," I said again. "I am so sorry about this. I hate to keep you waiting."

"Really, I don't mind." He smiled at me, and my heart lurched.

Cell Phone Boy chatted easily while waves of anxiety churned in my stomach. We talked about skiing (during the winter I was a ski instructor), his mission (in Louisville, Kentucky—he loved it), my family (of nine), his family (of *eleven*!), and more. We talked for an hour and could easily have chatted for another, but I suggested he reschedule with my dad. I regretted it the moment the words left my mouth. We made an appointment for the next day, and he left, flashing another heart-stopping smile.

I thought of him all afternoon. I was impressed with his easy confidence, and I was smitten by his smile. We both came from large families, and I was impressed that he'd been on a mission—to me, that automatically qualified him as mature and sophisticated. I couldn't wait to see him again the next day.

When my dad and brothers finally walked in, I stood up at my desk. "Where *were* you? Cell Phone Boy was here." I felt myself blush. "You had an appointment, Dad!"

"Did you get a date, Steph?" Andrew asked, and the four of them laughed.

"What? What do you mean?" I did my best to look indignant. "Of course I didn't get a date. He came to see Dad."

"Well, we were kind of hoping you'd get a date, Cubby," Dad teased as he sauntered back to his office. My dad had called me Cubby since I was a newborn, because they thought I looked like a baby bear cub.

"You mean you ignored my phone calls?" I yelled at his back. "You left me here for an hour with that guy *on purpose?*"

My dad chuckled and kept walking.

"That is so embarrassing!" I called down the hall. "Don't you dare tell him that!"

Later that day, after being teased mercilessly by all three brothers in the office, I was talking to the full-time receptionist, Sherry. She said, "Looks like we're all getting new cell phones from Christian."

"Oh, that's Cell Phone Boy's name?" I asked. "Christian?"

I couldn't help but smile. Christian had been one of my favorite make-believe husband names when I was a little girl. "Christian." I said it aloud again for no apparent reason. Sherry just grinned.

I spent the next afternoon watching the door, and when Cell Phone Boy—*Christian*—finally walked through it, a burst of adrenaline shot through my heart and spread throughout my body. After he met with my dad, he came back to my counter. My heart raced.

We talked about the weather, our jobs, my summer plans, and then were interrupted by the beep of the intercom on my desk. It was my brother Andrew.

"Steph, did you get a date?"

I slammed my hand over the intercom.

"What did he say?" Christian asked, smiling.

"Nothing." I shook my head. "I don't know. Nothing." I couldn't bring myself to look at him.

"Come on, he said something," Christian teased. "What did he say? It sounded like he asked if you got a date."

My face flushed and my heart leapt into my throat. "Oh, is that what he said? I couldn't tell." I looked out the window, willing myself to disappear.

"Actually, Stephanie, I did want to ask you out. How about Friday at eight?"

In a moment of bravery, I looked directly into his brown eyes. "OK, but tell me it's not because my brother just said that."

He laughed. "No, I really wanted to ask you out. Eight o'clock? Friday?"

"Well, in that case," I said, hoping my smile wasn't too revealing, "I'd love to, Christian."

Four

I've always been an avid journal writer, and wrote faithfully every day for years. In my journal the day I met Christian, I wrote:

Dad and the brothers talk about a boy that comes into work. His name is Christian. He is darling and I love talking to him. He has shown some interest in me. I can't decide if he REALLY does or if the brothers are teasing him about taking me out?! Anyhow, he is making my stomach turn.

Not exactly the stuff of steamy romance novels, but even in those private pages I was afraid to admit anything more. The previous days and months of my journal had been steeped in how much I missed Graham. It seemed so suddenly disloyal to be writing about someone else. I didn't write anything about the revelation I'd had that Christian and I would marry, but as I prayed that night, I asked God about the feeling I'd experienced at the office. Another electric feeling radiated through me. It was the warm and loving feeling I often felt when I prayed, but magnified. I knew this was real, and I was thrilled to feel my hope of marriage and family could be near. It didn't take me long at all to begin dreaming of the summer that lay ahead, and how Christian and I would spend it together, falling in love.

I didn't know what to think of Graham now. Of course I still cared for him, but I hadn't seen him in nine months. Things could change, couldn't they? I thought about the letter I would have to write—"*Dear Graham, I've met someone else . . .*"—but then pushed the thought away. I'd just wait and see. It wouldn't be long before I'd know.

It sounds silly to say it now, but I did imagine that Christian and I could be engaged by the end of the summer. In Provo, this would not have been unusual. It's common for young Mormon couples to marry after short engagements. The Church emphasizes the sacred responsibility of family and raising children as central to our purpose on Earth. With these beliefs, marriage naturally becomes a greater priority than in the world at large. Once you decide you're committed to another person, you commit completely. I don't speak for all Mormon girls, but at nineteen I wanted to be a wife and mother, and I saw no reason to wait. If I knew Christian was the one for me, once he figured it out, I didn't see any reason why we'd postpone the next chapter of our lives.

A few days before our first date, I confided in my mom about the future that I believed lay ahead with Christian. She'd always been supportive and shared my joys and sorrows. She listened lovingly but worried about Graham.

"I'm confused, too, Mom, but the feeling I had was so strong. I really think I'll marry Christian."

"Well, sweetheart, you'll do what's best," she said, with characteristic confidence in me. "I just hate to see Graham get hurt. But if this Christian is the one for you, then I can't wait to meet him."

When I called Page for advice, she suggested that a relationship with someone else could ultimately strengthen my relationship with Graham. I'd never know until I moved forward.

By Friday night, the rest of the family had heard about Christian and my feeling that he was "the one." My older sister Courtney and her husband as well as my older brother Jesse and his fiancée, Lindsay, came over. My younger sister, Lucy, and her boyfriend were also home.

I started getting ready at six o'clock with a lavender-and-jasmine scented bath. I was just getting out of the bathtub when Christian called to tell me he'd be an hour late. My heart sank. I didn't want to wait another minute to see him. An entire hour seemed torturous. And my entire family waiting around for his arrival was not helping my first-date nerves.

I chose my outfit carefully, hoping to highlight my best features: my legs, my bum, my boobs. I debated between a great skirt that showed off my legs and my Banana Republic wide-leg khakis that made my bum look good. I decided to go with the khakis and my blue Salt Water sandals. All the women in my family had inherited Grandma Clark's big chest, and I chose a blue tank top that looked good (but not *too* good) to wear under my favorite jean jacket with flower appliqué and embroidered orange stitching around the hem. I took the whole thing very seriously. After all, this was the man I wanted to marry.

Just before nine o'clock, I took one more look in the mirror. Freckles covered most of my body, and a fresh smattering danced across my face from the day I'd just spent boating. I loved my freckles and thought that having a few new ones was a good omen for the date. My green eyes stood out against my short dark hair. My skin was porcelain pale underneath my freckles, but my cheeks were flushed with a natural pink. Along with my grandmother's chest, I also inherited her plump red lips and round hips. I smiled at myself in the mirror, and my green eyes sparkled back. I was ready. I turned out the lights in my upstairs bedroom and watched out the gabled window of our white Cape Cod–style home for Christian to arrive. When he pulled into the driveway, I ran downstairs. Typically, our staircase was used for a grand entrance once the date had arrived, but I was too self-conscious to have anything like a grand entrance tonight. It was embarrassing enough that my family had all gathered to meet Christian. Truthfully, though, my gratitude for such a caring family overshadowed my embarrassment. I was flattered they had taken me seriously enough to make the effort to meet Christian, and I hoped he wouldn't mind too much.

Lucy's boyfriend answered the door and introduced himself. Then Lucy came to say hi and then Courtney, her husband, and Lindsay wandered in from the kitchen. My dad and Jesse were in the family room watching a game and didn't get up, but Dad called out, "Hey, it's Cell Phone Boy!" and waved.

My mom had just had her gall bladder removed and was resting in bed, but more than anyone else in the family, she really wanted to meet Christian. He said he didn't mind, so he shook hands with my mother while she wore a nightgown and smiled approvingly from her bed. He impressed us all with his kindness and ease in what could have been an awkward situation.

When we finally got out the door, Christian asked, "Does every date start that way at your house?"

I laughed and shook my head. "Oh, no, not every date. Sorry about that."

Christian laughed. "That's OK. They were great. You come from a great family."

At the theater box office, Christian's debit card didn't work. Puzzled, he tried again. "Oh, that's right," he finally said. "I emptied my account prepping for this trip. I'm going to Africa for the summer. I leave in the morning."

Africa? All summer? The fact that my date couldn't pay for our movie tickets took a quick backseat to the fact that the summer of falling in love I had begun to plan was disappearing before it had even started. He was supposed to sweep me off my feet that summer. He was supposed to propose to me. We were supposed to start our lives together. My heart sank.

"Wow, you're going to Africa? What a great opportunity," I lied through my teeth. "That's really fantastic."

He tried a credit card, but the theater didn't accept them. As he looked through his wallet for some other way to pay, he talked about the reason for his trip, to film a documentary about childbirth in Africa. The purpose was to educate African women and reduce infant mortality. Weeks later, when I got over being so disappointed that he had left, I admired the project and Christian's desire to go.

He looked up from his wallet and grinned. "I have an idea. Let's go get some cash." We drove to a grocery store where Christian planned to buy the most expensive thing we could find using his credit card, and then return it for cash. First he took me to a row of sodas and juice. "Go ahead and get a drink. Pick any drink you want," he offered. I got the impression he was splurging and still smile to think that his generosity extended only to beverages. I learned something that night that would play out for the rest of our lives. We had very different ideas about splurges.

I was too embarrassed to watch Christian return the cooler he had purchased one minute earlier, and instead I drove his car around the parking lot while I waited for him to come out. Just a few minutes later, he got in the car, laughing, and we went back to the theater with cash.

The movie had already started when we arrived. The theater was dark as we walked in. Christian reached for my hand and led me to our seats. We sat down, and he lifted the armrest between us. He put his arm around me, and for a moment, I forgot all about Africa. *This* was what I had hoped would happen.

Christian took me home at midnight, and as we got out of the car a gentle breeze met us. It carried the fresh smell of early June with the promise of summer in the air. The night air was sweet with the scent of Russian olive trees—my favorite. I invited Christian to talk in the backyard. We dragged two wooden lounge chairs next to each other and reclined the backs so that we could lie down and look up at the stars. I explained why I loved the Russian olives so much, how they reminded me of the absolute freedom of childhood summers. Every breath of their lovely scent made me smile. Above us, the fifty-year-old trees in the backyard made a canopy around us, leaving just a circle of open sky where the stars sparkled above. The whole neighborhood was dark and quiet, and it felt like we were the only people in the world.

"I've been in Provo for a while now," Christian said, "and this is the prettiest place I've seen. These trees are amazing."

I agreed that they were special and told him about my grandfather, who planted the trees when the house was built in the 1950s. Five years after they moved in, my dad's father was killed in a small airplane accident when my dad, the oldest of eight children, was just sixteen. My dad had lived in that house ever since.

"When I have a house of my own, I want trees like this," Christian said. "What about you? Do you see yourself in a house like this when you're married?"

"Yes, we'll have a yard full of trees." *We?* I said it without thinking. Embarrassed, and wondering if he had noticed, I quickly switched back to *I*. "I want a house with a wraparound porch, too."

"That's exactly what I want," Christian said. "A big comfortable porch across the front of the house."

I looked at him and nodded. That got us started on a conversation about the future: what types of houses we liked, where we wanted to live, even the names of future children. We discovered we both loved the name Claire. It all seemed almost too idyllic, but truly every element of that conversation seemed to confirm that we shared the same dreams, not just of a loving and happy marriage centered on God and family, but we also shared the same approach to life. I wished for some miraculous way to keep him from going to another continent the next morning. The night air got cooler and I would have put on my jacket, but I remembered I had left it in Christian's car. I decided to leave it there, figuring it would give him a reason to visit me when he got home from Africa.

At three in the morning, we said good night, and Christian drove away. On the one hand, I was elated. Our three-hour conversation had revealed so much, and I felt the beginning of the type of connection I'd always wanted. On the other hand, I was crushed to my teenage core that I wouldn't see him again for another two months. This seemingly perfect boy had come into my life just in time to leave again. The thought that I wouldn't hear his voice or see his face all summer was more than I could bear. The next morning, I got in the shower and just couldn't hold back the tears. I sat on the tile floor and cried.

A minute later, Lucy knocked on the door. "Steph, Christian's on the phone!"

I stood up and jumped out of the shower. Maybe he hadn't gone to Africa after all? Everything brightened.

I took the phone from Lucy and stood there, dripping wet, in a towel. "Hello?" I tried to sound calm.

"Hey." Hearing his deep voice say that one word was *almost* enough. "I'm in your neighborhood. I wanted to return your jacket. You left it in my car last night."

"Oh, I did?" I tried to sound genuinely surprised.

"I'm just on my way to the airport. Can I bring it over?"

I quickly fixed my hair and dressed and rushed around my room, wondering what else I could give him. I wanted him to have something to remind him of me. *Think, think, think.*

A Farewell to Arms lay on my desk. I had just read it for the second time. Henry and Catherine's romance spoke to my heart. Their commitment to each other was so beautiful. I still love their story and read it every few years. I hoped Christian would read it and think of me.

When he handed me the jacket, I handed him the book. "Something to read on the plane," I explained.

He took the book and looked at it. "Oh, thanks. Hemingway, huh?"

"I love Hemingway. *A Farewell to Arms* is one of my all-time favorites."

"Great. Thanks. I'll read it."

"Promise?" I said.

"Promise." He looked at me, and I felt sure he could see the obvious adoration on my face. "I'll be back at the end of July. I'll call you."

I walked him to the door, and we hugged. Then I stood in the doorway and waved good-bye. He turned to wave again before he got into his car, and I closed the door. I ran upstairs to my bedroom window and watched through my tears as he drove away.

I grabbed a notebook and lay on my bed. I wrote each day he would be gone in columns down the page, June 8, June 9, June 10, all the way to the end of July. Then I added a few more days to give him time to get settled. My countdown ended August 5. I taped the paper to the inside cover of my journal. Fifty-nine days lay ahead, and in my very comfortable life, that seemed like a lot to ask. Tears welled up in my eyes again.

Christian Mark Nielson, be safe in Africa. And please call me on August 5.

Five

I had thought I'd missed Graham when he left, but I took despondency to a whole new level when Christian went to Africa. It's the heartache and melodrama only young love knows. I knew I was being dramatic, but, boy, was I in love. I thought that summer would never end as I pined day after day, waiting, waiting, waiting for love and trying the patience of my entire family. I knew in my head that it didn't make sense to ache for someone you'd only been out with once. But the feelings in my heart were a different matter. I believed in the connection I had felt with Christian and wanted nothing more than to further it. But every so often I considered how ridiculous it sounded to suggest that I knew I would marry him, and I'd worry that something as wonderful as the fairy-tale love story I was imagining could really happen. Then I'd remember the night I had prayed about Christian and that powerful witness of truth. Yet I had no idea what Christian thought, and that kept the worry alive. It was the perfect storm of teenage romance. Two things kept me sane: exercising and my journal.

I had lived in the shadow of the Wasatch Mountains all my life, and every rugged line and canyon was familiar, their silhouettes comforting and protective. Y Mountain has a huge white *Y* on its face, for BYU, and I'd driven to the trailhead and hiked the Y every day since I got my license. The trail to the Y switchbacks up twelve turns, just over a steep mile. I spent many days on the well-worn trail that summer. I knew the terrain and every turn. Even the scent of the mountain was familiar and grounding. My worries faded when I hiked. I found a peace that came with putting one foot in front of the other, pushing myself to go faster and be stronger. Being on the mountain was a gift from God, and I felt close to Him there.

Sometimes I'd hike Rock Canyon, another rugged beauty of Provo's natural skyline. Or I'd walk or run through the familiar streets of our neighborhood. The Mormon temple was close to our home, and I often ran the loop around its hill. The temple was a sacred landmark in my life—it represented the promise that my family could be together forever, the surety of God's love for me and my potential as His daughter. In the temple, you learn about God's eternal plan and make promises to be faithful to Him. Temple attendance is qualified by keeping high standards of purity, honesty, and faith. The temple hill was not only a great place to push myself hard as a runner, but also a place I loved because of what it represented. To me, it was just as it's described in a children's song I'd grown up singing in church, "the house of God, a place of love and beauty." I felt that when I was near it, or when I could see its spire across the valley. It was a fixture of my life, like the mountains that had always surrounded me. And it was the place where I planned to be married.

When I wasn't hiking, I was filling my journal with pages and pages of longing. My journal was my closely guarded best friend, where I wrote every hope of my teenage heart—so earnest it hurt. I had recorded every detail of my first date with Christian. I made notes in the margins of some of my favorite things he had said, like how he had commented that my name, Stephanie Aurora Clark, was like a "storybook fairy-tale name." Of course, I loved that. He noticed my green eyes and dark hair and commented on that unusual combination. At one point, I even designed an elegant wedding invitation in its pages. *Mr. and Mrs. Stephen Clark are pleased to announce the marriage of their daughter Stephanie Aurora to Christian Mark Nielson.* I even made a note that the invitation would be engraved, a distinction I had learned from my mother. As the summer wore on, and the reality of my feelings about Christian began to settle, I wrote it all in my journal.

I have this crazy, divine feeling that I will marry Christian. It is a crazy sensation, a strong, powerful feeling. We have only been on one date, but I feel so strongly that we will be married. Somehow I feel a close relationship with this Christian Mark.

I have wanted to be married all my life. I want a husband. I feel in my heart it is Christian. I have never been so sure.

In another entry I wrote, *I just want to be married and start having my dreams come true. I especially want children, and a lot of them. I can't wait to start. I feel the truth of it when I think about that. I know it's so right and so true. My dream is my husband taking me to the temple. I can't wait to begin a true and honest life with him.*

It's true; I was young, naïve, and sappy. But I was also very sure about what I wanted. As I considered a future with Christian, my goals became more and more focused. I wrote, *People say to enjoy this time in my life, and I do. I am just ready to move on and discover a new and more meaningful life with the man I love.*

Finally, almost unbelievably, August rolled around, and I began counting the days until I would see Christian again. Soon every day on my chart had been crossed off and I still hadn't heard from him. My heart actually ached. It had been one week and one day longer than I'd expected. I'd waited, worried, and hoped all day, and finally, at about 10:00 P.M., I couldn't take it anymore. I had to know if he was home.

I walked to the pay phone just down the street. I dropped my quarters in and pushed each number deliberately. I wanted more than anything to hear his voice. But then, what if I did?

The phone rang two long, slow rings and then connected. My heart raced. His familiar deep voice, the one I had longed to hear, answered. "Hello." It was such a relief to hear that voice that I was quite sure I loved. But then it hit me: he was back and hadn't called. I gasped. "Hello?" he asked. "Hello?" Tears stung my eyes as I slammed the receiver back on the hook. I sped home and burst out crying as soon as I walked in the door. "Mom, he's home. He's home." She hugged me and let me cry on her shoulder. "He's home and he hasn't called," I sobbed.

My dad came in and asked what was wrong. Through my tears, I broke the terrible news that Christian was back and hadn't called me. My dad, whom I rarely heard curse, put one hand over his eyes and shook his head in exasperation. "Oh, hell," he said. "Cindy, you deal with this." He was still shaking his head as he walked out of the room.

A few days later, I was languishing on the trampoline in our backyard, still agonizing over Christian, when my dad walked outside. "Stephanie, you're going to make yourself sick."

"I just really love him, Dad. I think I really love him."

He sighed. "I need to talk to him about our cell phones. He sold us piece-of-crap phones. I'll call him and find out where he is."

I was at first slightly offended—Christian would never sell crappy phones. But the plan my dad was brewing offered the hope of deliverance. "You will, Dad? That would make me really happy!"

He smiled and kissed my forehead.

I didn't know it at the time, but when my dad spoke to Christian, he asked Christian to call him back at work, and then was conveniently not in the building when Christian called. When I answered the phone, I recognized his voice in an instant. "Stephanie?" he asked.

"Christian"— I feigned surprise—"are you back?" He told me about his trip and then he asked me on a date. After all the agony of waiting, I was obviously thrilled. Until he told me where we were going. "Roller-skating? Are you serious?"

He was serious, and I think I offended him, but I couldn't believe the man of my dreams was inviting me on a group date, roller-skating. It was the last place I would have chosen. I certainly didn't want to make a fool of myself on roller skates, but worse, I didn't want *him* to make a fool of himself. I didn't want to be forced to change my mind about him.

I felt out of place from the moment the date started. I thought the other girls were silly, and roller-skating was silly, and I endured it but did not enjoy it. Afterward we watched *Xanadu* on the roof of Christian's best friend's brother's house in Salt Lake. The setting was lovely—a gorgeous summer night and an amazing view of the city—and I did get to sit close to Christian, but I still felt a little disappointed. When the movie ended, though, Christian called me away from the others and told me he had something for me. He pulled out a grapefruit, a knife, and two spoons.

"*This* is how you slice a grapefruit," he said.

Later that week my dad was hosting a party at our cabin in Wallsburg, an hour away, and he needed someone to help saddle and supervise the horses for his guests. Christian had told me he had experience with horses and I wanted to invite him to come, but I was so nervous. I paced my room for hours second-guessing myself. When I finally got the courage to call, he said, "I wish I could, but I have other plans."

I jumped immediately to a number of heartbreaking conclusions. He didn't have a good time on our date. He didn't like me. He wasn't interested in seeing me again. I saw those words *other plans* as the end of my story with Christian.

Days went by and I didn't hear from him, confirming my fears. This was worse than when he was in Africa; at least then I had hope. But now he was back, we'd been on a date, and he didn't want to see me anymore. A bit of patience, trust, and perspective would have served me well, but I was carried on the wave of every emotion that washed over me. I was shattered to think that we were not destined to be together as I had hoped, and disappointed that the feelings I'd been so sure about weren't true. I felt rejected by his disinterest and mortified to think that I'd told my entire family that I would marry him.

Just a few days later, I was making peach cobbler on Sunday afternoon when he called. I was completely surprised and hope flickered again in my heart. He asked if he could come by. *Of course* he could come by. I hung up the phone, elated.

"Christian is coming over," I announced to my family. "Just be normal. Don't act like I've been crying for days."

Christian was still wearing the suit he wore to church. Boy, that man looked good in a suit. He joined us for peach cobbler and said it was the best he'd ever tasted. My mom, ever my ally, suggested that Christian and I go for a drive in the canyon. I would never have been brave enough to suggest it myself, which she certainly knew. She put the keys to her Audi convertible in my hand and practically shoved us out the door.

We drove with the top down on that faultless August evening, the road a ribbon winding through the steep mountains of Provo canyon. We pulled over at dusk and walked through a field of wild yellow sunflowers. I'd be lying if I said I wasn't hoping for something more than conversation. A kiss would have really made me happy.

But conversation it was, and that satisfied me, too. We walked and talked as the sun slipped behind the horizon. Christian told me about his family: his parents, Russ and Mary; his ten siblings; growing up in Arizona; and their family ranch in New Mexico where he'd spent summers and vacations all his life. I hung on every single word, captivated. I was laughing one moment and swooning the next.

He described how big the sky seemed at the isolated ranch, and the acres and acres of nothing but land that had belonged to his family for generations. I felt his loyalty as he talked, his love for the land. Darkness hid the mountains around us, but in my mind I saw the noonday sun blaze over the prairie grass and rolling hills of Bluewater, New Mexico.

Christian revered his ancestors, who had settled in the high plains and carved out a life and livelihood ranching cattle. He told me about his grandmother, whose paintings of the rugged mountains and gnarled pinyon trees hung in the ranch house. Once, when his grandfather was a little boy in Sunday school on the ranch, the class was interrupted by the buzz of an engine overhead. The low-flying plane landed on the property and none other than Charles Lindbergh disembarked—to relieve himself. He climbed back in the airplane and took off without so much as a word to the stunned churchgoers.

"When I was fifteen," Christian told me, "my grandfather promised me his bright yellow 1980 two-door Chevette if I could shoot one hundred prairie dogs. It took me all summer"—he laughed— "and hundreds of boxes of bullets, but I did it. And I drove that car all through high school." Christian told story after story of ranch life: hard work, rattlesnakes, four-wheelers, shotguns, dust, and cattle herds.

He talked about quiet mornings on the ranch, and how close he felt to God in that untouched, wide-open space. He told me how much he looked forward to taking his children there, and how he hoped they would feel God's love in the natural world, just as he did. I knew just what he meant. It was exactly how I felt when I was in the mountains I'd grown up loving.

"I love that ranch, Stephanie." He looked at me. "I'll take you there sometime."

It wasn't just that he loved his ranch that drew me in, but that he loved God and his family and took hard work in stride. I saw how he would take care of me, or anyone, really, who needed him. So many words came to mind while he spoke. *Rugged, masculine, capable, spiritual.* And *very sexy.* Not even the image of a bright yellow Chevette could change my mind.

After all those weeks of waiting, it was another splendid night. The hope that had flickered when he called that evening was blazing now, and I couldn't have been happier. Even that early in our relationship, I already knew that what I was feeling with Christian was different from what I had felt with Graham. It was in the way he treated me, and the way I felt about myself when I was with him. I became even more certain of my feelings.

Over the next few weeks, though, his signals were mixed, and I impatiently waited for him to realize that I was not just another girl, but *the* girl, and that he could stop looking at other girls, and stop worrying so much about his friends, and simply spend every waking minute with me. One night Christian sensed my frustration and asked what I wanted. As bold as I dared to be, I said, "I just want to see you tomorrow and every day after that."

I did see him nearly every day after that, and while I occasionally still worried if he would really love me the way I hoped he would, I also discovered it was not just exciting to be with him but also comfortable and satisfying. My insecurities slowly disappeared; I felt safe and accepted. When we talked, he looked at me in a way that was more than attentive. He *really* looked at me, as though he was intent on discovering the real me—what I cared about and what I really wanted. He told me I was beautiful and he loved my short hair. He made me laugh. For every hour we spent together, I wanted another and another and another.

I hadn't written to Graham for several weeks, but I couldn't put it off any longer. I had to tell him I'd met someone else. I hated the thought of hurting him, which was why I'd avoided it, but I knew I had to tell him. *Dear Graham, I'll always be thankful for you in my life, but . . .* I put a stamp on the letter and mailed it off to Argentina.

When fall semester started at BYU, Christian was busy with classes and a job. I took a couple of classes, too, but didn't have the same load he did. Sundays were my favorite, because we could spend the afternoon together. One Sunday afternoon we walked the few blocks from my parents' house to the Provo temple. My heart was heavy. There was something I needed to talk to Christian about, and I was nervous. We had enjoyed a magical courtship and confided many secrets in each other. We'd shared our fears and cataloged our flaws. I felt closer to him than ever, and we'd begun to talk about marriage, but there was still something I'd been afraid to tell him. Today was the day to explain.

We sat down on the temple lawn at the top of the hill, and I stared at the grass. I took a deep breath.

"Christian, I am not interested in school like you are. Even though it's my first semester, I don't think I will finish college—well, not now, anyway. What I want now is to be a wife and be a mother." I nervously twisted blades of grass. "I don't want to wait for those things. I want to get married soon and start a family right away."

Confessing this was agonizing. I knew the other girls Christian had dated had been academically ambitious, and I was worried he would be disappointed by my lack of interest in school. As much as I loved Christian, though, I didn't plan to change for him. If he accepted me as I was, we would move forward. If he was committed to having a wife who wanted a degree and a career, he would have to marry someone else.

When I'd said all I needed to, I finally looked up from the grass. Christian was looking at me with that brilliant smile of his. I was relieved before he even spoke.

"Stephanie, you'll be so good at those things. You'll be the best wife and the best mother. That's the kind of life I want, too. I wouldn't want it any other way. I wouldn't want you any other way."

As we walked down the hill, I felt like a burden had been lifted from my shoulders. Now Christian knew everything about my intentions and desires. I wanted to raise a family above all else. And I wanted to raise one with him.

It had been weeks and Christian still hadn't kissed me. He hugged me. He held me close. He put his cheek against mine. But our lips hadn't touched.

"Christian, why don't you kiss me?" I had to know.

"Because you're perfect, Stephanie, and I don't want being physical to get in the way of getting to know the real you."

It was a good answer. I was flattered, impressed, and satisfied. For a while.

One night soon after, he drove me home after one of our dates, and we stayed in the car and talked in my parents' driveway. I teased him about kissing me, and put my face close to his. He closed his eyes to avert the temptation.

"Hey, come on." I put my face even closer, to torment him a little.

He laughed. "OK, I'll kiss you," he said and leaned toward me.

This time I pulled back, laughing. "That was a close one, Christian. Are you sure you want to kiss me?"

Christian got serious. "Stephanie, close your eyes." He took my face in his hands and pulled me close. Our lips touched. Time stopped and the world around us disappeared in those few breathtaking seconds.

Sometimes, when you wait a long time for something, and then finally get it, it's not as great as you hoped it would be.

This was not one of those times.

Our first kiss lived up to every romantic ideal I'd ever had. I had never written truer words when, in my journal that night, I described that kiss as *absolutely perfect*.

After that, there was no shortage of kisses, but Christian and I shared the belief that sex is sacred and intended for marriage. That commitment to wait is so widely accepted and understood among Mormons that it didn't even come up in conversation between us. We would wait because we believed in waiting. We didn't think about what we were missing. Instead we thought about what lay ahead. It wasn't that we weren't interested or eager—I'd never felt such a powerful attraction, and we had more than a few naïve conversations about sex. But Christian had a sense of responsibility for me, and he was a perfect gentleman, always. We spent plenty of time making out, but it never went further than that.

At the beginning of September, Christian and I drove to Lake Powell with my sister Courtney and her friends. Most of our group rode in a Suburban ahead of us, but Christian and I drove Courtney's car and talked and laughed the whole drive. When the odometer hit 11,111 miles, we thought that deserved special recognition, so we pulled over and kissed for a few minutes. At Lake Powell, we boated and camped in tents on the sandy shores. On the last night of our trip, Christian and I put our sleeping bags in the boat and lay under the bright stars. The night was still and quiet except for the sound of the water lapping against the boat and our hushed conversation.

We leaned our heads together and Christian put his arm across me.

"Stephanie, I think I love you. I'm pretty sure I love you," he stumbled. He gained some footing with the phrase and said it again, certainly. "I do. I love you. I love you."

"Christian, I love you, too!" I needed exactly no time to feel comfortable saying it back. Of course I loved him. And he loved me!

"I've never said that to anyone. I never wanted it to mean anything less than my whole heart." He looked at me intently. "But I love you. Stephanie, I love everything about you. I love your body and your mind. I love your eyes and your freckles. I love your kindness. You make me laugh. You're gentle and compassionate. You're beautiful. You're so beautiful. I love you. I want you to come to Arizona and meet my family."

"I would love that." I smiled.

"Stephanie, I am so happy we're together. I want us to spend our lives together. We'll be so happy."

"Christian, I want that, too. I love you so much." After weeks that had felt nothing short of years, he finally knew what I had known all along.

"Let's have a little girl and name her Claire. Let's live in a house with a big front porch. Let's plant you Russian olive trees." It was everything we'd talked about on our first date, but this time it wasn't abstract—we were talking about *our* future. We lay under the stars and dreamed of our life together.

Six
....

At the end of September, Christian invited me on a trip to Arizona to meet his family. I also suspected (hoped!) that he might propose over the weekend in Mesa. I went shopping for new clothes. It was autumn in Utah, so I bought wool dress pants and classic fall sweaters. I wanted to look my best when I met Christian's family.

Christian's parents were having the whole family over for dessert my first night at their house. Christian and his brothers had helped their dad build the house the summer after Christian's junior year in high school. It was a lovely and comfortable home. The main thing I noticed was the large circle of chairs set up in the family room adjacent to the kitchen. There were two chairs clearly at the head of the circle, and I soon learned those were for Christian and me.

I was used to a big family, of course, but Christian's family seemed enormous. I had met his parents, Russ and Mary, a few weeks earlier when they had been in Utah, and it was lovely to see them again. But I'll admit I was unnerved by the steady stream of people coming through the door. So many people. They said hello, shook my hand or gave me a quick hug, and eventually filled the circle.

Just as we settled in our seats there was a chorus of voices around the circle. "Tell us about your family." "How many brothers and sisters do you have?" "Where were you born?" "Are you going to college?" "Where?" "What are you studying?" "What do you like to do?" "How did you meet Christian?" "What do you like about him?" I felt like I was being interviewed for the position of "a Nielson."

I had not expected to be grilled like this. I knew Christian loved me, but this was his family, and I knew their opinions would matter. I wanted so badly to make a good impression, but the questions just kept coming. I responded, and then there was another question, then another and another and another.

It didn't help at all that my beautiful wool pants and fall sweater turned out to be exactly the wrong thing to wear. *Why didn't someone tell me it was going to be 120 degrees?* My stomach was in knots and my hands were sweaty. Christian, who was holding my hand, let go of it every few minutes to wipe his hands on his pants, and then he'd gently take my hand again. I did the best I could to answer all of their questions. I wanted to impress them but wasn't sure I had.

The next evening Christian and I dressed up for an elegant dinner at Gainey Ranch, an upscale resort. After dinner, we went out to the lush gardens of beautiful flower beds and towering palm trees. It was a warm night, of course, but had cooled off considerably from the earlier heat of the day. We took a gondola ride and walked through the impeccably manicured gardens. Christian started coughing, then sneezed, then got the hiccups, and started coughing again. I wondered what was going on. I noticed his hands were sweaty and couldn't figure out why. He'd taken me to a jewelry store earlier in the day to look at wedding rings and we left without buying one, so I knew he wasn't going to propose. At least I thought I knew.

Finally, Christian stopped me on a bridge that crossed a little stream. The lights in the garden cast a glow over everything near us. We wrapped our arms around each other, and I leaned my cheek against his chest and looked out over the palm trees and flowers. They were beautiful, but I would have been just as happy looking out over a cactus and a sand dune as long as I was close to Christian.

He coughed again and cleared his throat. "Stephanie, you know I love you very much. I want to be with you forever."

My heart started beating faster. Could this be what I thought it was?

He continued, "Stephanie, I love you—so much—and I want you to be mine. I am so in love with you. I want us to be together all the time. I am confident that marriage is part of God's plan for us. I want to create a family with you."

My arms were still wrapped around his neck when he slipped the ring on my finger.

"Stephanie, I want to ask you to, and I hope you will . . . marry me?" he asked.

Beaming, I put my hands on his face and practically shouted, "Of course!"

I wrapped my arms around him again and glanced over his shoulder at the solitaire diamond ring he had chosen for me. My engagement ring! I definitely approved.

Over the next few months we planned a winter wedding, which we'd have during Christian's semester break from BYU. We bought our first home in downtown Provo, close to campus and close to my parents' house. It was a little brick pioneer house that was just a few months shy of its hundredth birthday when we moved in. Christian turned twenty-two in November, and believing every family should have a dog, I gave him a Brittany spaniel for his birthday. He named it Jimmy after his favorite band, Jimmy Eat World.

Christmas, already rich with nostalgia and family traditions, was the perfect time for a romantic wedding. I pictured cold temperatures and deep snow and I would be cozy and warm and complete, as Mrs. Stephanie Nielson. I pulled out the issues of *Martha Stewart Weddings* that I had been collecting since I was fifteen and got to work.

Our wedding would be simple and sublime. The ceremony would take place in the Provo temple, where Papa Jones would marry us since he had the special role in the temple of performing marriages. It would be a unique privilege and honor for me to have my grandfather marry us. Then we'd celebrate with a wedding luncheon at The Homestead, a cozy mountain resort. I planned woodsy details and made beautiful mirrored garlands to decorate the tables. I sewed little purses for each of our nieces, using the same fabric I'd used to make pillows for our new couch. Our family friend Vanessa made my gorgeous wedding dress, inspired by a picture of a Vera Wang dress I'd torn out of a magazine. And of course the engraved invitations went out to our family and friends.

The night before our wedding, a snowstorm covered everything in a thick blanket of fresh snow. Christian and I couldn't have asked for a better wedding gift than the beautiful, bright white snow. Page and her family had come from California, and our house was full of people, sleeping everywhere, that morning. The full house, the Christmas season, and now new snow made our wedding day feel even more magical.

Our family and friends had joined us for the sacred ceremony in the temple, but we were the last to walk out. They gathered outside the doors and greeted us with cheers and applause when we came outside. I was so proud to be on Christian's arm, and so thankful to share the day with the people we loved most. I wore a red shawl over my white wedding dress, and when I hugged Christian's dad, he told me I looked like Snow White, something Christian called me for years afterward.

At the luncheon, we carried out the Clark family tradition of wedding day tributes, a custom of affectionately teasing the bride and groom. Stevie went first. He gave me a box of Toaster Strudel, since I had once eaten a whole box when I was babysitting for him and his wife, Suzanne. Matt gave me a back scratcher, in loving reference to my nickname Baboon. Page gave me a wreath made of dried flowers that I had made for her when I was little. Christopher had saved a letter I'd written him on his mission about a terrific crash I'd had while skiing. Lucy gave me a framed photo of the two of us as little girls, to remember all the great times we'd shared.

That night, Christian and I drove down Provo Canyon together. Alone for almost the first time that day, we said over and over again, "We're married!" We arrived at our little home, and our life as husband and wife truly began. Christian carried me across the threshold and into our bedroom. As he tenderly unzipped my wedding dress, he kissed the back of my neck. My dress fell to the hardwood floor next to Jimmy, who slept peacefully in the corner. The moment we'd both been waiting for was the perfect end to our wedding day.

The next morning we flew to Florida to embark on our honeymoon cruise. On the way to the airport I asked Christian to stop at my parents' house, just to say good-bye to everyone. He was hesitant but didn't want to upset his new bride. There was a fire in the fireplace and all my brothers and sisters were there, sitting in the living room and kitchen, eating my wedding cake. As I walked in, I felt enveloped in that familiar, loving world of my family, and I wanted to delay the honeymoon just for a while and sit down at my parents' kitchen table. Christian stood near the door, waiting.

My mom pulled me aside. "You feeling OK?" she asked.

I nodded.

"Then what are you doing here? Go," she said, and pushed me out the door. "And have a wonderful time!"

I called home once more on our way to the airport to thank my mom and dad for all they had done to make sure I'd had the wedding day I'd dreamed of. I was overwhelmed by all they had done for me, on that day and my entire life.

Our honeymoon was exactly what I'd hoped it would be—uninterrupted time dedicated to Christian and me. We could do whatever we pleased, and we did plenty of it. Intimacy was brand-new for both of us, and being together was beautiful and exciting. We spent hours in bed, and talked for hours more. We swam and talked and kissed and went back to our cabin, where we'd lie in bed for hours again. One evening we rented a scooter on Key West and I sat behind Christian and wrapped my arms around him as we drove around the island while the sun set. *Mrs. Nielson*, I thought. *Can that be real?* I held Christian a little tighter. Yes, apparently it was. And being Mrs. Nielson was certainly lovely.

When we returned from our honeymoon a week later, a bright little Christmas tree, complete with decorations, was waiting for us in our living room. My brother Andrew and his wife, Megan, had gotten the keys to our home and decorated the little tree for us. Andrew also made sure there was a fire in the fireplace when we arrived. It was such a cozy welcome home.

We settled quickly into a contented married life. I loved grocery shopping to fill my own cupboards. Our $100 grocery budget was the first time I'd had a budget in my life, and I looked forward to making Christian proud. I did my best to make sure he came home to a great dinner after his long days at school and work, and I loved taking care of him like that. I delighted in making the bed in my own house, and fluffing the pillows that I had made for us. For the first several weeks of marriage, we still occasionally looked at each other in wonder and said, "We're married!" The complete joy of that, and all that it meant, didn't wear off.

I n February 2001 I visited Christian at work with a special gift. He worked at a home improvement store called Anderson Lumber, and I found him on aisle three among the nuts and bolts and handed him a small rectangular box from Victoria's Secret, left over from my wedding shower.

Christian took the box. "Stephanie, what's this?" He looked around. "Are you sure I should open it here?"

I smiled and nodded. "It's safe."

He took the lid off the box and looked at the positive pregnancy test I had placed inside. His face lit up. He grabbed me and held me tight. "Stephanie, really? You're really pregnant? This is the best news!"

He pulled me away to look at my face, and tears of joy welled up in my eyes. He brought me close again, and the smile on my face felt permanent. I couldn't imagine anything that would keep us from being this happy always.

And then the nausea hit. My entire pregnancy was a blur of queasiness and vomit. I was in rough shape, and nothing seemed to help. Sometimes I could keep grape Gatorade down, but that was about it. Christian was as busy with work and school as I was miserable. I didn't know what could make me feel better, but Christian doting on me would have helped. Unfortunately he was often too busy to meet my, admittedly, bottomless need.

And Jimmy didn't help a bit. I often wondered why I'd bought that dog. He peed in the house and constantly got into the trash. That dog chewed everything in sight—pillows, socks, even my fancies. It was something I could handle before I got pregnant, but once I got sick,

Jimmy's bad habits were intolerable. When Christian would remind me that I had bought the dog, I would say, "Yes, and I can take him away, too!"

Thank goodness for my mother, who pampered me in ways Christian couldn't. I spent hours and hours at my parents' house, and when we weren't together, they or Lucy would bring lunch to my house. Eating breakfast was out of the question. By lunch I was hungry enough to eat, but I couldn't make anything edible. Every smell was an assault. Even the smell of Christian, which I normally loved, was overwhelming and hostile. I was happiest in my bedroom with my head stuffed in a pillow.

But I wanted to continue making dinner for Christian as I had every night since we'd been married. I had to learn to function feeling awful. I folded a stick of mint gum over my nose, and that helped. It didn't stop the world from spinning, but it slowed it down enough for me to move. Sometimes I would pin a clothespin over my nose while I made dinner. I often threw up in the kitchen sink while I cooked.

Even if I'd made it, the smells of dinner were too much, so I'd sit in the living room while Christian ate. The carefree times of our newlywed days were over, abruptly.

One night, I had a plain old breakdown. "I'm so sorry," I sobbed. "I'm sorry I'm so sick, I'm sorry I can't do anything. I'm sorry I'm not a better wife."

Christian came to sit by me on the couch, but he brought his plate of smelly food with him, so I had to send him back to the table. "Stephanie, it's OK. This will pass, and you'll get better. We're going to have a baby. This is what we want, but it's life. Sometimes you get sick." I appreciated his words but wanted more. I wished that he could change his schedule, quit his job, cancel his classes, and just take care of me. He probably wished I could just get up in the morning and make his lunch, like I had before, then send him on his way with a kiss and a smile.

We both had some growing up to do and nothing developed our unselfishness—and perspective and patience and compassion and gentleness—like becoming parents.

Seven

....

I t was a glorious autumn afternoon at the end of October when my labor started with dull, manageable cramps. As they steadily grew into earnest, full-fledged contractions, I grew more and more anxious about the pain of labor and the possibility of complications. When the contractions were seven minutes apart, we got ready to go to the hospital, but before we left I asked Christian for a priesthood blessing for comfort and protection.

A priesthood blessing is a bit like a prayer in that it's a way to receive counsel, comfort, or healing from God. In this case, I needed all three. Christian and all the men in my family, as well as almost every man who is active in the Church, hold the priesthood, which gives them the authority to act in God's name. When Christian gave me a priesthood blessing, I knew he was taking seriously his responsibility to seek God's will and communicate it to me.

He laid his hands on my head. "Stephanie Aurora Nielson, by the power of the priesthood which I hold . . . ," he began. Throughout the blessing Christian paused, and I knew he was listening to the impressions he was receiving to be sure he was telling me, the best that he could, the blessings our Heavenly Father wanted me to hear.

As Christian blessed me, I felt a warm peace wash over me, in spite of the contractions. I expected labor would still be difficult, but I faced it with calm faith that everything would go well. And everything did go well for me. Christian had a slight setback when he fainted as my epidural was administered, but he recovered quickly.

The morning after our Claire Elizabeth was born, a rainstorm pummeled my hospital window. Outside, the world was cold and wet. Inside, the world was warm and wonderful.

Claire's first few days on Earth were some of the most joyous days of my life. I came home from the hospital feeling great—the sickness that had plagued me for nine months was gone, and I had the most gorgeous baby girl. Christian and I had found a rocking chair at a thrift store that we'd painted white and put in our living room, right in front of our big picture window that looked out at the walnut tree in our yard. Claire was born on October 29, and when I came home just two days later on Halloween, the maple tree had turned an even brighter, more brilliant yellow. I thought of its glory as a greeting for Claire. I would sit in the rocker with my baby for hours, looking at the tree and nursing her, admiring her perfect little ears, the delicate curve of her hairline, her soft plump cheeks. I knew the world outside our four walls was moving along at its usual hectic pace, but there was a stillness in our house. Life was in slow motion, and I was being given the gift of savoring every moment. Nursing was a tremendous gift—it seemed miraculous and at the same time natural—and I cherished the time I spent in that rocking chair.

As I rocked baby Claire and stared at the trees outside, I thought about how I had become a woman. I had left girlhood behind, and the change felt wonderful and sacred. I was so proud to be a mother, so thankful I could bear a child. The purpose I'd always known was waiting for me in motherhood began to settle in my soul. In Claire's earliest days my mother and sisters brought aunts and cousins to meet the newest member of our family. They came to visit us and love us, to delight in my baby and my new stage of life.

"Oh, Stephanie," Aunt Lisa said. "She's perfect! Look at her. What an angel." She took the baby from my arms and rubbed her cheek against Claire's fuzzy head. Then she looked up matter-of-factly. "How's your bleeding?"

"And how's nursing?" Page asked. "Are you doing OK?"

Aunt Judy chimed in. "Oh, I remember how bad it hurt when my milk came in with Jake!"

They brought meals and did dishes, vacuumed and loaded laundry. They waited on me like I was a queen. It felt biblical to have the women who had always loved and nurtured me come to acknowledge my new role. I felt bound to them in a deeper way as I thought about loving and nurturing my own family. I was one of them now.

The birth of each of our children has been sacred, and a time of gratitude and spiritual wonder. But something—the response from the people around me, the beautiful autumn, our brand-new roles as mother and father—all of it together, probably, made the first days of Claire's life distinctly serene.

The possibility of being the wife I'd wanted to be came into focus again as we found a rhythm in our life with Claire. Christian came home from his long days at work and school and held her while I made dinner. Whether I was consumed with love for my angel baby, or just inexperienced, I couldn't both hold Claire and make dinner at the same time. Christian was smitten with our beautiful baby daughter, too, and he'd scoop her up and zip her in his jacket, keeping her as close to him as he could. She seemed to like it as much as he did.

We'd just finished dinner one night when Claire was a few months old. She slept peacefully in Christian's arms. I sat next to him on the couch and put my head on his shoulder. Spring was beginning to hint at its arrival outside our window.

We both looked down at our sleeping baby. "Christian," I said, "I'm ready to do this again. Are you?"

"Have another baby?" Christian looked at me and smiled.

"I just feel it, Christian, I just feel like it's time."

"Then, so do I, Stephanie. I am ready, too."

When Claire was six months old, my family was gathered at my parents' house for Sunday dinner and Christian and I announced that we were expecting another baby. I so looked forward to the next little spirit who would join our home.

I was still nursing Claire when I got pregnant again and hoped to continue nursing her throughout my pregnancy. But the pervasive nausea was back, and I learned to grab a bag before I nursed, so I could just throw up in it while I fed her. When Claire was about a year old, I realized I could simplify this for myself. I didn't have to nurse anymore, and Claire would be fine. It was the first in a long list of expectations I surrendered. Maturing as a mother is a gradual, but steady, process, if we let it unfold, and this decision to stop nursing before I'd originally planned to was one of my first steps. *I can only do my best, and that's all that matters*, I'd tell myself. It wasn't the last time that the physical demands of motherhood overcame my ideals. I'd never let go of the truly important things, but my criteria for what the important things were often realigned.

On the day our second child was born, I had hiked my beloved Y trail, and I'm sure that's what got my contractions started. It was a cold February day, but when I got to the top, I was suddenly enveloped in warmth. I felt my great-grandmother Jane. I didn't hear or see her, but I felt her there, and a whisper of a feeling that this baby's name was Jane.

I had prepared for a natural labor this time—no anesthetic—and I had planned to labor for as long as I could at home. When the contractions started, I breathed through them and let nature take its course. When I felt it was time to go to the hospital, we called Lucy to come and stay with Claire. We felt confident in our decision to have our children so close together, but I still felt a twinge of guilt when I thought of Claire's short reign as the only child. I leaned over Claire, sleeping in her crib. I couldn't hold back the tears. "Claire, I'm going to have another baby right now, and I'm really sorry." It felt like the end of a chapter, the only time in our lives where I could devote my full attention to Claire. But I knew I would be bringing another wonderful gift home from the hospital in a baby sister. The girls would always be glad they had each other.

My contractions were strong and close together by the time we left for the hospital. Christian sped through the streets of Provo. Soon, the lights of a siren flashed in our rearview mirror.

"You can't stop!" I shouted. "I'm having a baby!" I was already pulling my pants off. This baby was coming.

The officer barely had time to shine his flashlight in our faces before I yelled, "I'm having a baby! We have to go!"

He nearly dropped his flashlight but gave Christian permission to get to the hospital as fast as he could. Our redheaded baby, Jane Bronwyn, was born just five minutes after we arrived.

Jane and Claire were just fifteen months apart, and those were very busy days when Jane was brand-new. Just before Jane's first birthday, she woke up crying late one night, or maybe early one morning—when you're mothering babies you're never quite sure. I went to her room to comfort her when two-year-old Claire called out for me. I brought Claire into Jane's room and sat on the floor to nurse Jane. Claire curled up in my lap and fell asleep. I stroked her dark hair with one hand and held Jane's red head close to me with the other. I thought about all that was ahead for our little family. Christian would graduate from BYU in just three weeks, and he was looking at jobs all around the country. We'd soon be leaving Utah. I knew I'd miss it immeasurably, but as I looked at our little girls, I knew the things that mattered most would be coming with us. In the quiet of that little moonlit room, I silently savored the gift I'd been given—the chance to be a mother to these two gorgeous girls, to comfort and protect them all their lives.

The next morning, we got the call about Christian's job. He hung up the phone and smiled. "Stephanie, how do you feel about New Jersey?"

Eight

Provo has always been home to me in the most robust, complete sense of the word. I was born and raised there, married there, and my own children had been born there, too. My parents and siblings practically lived in my backyard, not to mention the nieces and nephews, cousins, aunts, uncles, and lifelong neighbors and friends who surrounded me. And the mountains and canyons that I felt were truly a part of me. As we packed up our house, I dreaded the homesickness I knew awaited me, but I also looked forward to the adventure of living across the country. Almost all of my older siblings, always the standard by which I measured my life, had settled in Utah with their own little families. I felt like a pioneer leaving what we called "the Clark compound" and heading out East. I remembered those young mothers from church whom I'd always admired. They had left their far-off homes and come to Provo. Now I would leave Provo and have my own adventure.

Christian found our home on Harvey Circle in New Brunswick, New Jersey, when I was still in Utah with Jane and Claire. He called to say he'd found a great house in a great neighborhood, close to work and close to church. And then he sent me a picture. I confess, I cried when I looked at the drab brown rambler. It was a downright ugly house, and the lawn was covered—*covered*—in lawn ornaments of the Virgin Mary and Jesus on the cross. You could barely see the grass. The pictures of the interior were no better, especially when I compared it to our lovely, hundred-year-old house in Provo.

A few weeks later, when I stepped inside, my heart sank as I realized that the pictures may have actually been generous. As she handed us the keys, the sweet little old woman who sold us the house said with genuine delight, "I left a few items for you at the house that I think you will be happy with. Things I thought you could use." What I believe she meant was that she decided to save time by packing only half of her stuff, and leaving the rest for me to worry about. In the bathroom we found an old bar of soap, a razor, toilet paper, women's personals, and even her deodorant. I couldn't hold back the tears as I discovered things she'd left behind in every cupboard, closet, and bedroom. And worst of all, the whole house smelled like mothballs.

A lovely home had always figured prominently in my daydreams of married life, and our new home left much to be desired. I would have loved to do a full remodel, but we didn't have the money, and Christian certainly didn't have the time. I was also pregnant again by the time we left Provo, and therefore sick. But despite those obstacles, I was determined to make our new home a place that felt like us and not the elderly couple we'd bought it from.

I would build us a happy little nest.

The heat was intense that summer of 2004, with humidity like I'd never known in Utah, and I bought the girls a kiddie pool and filled it with just a little water. I slathered them with sunscreen, and they played for hours in the backyard while I worked inside, tearing out carpet, removing panels of fake brick, and hauling away piles and piles of things the previous owner had left behind.

As the months wore on, my determination deepened. This house would look great—or as great as it could with every ounce of effort I had—before we had our baby. Every night when Christian came home from work, the pile of items for the weekly trash collection had grown. Our garbage truck would arrive to pick up the can, and the drivers would kindly get out and pile my junk into the truck. I would call the girls to the front window, and we'd wave good-bye to an old mattress, the fake brick, and ratty carpet one week. The next it was a beat-up side table, a box of costumes, and a pile of drywall. I threw away loads of expired canned food, framed prints, coffee mugs, and a collection of Virgin Mary figurines.

Christian worked hard after work and on Saturdays, even when he probably didn't want to, to finish projects I'd started. I was great at demolition and big ideas, but I needed Christian's skills to saw, nail, patch, assemble, and install. But we met my big deadline, and before my due date our home had changed from a place that made me squirm to a place I—mostly—loved. We'd saved our bedroom for last and painted the walls a pale shade of blue just two weeks before I delivered Oliver there, on our very own bed.

Years earlier, when Christian had returned from Africa, he'd told me how much he admired the home births he'd seen while he was there. He told me he hoped his wife would be interested in home births, and I laughed in his face. But after two hospital births, I was ready to try Christian's idea. We found a lovely practice of midwives who took excellent care of us. When the pain threatened to pull me away, Christian brought his face close to mine and anchored me with his dark brown eyes, his soothing voice. But even with his loving care, I couldn't contain myself for those last few pushes. I screamed so loud I surprised myself and affected Christian's hearing for the next several minutes. But, oh, how good it felt to scream.

Our new baby boy, Oliver Christian, was delivered in our home on January 2, 2005. From the very beginning, he was a gentle, easy soul, a most welcome addition to our family.

After Ollie's birth, there was no throng of welcoming relatives, as with the girls, but our church community, or ward, celebrated with us. They brought meals and visited and doted over our new son. They helped us feel anchored in our New Jersey world. Wards are organized by geographic boundaries, so our Utah ward had been full of the young married couples with small children that lived in our neighborhood. Our ward in New Jersey was very different from the one in Provo, but we found the comfort of people who understood our decisions and values and who embraced us instantly. Many people at church became our dear friends. Our paths wouldn't have crossed in the same way if we'd met in Provo, where I would naturally have gravitated to the women my age or the mothers with young children. But in New Jersey our shared beliefs brought us together, despite age differences. I was thankful for those connections, and the church community that supported and loved us, because our neighborhood was a different story.

All my life, I had grown up knowing pretty much every single person in my community. I'd been born into that neighborhood; it was a fixture of my life, like my family and my home. Whether they were especially friendly people, or just friendly because we shared so much in common, I'm not sure. But, in comparison, I found our life in the East to be very lonely. I was so different from other twenty-three-year-olds in New Jersey, a stay-at-home mother who just gave birth to her third child—on purpose. Strangers were not afraid to comment on how unusual I was.

I soon found that the easy, doors-open approach that seemed natural to me, the way I'd watched my mother interact with neighbors, was not the standard here. Case in point: after a week in our new home, we still had not met our neighbor to the right. Christian needed to have a shirt ironed for his first day of work, but our iron was still packed and I couldn't find it anywhere. The obvious answer was to just run next door and borrow an iron from the neighbor. When she opened the door, I introduced myself and asked my favor. The middle-aged woman looked at me for a moment, this stranger from Utah, and then reluctantly agreed. I stood on the porch while she went to get her iron, feeling an unaccustomed sense of awkwardness. I waved good-bye, proud of myself for reaching out to a neighbor, and getting an iron. But as I got to know the neighborhood and the New Jersey norm, I realized this was a very unusual request, and my neighbor probably thought I was crazy. In fact, I'm sure she did, but I was naïve and I needed an iron.

Granted, I didn't expect long chats or deep friendships to develop overnight, but I was always surprised that even after we'd introduced ourselves to our neighbors, some of them never waved or smiled again. Once when Christian had wheeled our overfilled trash can to the street, three empty soy milk containers fell out. Christian noticed that the garbage can that belonged to the older couple across the street was just half full, and so put the containers in their can. The next morning, the three containers were on our front lawn.

Events like this baffled me. This was not how my mother had raised me. My mom is effusive, with open arms and an open heart. She always kept us kids waiting after church—it was terribly inconvenient for us—so she could catch up with friends and chat with ward members. She loved visitors in our home, welcomed friends, had warm conversations with almost everyone she had contact with in a day. I remember once as a young girl I watched her speak to her cousin's daughter, who was mentally disabled. As a child, I didn't understand her disability; I just knew there was something different about this girl. But there was nothing different about the way my mother spoke to her, with such genuine love and kindness. I always remembered that. When I thought it might be easier to ignore my neighbors as they had ignored me, I remembered my mother's friendliness and care. It pushed me forward.

I visited the women who lived on either side of me. At first they were guarded and maybe even suspicious, but ultimately they saw my friendliness for what it was, and opened up to me. My choices in life had been wildly different from theirs, but at separate times each of them surprised me by telling me they admired what I was doing with my life. "I wanted to do exactly what you're doing—stay at home and be a mother—but I couldn't, my mother discouraged me." I was touched to think that they looked at my life and respected it.

One afternoon the children and I were out on the front lawn, having a picnic. The girls were pretending they were "lost and lonely" on a boat, the boat being the picnic blanket. We hadn't met the older couple across the street, although we were bound by the soy milk incident. They happened to be outside while we picnicked, and the woman tentatively walked over. She introduced herself as Adele but didn't give her last name. I remembered my mother and responded with all the warmth I had. She told me she had lived in that same two-bedroom house for forty-four years. When I asked her about her next-door neighbor, she shrugged in embarrassment. She didn't know them, and then I was astonished to learn that she didn't know anyone else on the street, not a single other neighbor. She and her husband worked in their garden, and kept quietly to themselves in their house.

It was a life I couldn't imagine. We decided we wouldn't worry too much about not fitting in. Like the neighbors around us had, we just decided to be ourselves, and that meant waving, and visiting, and sharing cookies, just like we would have done with our neighbors in Utah. Some of our neighbors were drawn to our openness and friendliness; others, I believe, thought of us as a strange young family during the entire time we lived there.

Feeling so out of place was hard though. I felt a constant undercurrent of homesickness, and I longed to feel closer to my family despite the miles that separated us.

Nine

I t was my brother Christopher who introduced me to blogs, and my first honest thought was, *Who would do that?* Then I realized it could be the perfect way to stay in touch with my family and friends and soothe my homesickness. It wouldn't be Sunday dinner with the family, but it was something, and I was desperate.

In May of 2005 I headed down to the computer, which for some reason we set up in our dark, windowless basement, tucked away on a desk in the laundry room. Frankly, it was stinky and ugly. I didn't have any fear of spending too much time online because I didn't even like to be in that room. But I created a blogger account, gave my blog a clever title (which I abandoned once I discovered the repetition in my name and began to call it NieNie Dialogues), and started my very first post.

> Hello and welcome to my blog. This is fun; too bad I don't know what it is.

Writing the blog quickly became an important outlet and connection for me. I loved sharing our life with my family and friends in Utah, or posting something that I knew would make Christian laugh.

I was especially pleased to document the dress and grooming of our neighbors' porch-dwelling cement goose. "Look, girls, come here," I'd call to Claire and Jane. "Come look out the window. Stanley is changing the goose!"

The girls would hurry over, and we'd watch while Adele's husband removed one seasonal outfit and replaced it with another. On one memorable day, Stanley brought out a Pilgrim ensemble with a peaked Pilgrim hat and a stiff white collar on a black frock. He paused and put a thoughtful hand to his chin while circling the goose. Then he snapped his fingers and went back inside.

What had he remembered? The anticipation was killing me!

His wife came to the porch, took one look at the Pilgrim costume, and threw her hands in the air. She disappeared inside the house, too, and a few minutes later they both came back and redressed the goose, this time in a black braided wig and brown fringed dress à la Pocahontas. Together they nodded in approval and then went back in the house.

I couldn't wait to write about this scene with the goose. I knew my readers (my mom and siblings) would get such a kick out of the episode. Whole conversations would develop in the comments after my posts among my mother, Christian, Courtney, Christopher, his wife, Lisa, and a handful of other friends. It wasn't quite the same as sitting around the kitchen table together, but my blog felt like a bridge from Utah to New Jersey that allowed me to laugh with family a few times a week. Sometimes Courtney would leave a comment with a long-standing joke between us that made me smile the entire day.

One afternoon, not long after I started blogging, I found yet another box of mothballs in a closet in our home, and something about those mothballs plunged me into a despairing homesickness. I poured out my heart on my blog.

Simply put, I miss home . . . I realize that home is where the heart is, and if that is the case my heart was left on the mountains of Utah. I will always be home wherever my love Christian is, but deep down I long for Utah.

I miss listening to the BYU marching band practice on those lazy late summer afternoons. I missed the whole season of BYU football. Not that I really enjoyed going to the games, I just missed the anticipation in the air on those Saturdays. I miss hearing the bells chime on campus. I miss driving past Wasatch Elementary School; I miss seeing all of my dear nieces and nephews. I miss sluggish days at Page's house having lunch in the backyard while enjoying the breeze that blows from Rock Canyon. I miss calling Courtney to see if she wants to meet me for dinner, then we end up chatting for hours about everything. I miss my mom. I miss packing up the kids and headed to Umi's house when I get bored or need advice, or want to see what Lucy has in her closet for me. I miss getting into Dad's hot tub at night with Christian while Dad watches the kids. I miss the holidays, all of them for every reason imaginable. I miss Café Rio, Ottavio's chocolate cake, cheap dates, canyon drives, The Good Earth store, Great Harvest bread, walking to the temple, family parties, and I miss the mountains.

My mom always called after she read my posts. When they were about the girls or our outings, she'd call to hear more about the story I'd shared. Before she hung up she always asked the most sincere question: "How are you really doing?"

On "Mothball Day," that question left me a tearful, snotty mess. I sobbed about how much I missed my family, and the mountains, and how tired I was with three little ones, and how much Christian worked. My mother, as always, listened and offered soothing words of comfort until the stuttering breaths of my sobs slowed and my breathing was normal again.

Blogging became a bit like putting a message in a bottle and tossing it out on the ocean. I never knew exactly who would find it, but I loved what happened when they did. Some days, it was truly a lifeline. Thus, despite the dark and smelly laundry room, I spent more and more time at the computer. I ran up and down the stairs several times a day, checking comments and e-mails. I'd get the children breakfast and then run downstairs to check comments. I checked first thing when we came home from the grocery store, right after I put Ollie down for a nap, just before dinner, again before bedtime, and any other moment I could spare. There would always be a few new comments to read and respond to, and often I'd have e-mails from readers who had questions or just wanted to introduce themselves. Much to my surprise, they had started coming in from all over the country. I'd respond to the comments and e-mails and then look through the links they had sent. I could say *I'll only be a minute* all I wanted, but it was never true.

One day I put Ollie down for a nap and then put on a movie in the guest room next to my laundry room office for the girls. I pulled out markers and paper to keep them occupied, and then went to the computer. I was busy at work designing new banners for my blog, downloading and editing my latest photos, putting the finishing touches on a post. I felt like the CEO of my own little magazine. My blog gave me an outlet to share all of my interests—parenting, photography, style, cooking, crafts, plus personal elements like my faith, my charismatic husband, and our neighbors' cement goose—and people seemed to care. But before I knew it *Beauty and the Beast* was over and the girls were asking to watch *Cinderella*. *Only for a minute*, I said to myself. But then all of a sudden the credits were rolling on *Cinderella*. My children had just spent another afternoon watching TV.

I pushed the chair away from the computer desk and went to gather Claire and Jane. Oliver was just stirring from his nap as we walked up the stairs. I picked him up from his crib and mugged on his little neck, then went to the couch in the living room. "Girls," I called, "come here." My little girls came running, and I gathered them close to me. "Come say hello to baby Ollie." The three of us tried to get a smile or laugh out of Oliver. Jane was the best at silly faces, and soon we were all giggling.

I couldn't sacrifice time with these beautiful children for blogging, and yet I loved it and didn't want to stop. I couldn't stay balanced if I was constantly running downstairs to find out what people thought about my latest post. I loved the interaction but decided that closing the comments was better than giving up blogging altogether. Because one thing was certain: I did not want to give it up.

Ten

Living in New Jersey made me tougher and more tolerant. Our little family grew, and we made friends we loved. But when Christian found a job opening in Arizona at Boeing, there was very little discussion about whether or not he should apply. We both knew we were ready to live in the West again. Claire would be starting kindergarten the next year, and we loved the idea that she would start school in Christian's hometown. Out of habit, I still called Utah home, but Arizona was close enough.

When we arrived in Mesa, we moved in temporarily with Christian's parents, Russ and Mary. They were gracious enough to let us stay in their home while we looked for a home of our own to buy. The month that we had planned to stay turned into a year, and they continued to be welcoming and understanding throughout that time. Even after six years of being married to their son, I couldn't say I knew Russ and Mary well, so living in their home brought a new dimension to our relationship. My love and admiration for them grew, as loving parents and grandparents, and as individuals. They loved me like a daughter, and we forged the kinds of bonds that carry you through good times and bad.

I was pregnant with our fourth baby when we moved to Mesa, and Nicholas Jones was born that October in Russ and Mary's home, in the bedroom where Christian's twenty-six-year-old sister Charity had passed away nearly five years earlier. Cancer had taken Charity's life, and I was honored to give birth in that very same room. The labor was long and difficult, but Christian kept me looking into his dark brown eyes, and I stayed strong. Well, *afterward* I felt strong, but during labor, I did think I might die. Nicholas was almost nine pounds, but when the midwife laid him on my chest, I forgot about the extraordinary pain and marveled that God had blessed us with another healthy baby.

We found a lovely house in Mesa in a neighborhood near Christian's parents and eagerly made an offer—I was desperate for my own home—but the sale fell through. We loved that little house, and I was so disappointed we wouldn't be moving in after all. A few months later, though, it was up for sale again, and this time it was ours. We moved into our ranch-style home in March 2007 and got to work right away making it our own.

I'd always been passionate about decorating, and I shared pictures of our home on my blog. Our home was featured on *Cookie* magazine's online home tour, and my pictures had been used on Martha Stewart online (Martha Stewart!) and the Web site for her *Blueprint* magazine. All of this was such an honor, and I beamed about it for days.

When I first started blogging, I set two important guidelines for myself. One: I would post my own projects and ideas, and not recycle what I had seen around the Internet. Two: I wouldn't complain. There was enough bad news in the world, and I knew I could add something positive or beautiful or funny. Apparently people liked what I was up to because they kept coming back. That fueled my creativity, and I thought up more and more projects I could share. It also motivated me to write openly about the things that mattered most—my role as wife and mother and my faith.

I devoted a whole week to honoring mothers and their divine role. The posts centered around one of my favorite talks given at General Conference, the twice yearly two-day conference packed with messages of hope and faith from the Prophet, Apostles, and other leaders of the Church of Jesus Christ of Latter-day Saints. In Mesa, and all over the world, General Conference is broadcast via satellite, and we always eagerly watched, knowing we would be inspired. My favorite talk that year was given by Sister Julie Beck, who celebrated the responsibilities and blessings of motherhood—bearing, teaching, and nurturing children; honoring covenants; being leaders; doing less instead of more; and standing strong. As she spoke about motherhood, my own little family was gathered close around me. I held Nicholas and he nursed contentedly with his eyes closed. Ollie played with blocks at my feet, and Claire and Jane were snuggled on the floor whispering to each other and laughing quietly. Christian sat on the carpet near the girls.

I had always believed in the divine purpose behind my desire to be a mother, and here I was, surrounded by the family I had always dreamed of, with the father of my children, my protector and provider, sitting next to me. My tears fell quietly on Nicholas's head as I felt the power of Sister Beck's message.

Her words moved me not only because they aligned with the truth of my life, but also because they inspired me to be a stronger, more deliberate mother as I tried to teach my children about God's plans for them. During that week of honoring motherhood on my blog, I celebrated every effort and aspect of motherhood to show my love and respect for mothers everywhere. The things I shared resonated with other women around the country and the world. I could hardly believe the attention I was attracting and found it enormously gratifying.

I was first and foremost a homemaker and hadn't sacrificed being the kind of mother I'd always wanted to be. Yet I'd also been able to build this little enterprise based on my passion for homemaking and motherhood. Passions I learned my readers shared, as more and more kind notes filled my inbox and delighted me. Notes like this:

> I just HAD to tell you that your blog has been so inspiring to me. I don't remember how I came across it, but while my little girl was napping last week, I could not help but read almost all of your posts (she is a good napper). I found myself laughing, crying, and smiling like a mad woman! Your style, grace, humor, photography skills, and ability to express yourself have helped me look at my own life and just be so grateful for all that I am blessed with. Not to mention your delish pizza dough recipe which I made Saturday! I want to thank you for your honesty and sincerity. I can just feel your love for your children and your husband. It is absolutely precious. Thank you thank you thank you.
> —Katie

I absolutely LOVE your blog, and your commitment to
motherhood and family. Your relationship with your
husband is such a thing of beauty that it actually is one of
the things that convinced me to break up with my
boyfriend of four years because I know I deserve the kind
of relationship that you have with Mr. Nielson.
—Jessica

Not every e-mail was flattering, that's for sure. Readers also sent
fierce criticisms about me, my taste, my beliefs, my family. I'd never
expect everyone to agree with me, or even like me, but I was surprised people would take the time to tell me how much they disliked
me or my blog. Those comments hurt, but I tried to take it all in
stride. To feel a little better, sometimes I'd write a scathing response
and just delete it.

Overall, though, the feedback was largely positive and it was all
very humbling and something I appreciated very much. It was also
terribly fulfilling to think that my blog—this project that I loved so
much—was touching other women. They told me I was blessing their
lives, and they were certainly blessing mine.

At the checkout line at a Target in Mesa one day, a woman approached me. She shyly asked, "Um, are you Nie Nie? I think I read
your blog." She introduced me to her sister, who also knew who I
was, and asked me a few questions about the paper fans I'd made for
my girls' room. I had posted pictures of them on my blog.

I managed to answer her questions and finish a pleasant conversation before hurrying out to the parking lot to call Christian. "Guess
what?! Someone at Target just recognized me from my blog!"

On the way home, Claire looked thoughtful. She asked, "Mommy,
do you know her?"

"The woman at Target?"

Claire nodded.

"No, I just met her. But she looks at my blog—you know, on the computer where I put pictures of what we do together. That's my blog, and she looks at it on her computer, so she recognized me. She likes the projects we do, Claire."

"Mommy"—I could see the wheels turning in her head—"are you famous?"

I'd begun calling Christian Mr. Nielson on my blog after I saw the 2005 version of *Pride and Prejudice*. Mr. Darcy was great and all, but I had my own guy, the dashing Mr. Nielson. In April 2008, I shared his next big adventure on my blog.

> Did you know that Mr. Nielson becomes Mr. Pilot Nielson on Wednesday?
> Around 4:00 the family watches the father of our home fly around Mesa in a very small airplane.

We had driven to the airport to watch Christian fly and got there in time to watch him do the preflight checklist. That gave Jane and Claire a chance to climb into the airplane. They pretended to fly over an enchanted forest and through colorful rainbows. But then they started fighting over who got the headset and who got to be named "Kalee," so that was the end of that.

From the car we watched Christian practice takeoff and landing maneuvers. Oliver watched, mouth open, terrifically mesmerized. Nicholas squirmed and screamed until I unbuckled him from his car seat for a better view.

I finished the report on my blog:

And NO, Mom, Mr. Pilot Nielson didn't crash.

In fact, my heart swelled nice and big as I watched him soar in the sky. He is fulfilling a 29-year-old dream. Did I ever tell you about the time when Mr. Nielson was 6 and he ate birdseeds because he thought he'd grow wings and fly away?

He was made for this.

I am so happy for him.

When he began his flight lessons that spring, studying flight procedures became part of our nightly routine. After our children were asleep, I sat next to Christian in bed, a Cessna manual propped against my knees, quizzing him.

"Okay, starting the engine." I read the heading from the airplane manual. "Mixture?"

"Rich," he answered.

"Carburetor heat?"

"Cold."

"Master switch?"

"On."

We went through the entire list, everything from starting the engine to securing the plane when it was back on the ground.

"Wow, I am really impressed." Christian knew every procedure. There was so much to learn, and he was learning it.

Eventually we put away the Cessna manual and turned out the lights, but we lay there in the dark, practicing the phonetic alphabet. Pilots use the phonetic alphabet—words instead of letters—to spell things out so there's no confusion over the radio. Instead of just saying "sky," a pilot would spell out "Sierra Kilo Yankee" and there would be no confusion in the control tower.

"Alpha, Bravo, Charlie . . . ," Christian started. I lay my head on his chest and felt the familiar vibration of his voice.

"Delta, Echo, Foxtrot, Golf," I answered, going through the entire alphabet.

"You're officially promoted to copilot, darling." He kissed the top of my head.

"Kilo India Sierra Sierra me, right here," I said, pointing to a certain part of my anatomy.

"Wilco," Christian answered, pilot-speak for "will comply."

It's important for a pilot to be able to follow clear directions. "And Hotel Echo Roger Echo, please."

He was very good at following directions.

"I Lima Oscar Victor Echo you, Pilot Nielson."

"Roger that," he said, pulling me closer.

T hat July, as Christian was wrapping up his training, the kids and I visited my family in Utah. At our annual Fourth of July picnic, I told everyone about Christian's plan to become a pilot. My mother's father, Papa Jones, came over to me and took my arm. "Don't you get in that airplane with him," he warned. "They aren't safe."

I knew I would fly with Christian, but Papa Jones's warning shook me. I felt suddenly anxious and went over to sit with my brother Jesse. Suddenly I blurted out a strange question for a merry Fourth of July picnic. "If something happens to me and Christian, will you take our kids?"

Jesse looked at me. "Well, that's something I'd better ask my wife about."

That got Lindsay's attention, and she sat down, too. I asked them both, "If something happens to us, will you take our kids?"

"Of course we would," Lindsay said.

Someone brought out dessert, and the children crowded around, and any grim possibilities we may have entertained were drowned out by the joyful shouts of our children.

I n Out of Africa, *a movie I'd always loved, Robert Redford* dazzles Meryl Streep with a flight over the African landscape. "A glimpse of the world through God's eye," she says. As Christian prepared to become a pilot, I thought over and over again of the scene where Meryl reaches for Robert's hand midflight. She is breathless, smitten.

Christian successfully completed his solo flight and became a licensed pilot by the end of July. For our first flight together, Christian and I planned to take off at dusk and watch the sunset over the city. I wore a sunny yellow dress and sandals Christian had given me for my twenty-eighth birthday a few weeks earlier. I called my two little girls into my room as I buckled the straps.

"Daddy has worked so hard to become a pilot, girls. I'm so proud of him. We're going on a special date tonight to celebrate. We're going to fly in the airplane."

"You look pretty, Mommy," Claire said. "Are you going to put on makeup now?"

"Mm-hmm. Want to watch?" I loved showing the girls that a date with their father merited extraordinary style. Even though they were small, I wanted them to know how special I felt when I went out with Christian. I hoped they would feel that way about someone someday, too.

At ages five and six, the girls were transfixed by the wonder of makeup, all those colorful tubes and brushes. I applied blush, eyeliner, smoky eye shadow, and mascara. My girls watched, openmouthed. My finishing touch was glossy red lipstick.

Claire nodded. "Now you look *very* pretty, Mommy."

"So pretty," Jane agreed.

"Thank you, girls." I turned to look at them. "But you know who *I* think is pretty?"

Big smiles spread across their faces.

"You!" I tickled Claire's little tummy. "And you!" I did the same to Jane, and then held both girls in my arms and squeezed them tight. "Now help me choose the prettiest earrings."

Normally I felt stifled by the summer heat, but I don't remember a thing about that July evening at Falcon Field except pure magic. In the cockpit, we each put on a headset and listened to the radio for the latest flight information. The faint scent of jet fuel hung in the air.

"Falcon Field, Yankee," the recorded message began. "Time: 1749 Zulu. Winds: two-six-zero at five. Temp: three-one C. Altimeter: Two Niner Niner Eight." Christian checked countless switches and dials on the instrument panel and brought the engine to life. We started slowly down the runway. My stomach fluttered in delighted anticipation.

He radioed ground control to request a runway and permission to take off. In the pilot-speak he'd worked so hard to perfect he said, "Falcon Tower, Cessna 78 Bravo, on the ramp. Taxi VFR departure, westbound with information Yankee."

Surely they'd been impressed. ". . . runway two-two left, taxi via Delta," air traffic control answered back.

We taxied to our position on the runway, powered up the engine, and Christian radioed the tower. "Falcon Tower, Cessna 78 Bravo ready for takeoff, runway two-two left."

"78 Bravo, Falcon Tower, runway two-two left, cleared for takeoff."

Cleared for takeoff! I couldn't keep the smile off my face. The airplane accelerated, and we sped down the runway. Out my window, the pavement was a blur.

"Here we go!" I cried. The ground dropped away below us. "We're flying! Christian, I can't believe we're really doing this!" Just months earlier, this had been a dream, but now here we were, flying over Mesa. I looked out over the ordered streets and watched the buildings get smaller and smaller. "I am so proud of you." I said it over and over again.

Sure, we had four children and a dog, a mortgage and two cars in the garage, but sitting in the cockpit with my husband, *the pilot*, sure made me feel like a grown-up. This was bona fide adulthood, not just some wild adventure, but a real life we'd built together. And my partner in all of it, this charming man, had just lifted an airplane off the ground.

Golden evening light spread across the valley, and the lights below began to twinkle on here and there. We flew over the yoga studio where I taught on Saturday mornings and the beautiful Mesa temple where Christian's parents and my grandparents had been married bathed in white light. Then we circled over our home with its trim lawn and backyard tree house.

"I love to see our house like this," I said. "So small and tidy, with our little family inside. What do you think they're doing?"

"The babysitter's putting them to bed?" Christian hoped.

I shook my head. "She's probably texting while the children tear apart the house."

We flew over the city again and watched the summer sun sink below the horizon, burning a trail of orange and red all the way down. After the sun had set, the palest blue hung in the sky for another few minutes.

Christian got serious. "Now, if something ever happened to me, like I had a heart attack in the air, you would need to push this button right here, and set to seven-seven-zero-zero. Then use the radio on one-two-one-point-five and explain the situation. Someone would tell you exactly what to do, and you could fly us safely home."

I nodded. "Seven-seven-zero-zero. I'll remember that."

We talked about our plan to fly with our children to Utah for the holidays, once Christian was qualified to fly a big enough plane. We'd load the kids in the plane and arrive in two short hours instead of eleven. I pictured our kids in the backseat, reading and coloring, looking out the window at the earth from above. What an easy, efficient way to travel.

Christian cruised over to the mountains, and for the first time during the flight I got nervous. "What if we can't see the mountains and we fly right into them, Christian?" I was struck by the memory of my grandfather who had been killed in a plane crash. The fact that he left my grandmother a widow with eight children resonated with me even more now that I had children of my own.

"We're not close enough to crash, and I have instruments to make sure we won't, but we don't have to fly over here. Let's go somewhere else."

The score from *Out of Africa* played in my head as he maneuvered the plane away from the mountains, and we skimmed over Mesa again. The sky was inky black now, and the city lights were scattered like brilliant glitter across the valley.

What I wanted to do was sit on Christian's lap and offer up a passionate kiss from the depths of my soul, but I saved that for later. Instead I reached across the cockpit and put my hand on Christian's neck, beaming with pride.

"I'm so proud of you, Christian. You're flying!"

Christian smiled back. "I couldn't be happier, Stephanie. This is a dream come true being up here with you."

Maybe I should have been used to it by now, but I was smitten all over again, by Pilot Christian Nielson.

Eleven

·····················

C*hristian's love for his family's ranch hadn't changed since* he'd first told me about it in my mother's convertible. If anything, it had deepened when we began taking our children there. We hadn't been able to visit the ranch while we lived in New Jersey, and Christian was thrilled to be back within driving distance. The end of July marks Bluewater Days, as Russ likes to call the annual family reunion at the ranch. Christian's parents and ten siblings—most with spouses and children—had already arrived and were waiting for us at the ranch. Our children had fallen asleep about an hour after we left Mesa. Our tires hummed steadily over the asphalt.

After four hours on the road, we pulled off Route 66 into the village of Bluewater at 1:00 A.M. The village is just a handful of scattered houses, a Dairy Queen, and a gas station that doubles as a trading post. Even in the dark of night it felt familiar and nostalgic. Christian took a deep breath and smiled. I reached over and squeezed his hand. "Almost there, baby," I said.

As we drove through the village, though, the kids began to stir, like they'd detected the proximity of Bluewater on some internal radar in their genes. We turned onto the gravel ranch road, and when we stopped to open the gate Claire perked up. "Are we there? Are we almost there?"

I nodded and smiled. "Getting close!"

Jane and Oliver blinked awake, and a burst of last-stretch energy zinged through the car. Claire grabbed Jane's shoulders. "WE'RE ALMOST THERE!"

"Yaaaay!" Jane shouted. "We're here, we're here, we're here!"

Oliver joined in, and all three older children chanted together.

Miraculously, Nicholas stayed asleep. But even he had a serene smile on his face.

We rolled down the windows, and warm night air that smelled like sweet wet dirt and prairie grass floated into the car. The kids unbuckled their seat belts and put their heads out the window, gulping big breaths of Bluewater while they laughed and shouted. Christian and I exchanged a look of parental delight and then joined in the shouting ourselves.

The stars blazed in the dark sky, looking so much bigger than the stars at home. That multitude of stars was one sure sign we'd left the world behind. We bumped along the gravel road for almost twenty minutes, stopping to unlock both gates and crossing two cattle guards before we rounded the last corner and were greeted by the glowing lights of the ranch house.

A fresh cheer erupted from the backseat as we parked, and Claire, Jane, and Oliver scrambled out. Christian unbuckled Nicholas, and family came out to welcome us and help carry in our things. We had packed all we could bring for a week, and everything else we needed was already here: cousins galore, plenty of loving aunts and uncles, dear grandparents, and nine thousand acres to roam.

Our days at Bluewater were always relaxed and simple, and delightfully unscheduled. The women in the family kept an eye on the little ones, cooked and crafted and caught up on one another's lives as well as plenty of magazines. The men worked outside on ranch projects. This year they were finishing the inside of the barn they'd built the year before. The older children played continuously with their cousins. The girls were usually planning and performing elaborate musical productions based on the latest Broadway hit, and the boys were chasing lizards, throwing rocks, or playing with Legos. I spent a few afternoons swimming with the kids in the icy cold waters of the homemade swimming pool—two steel water tanks welded together. And you could always pick up a conversation with whoever happened to be lounging on one of the eight-foot porch swings that framed the front door. We also spent plenty of time riding four-wheelers all over the ranch. In the evenings, the whole family—all fifty-eight of us—met for dinner in the dining hall, and then we'd gather around the campfire to talk.

One of my favorite things about being in Bluewater was getting up early to go on a run. I'd quietly pull on my running clothes, careful not to wake Christian or our children, who were sleeping on the floor in our bedroom. They were still in dreamland, mild grins spread across their faces. I resisted the urge to kiss their peaceful little cheeks, and instead took a good long look at each of them and quietly closed the door behind me. The entire house was quiet and still, but I usually saw Russ outside, waiting for the rest of the men to wake up and get to work.

Christian had always described the big, big sky at the ranch, but it wasn't until my first visit to Bluewater years earlier that I had really understood the influence of that big sky. Now, as I stepped outside, I welcomed the familiar sight, that vast stretch of uninterrupted blue. I loved what it did to my soul, how it made me feel bigger and smaller at the same time. I took a deep breath of the clean, sweet air and set out on my run.

It was quiet except for the sound of my shoes on the dirt road. Little puffs of clay-colored dust rose around my feet with every step. A faint chill hovered over the morning, the last trace of the night air. Even though it would be gone in an hour, it was still a welcome change from the stifling heat of Mesa.

I looked out over the gentle hills covered in gray-green prairie grass as far as I could see. In the west, pinyon pines and junipers made a line of dark green just below the long, low plateaus that rose above the hills. About fifteen miles away, an early morning train made its way across the plains.

With every step, I left behind the pressures and distractions of regular life. In all that wide-open space, there was surprisingly little room for things that didn't matter. I offered up a silent prayer of thanks. First, that I could run. I thanked God for my healthy body, for His beautiful Earth, for my precious family. As I prayed, I felt more and more gratitude. I had so much to be thankful for. Our home in Mesa, the mulberry tree, the monsoons, air-conditioning, yoga, our tree house, a good school for Claire and Jane, our great friends, cars that ran, Christian's job. Blessings poured into my mind, as clearly as if they came from that enormous blue sky. I quickened my pace. My legs felt strong and steady, like I had the momentum of that far-off train.

Later that afternoon, Christian and I found a moment to get away by ourselves. After sleeping in the same room as our children for several days and sharing a house with fifty-six other people, we were excited at the prospect of an hour or two alone. I had just put Nicholas down for his afternoon nap, and our other children were busy with their cousins. Christian's sisters were more than happy to keep an eye on our kids, so I packed a picnic lunch and we drove a four-wheeler across the ranch to find a place for target practice.

Just a few weeks before we came to Bluewater, I had acquired both a gun permit and my own little pistol, a G26 "Baby" Glock. Our neighborhood in Mesa was truly charming, with big trees, wide streets, and friendly young families. But police helicopters circled regularly, their spotlights searching. One morning we had been awakened at two-thirty by *seven* police cars surrounding a house in our neighborhood. It scared me, and I wanted to be able to defend my children and myself if I needed to, so my friend Lindsay and I decided to get gun permits. I had attended the class, taken the test, and earned a CCW. I was officially certified to carry a concealed weapon, which I did when I went downtown to teach yoga. Fortunately, I hadn't needed to fire the gun to defend myself or my family or save the neighborhood, but the ranch was the perfect place to improve my aim.

The day had warmed, and there was a nice breeze and a line of puffy clouds low in the sky. Christian drove the four-wheeler and I wrapped my arms around him and leaned my body into his. We drove for about fifteen minutes and stopped at a stand of ancient trees where we found plenty of old cans to use as targets. We set them up on stumps, and Christian took aim.

He brought his gun to eye level with a steady arm and easy concentration. His stance was confident and self-assured. My heart began to beat a little faster as I watched my rugged husband fire away. His first shot blew the can off the stump with a metallic *ting*. Every time he took a shot, a can catapulted into the air. After ten rounds, he reloaded the magazine and fired ten more times, this time as the cans lay on the ground.

"Impressive," I said. "Very impressive." I swatted Christian's rear.

"Your turn," he said, with a quick kiss. "Let's put those cans back up and see what you've got."

We replaced the cans, and I loaded my pistol. I took a deep breath and wrapped my hands carefully around the body of my little gun, took aim, and then squeezed the trigger gently. *Ting*. My first can went flying. Oh yeah. I took careful aim at the second can and squeezed the trigger again. This time the bullet zoomed off into Bluewater. And the next one joined it, and the next one after that.

Christian came up behind me. "It's all about the stance, hon." He adjusted my hips and steadied my legs against his, then wrapped his arms around my sweaty aim. I can't help it—when I'm nervous, sweaty hands just come with the territory. "And you've got to keep this arm straight and steady, like this." He raised my arm a little. Then he kissed my neck and ran his hand down my back. This did nothing to steady my stance, which now required readjustment. Christian grinned. "OK, try it again."

I squinted a surefire aim, straightened my arm like an arrow, squeezed ever so gently, and, *ting*, the can flew off the stump. Eventually I shot all twelve of my targets and we spread out the blanket . . . but skipped the lunch.

Christian wrapped me in those sure-shot arms of his. "I like how you handle your gun, miss," he said, in a rancher drawl. "Seriously, I'm proud of you, Steph. You're getting good."

"I'll get even better," I said.

"Well, give yourself about another hundred prairie dogs."

Christian leaned forward, and I closed my eyes for a kiss the size of New Mexico itself. That first kiss led to another and another, and we were quite enjoying ourselves when I heard the rumble of four-wheelers in the distance. We both froze, not unlike a pair of startled prairie dogs.

I was dumbfounded. "How could someone find us here?"

"They're not coming here," Christian reasoned, pulling me down to the blanket. "What are the chances someone would come to this very spot?"

While he had a very good point, the rumble grew louder and the four-wheelers were definitely headed our direction. I scrambled to find and then put on my shirt. I straightened my hair, zipped up my jeans, and looked in the direction of the approaching noise.

Christian's parents, also out for a break from the family, arrived on the four-wheelers.

"Hi!" Christian welcomed heartily. "What are you guys doing out here?" *Why hadn't I smoothed his disheveled hair?*

"Oh, just out for a ride," Russ said. "Doing some shooting?"

Mary's eyes drifted to my shirt. I looked down, panicked. It was on backward. Our eyes met again for a split second and then I looked away.

"Yeah, Stephanie's getting really good with her pistol. You should see her hit those cans," Christian said.

"Oh, I'm not that good," I said, avoiding eye contact.

"I'm sure you're wonderful, Stephanie," Russ said. "Well, I think we'll keep going. You two have a good day. See you at dinner."

They drove away. Embarrassment hung heavy on the dust they left behind. Christian fell back on the blanket, laughing hysterically.

"It's not funny, Christian," I said. "That was so embarrassing."

"Oh, come on, we're married, Stephanie. We've had four children. I think my parents might suspect there's something going on between us," Christian teased.

"It felt like getting caught in high school."

"What would you know about getting caught in high school?" He pulled me down next to him on the blanket.

He had a point there. I'd never been in the position to get caught doing much.

"Anyway, they didn't know what we were doing," he said. "It just looks like we're out here having a picnic."

Unconvinced, but sure his parents were out of sight, I let Christian pull me into another fervent kiss. And another. And then just one more . . .

T he next evening we loaded the kids onto two four-wheelers at dusk and drove the short distance up the hill from the ranch house to the fire ring for a family dinner. Christian had fond memories of going there with his father and grandfather and was eager to create memories for our kids. Our children had played their hearts out all week—nonstop fun and games—and that was just as it should have been. But I looked forward to a quiet time at the fire ring, a chance to focus on reverent things.

Our children were thrilled that we were going to build our very own campfire, and they shouted questions at Christian while he built the fire. Meanwhile, I assembled tin-foil dinners, a family classic. I'd gathered produce from Russ's abundant garden and wrapped servings of potatoes, carrots, asparagus, and green beans into squares of tin foil. We cooked the packets of tin foil in the coals of the fire and enjoyed a delicious outdoor meal, which wouldn't have been complete without s'mores.

Our children practiced the art of roasting the perfect marshmallow. Over and over again, Jane's marshmallows blackened and Jimmy gobbled up each and every one that she threw on the ground. She kept working until she achieved the golden-brown marshmallow of confection perfection. The other kids were less discerning, and everyone consumed a great deal of marshmallows, chocolate, and graham crackers.

By the time we were finished with the s'mores, the kids' faces were coated with a fine, sticky layer of dirt, and they were as happy as could be. Nicholas had fallen asleep on Christian's shoulder. Claire, Jane, and Oliver were snuggled around me, wrapped in a blanket, still licking their fingers.

Christian told them about his second great-grandfather Frihoff Nielson, who had settled the ranch. He'd emigrated from Denmark with his family when he was nine years old, arrived in New York City, traveled to Salt Lake, and eventually to Bluewater.

"When he got here, there was nothing," Christian explained. "No ranch house, no barn, not even cows. He had to bring everything here and build everything himself. It was hard work and took a lot of faith and courage. I'm sure there were times when he wanted to give up, but he kept going, and worked really hard for a long time, and now we get to come and enjoy this beautiful ranch. I want you to know that's where you come from, that's who we are. Frihoff Nielson's determination and hard work are in your blood."

"He had blood?" Oliver asked. "Did he get blood at the ranch?"

"It just means that he is your family, Ollie," I explained. "That we come from a family of people like Frihoff Nielson who work hard and have faith."

"Oh. That's in my blood?" Ollie touched the scab on his arm.

I could see where he was going but chose the simple answer. "Yes, that's in your blood. Things were really different then," I continued. "No cars or lights or phones or four-wheelers. But some things were the same, the important things. Frihoff Nielson looked out over these very same hills and looked up at the stars, just like we're doing. He believed in Heavenly Father and Jesus. He prayed for help like we do. And I know he loved his family, just like we love each other so much. He was a great man, and that's why we want you to know about him."

Our children listened quietly as we told other stories about our pioneer ancestors and their faith. Christian and I took turns sharing our love for God and Jesus Christ. I knew our kids would probably not remember our words, but I hoped they would remember the feelings of that night around the fire ring.

"Families are part of God's plan for us. For everyone," I said, "not just people in our Church, but everyone. And nothing is more important to me than you." I pointed at each of them. "Daddy, Claire, Jane, Ollie, and Nicholas. You're the best things that have ever happened to me in my whole entire life. I love being your mother, and I love being a daughter and a sister, too. We have a wonderful family of aunts and uncles and cousins and grandparents that will always be there for us. If anything ever happened to us, they would help with anything we needed."

"Anything?" Claire asked.

"Anything," I answered. "Isn't that the best?"

Christian sat down next to me, and the kids snuggled a little closer around our feet. We watched the fire, and stars sparkled everywhere above us. I felt so complete. I had everything I needed, right here.

A s much as we enjoyed our trip to Bluewater, it was always nice to come home. The girls had just started school, and we were just getting used to our new schedule when Christian called me on a Tuesday afternoon.

"Hey, honey—I have a great plan for our date this weekend."

I put down the laundry basket I was carrying and fell backward on the bed in my apron. He had my full attention. I relished the time Christian and I got to spend together on the weekends.

"Oooo. Tell me more." I stared at the ceiling.

"I want to take Doug down to Bluewater on Saturday, show him the ranch."

Oh. A day trip with Christian's flight instructor? Here I was thinking of a romantic evening alone together.

Christian continued, "If we fly to Bluewater, I can get checked out in the bigger airplane." We'd been waiting for Christian to get certified in a big enough airplane to fly our family to Utah for Christmas, and this trip would provide more valuable experience. "It'll just be a quick flight up and back, but while we're there we'll take the four-wheelers out to show Doug around a little."

I wasn't crazy about the idea, but I could not ignore the enthusiasm in Christian's voice.

He noted my silence. "What are you thinking?" he asked.

"I'm thinking about those moccasins I wanted at the Bluewater trading post."

"Ah." I could hear the smile in his voice.

"How about I get a pair while we're there?" I negotiated.

"Great. You've got a deal."

That Saturday morning we got up early and hurried to get the children dressed and fed and over to Russ and Mary's by seven-thirty. I made the pizza dough for dinner later that night as Christian dished up bowls of oatmeal for the children. We rushed to get the kids in the car and raced to Christian's parents'. Christian and I always ran notoriously late, but Doug was the epitome of punctuality, and we didn't want to make him wait.

At Russ and Mary's, we gave quick hugs and kisses to Jane, Claire, and Oliver, and they ran off to play. But Nicholas clung to my shirt. Big tears traced down his cheeks and he held on for dear life.

"Gigs, Mommy will be back tonight." I spoke to him in my sweetest mother voice. "Remember we made pizza dough? Mommy will be back and we'll have pizza tonight. OK, my little Gigsie? Mommy will be back."

I peeled his hands off me and put him on the ground. He grabbed my leg and sobbed.

"Nicholas," I said, less sweetly, "Mommy has to go. I'll be back tonight."

Mary picked up Nicholas and waved us out the door. "You two go. Have a great time. Everything will be fine."

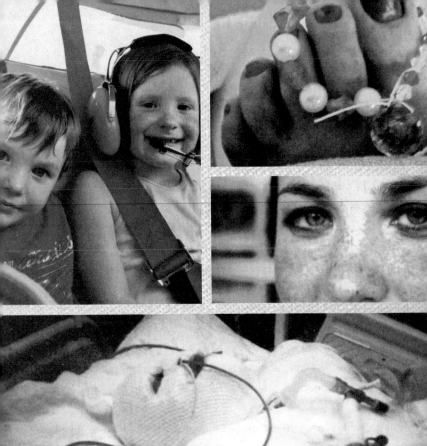
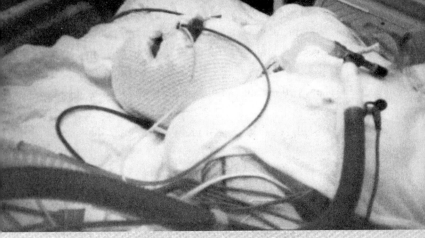

PART TWO

• • • • • • • • •

*There is in every true woman's heart a
spark of heavenly fire, which lies dormant in
the broad daylight of prosperity, but which
kindles up and beams and blazes
in the dark hour of adversity.*

—Washington Irving

Twelve

·················

I heard Courtney laugh. *Through half-closed eyes, I saw her* across the room, dressed in pink. She seemed to be wearing a costume.

I heard other people—I couldn't place their voices—talking about Halloween. *Courtney's dressed up for Halloween*, I realized. *She's in a pig costume. Cute.*

Small round circles dangled from the ceiling. *Those must be dough-nuts for a Halloween party.*

My eyes were so heavy. I couldn't keep them open as the voices swirled around me.

"Her eyes have been fluttering open all morning." My mother's voice. "And she's been moving her tongue, like she's trying to talk to us."

"Does that mean she's awake?" I heard my dad ask.

Were they talking about me?

"No, she's not awake," a stranger's voice said. "Her body is ac-customed to the medication, so she's not sleeping as deeply as she was. That's fine, though, because we'd like to begin the process of waking her up." I realized he must be a doctor.

"What will we say to her when she wakes up?" It was my dad again.

I was relieved to think my parents were close. *I must be at their house*, I thought.

"She'll be confused. You'll need to take it slow, especially at first," the stranger said.

The voices faded, as if I were suddenly at the opposite end of a long, dark tunnel. Sleep enveloped me.

S ometime later, I opened my eyes. I noticed a date written in blue marker on a white board on the wall. I strained to see it clearly. *Today is November 5, 2008.*

I stared at the words. *November?* There had to be a mistake. I looked around at an unfamiliar room. The ceiling was covered in white tiles, and there were fire sprinklers above my bed. The beige walls were blank, except for the white board. *Where am I?*

My mom and my oldest sister Page hurried into sight, their faces bright and eager.

"Oh, Stephy, hey, you're awake." Page smiled and spoke to me like I was a child.

Of course I'm awake. What a strange thing to say. But where am I?

Page and my mom smiled at each other. A knowing look passed between them and they leaned forward, grinning, almost giddy.

"Stephy," my mom said. "Oh, Stephy, it's so good to see you." She sniffed. "Oh, honey, do you know how long we've waited to see those green eyes?"

"Stephy, you were in an accident," Page explained gently.

Where's Christian? I wondered. *Where are the children?*

"Do you know where you are?"

I shook my head a fraction of an inch. I had no idea.

"Darlin', you're in the hospital. We're in Phoenix."

In the hospital. Not at my parents' house. I was disappointed, and then worried. If Page and my mom had both come to Phoenix, I must be very sick.

I blinked and tried to smile back at their eagerness. But a dense fog seemed to cling, thick and heavy, to my thoughts. *There has been an accident. I am in the hospital,* I repeated in my mind, trying to grasp this news.

And then, without warning, a deep and pervasive pain pushed aside every other thought. I closed my eyes against the weight of it. It felt as though my arms and legs had been stripped of skin, scrubbed with sandpaper, and then left raw and exposed to the sting of open air. The skin on my face seemed stretched across my bones, and every time I blinked, it felt as if it might tear. Throbbing spikes of pain pierced through me from head to toe. Every nerve in my body seemed to pulse with a sudden and steady beat of agony.

As though she realized the wave of pain that had crashed over me, Page said, "You're hurt, Stephanie. You're probably in a lot of pain. Tell us how you feel." She held up a piece of paper with a row of ten round faces on it. The face on the left was happy, and each face gradually became sadder and sadder. "Choose the one that matches how you feel, and the doctors can help with your pain." She spoke to me slowly, like I was a child.

The drawing second from the end, with the wrinkled eyebrows and frown, looked exactly as sad and confused as I felt.

That one, I tried to say, but nothing happened. The words hung in my throat; I nearly choked on them but couldn't make them come out. The terror I felt must have been obvious.

"Oh, Stephy, darlin' you can't talk," Page hurried to explain. "There's a tube in your throat to help you breathe and to feed you."

"You can't move your arms right now, either, honey," my mom said. "You're all bandaged up. Just use your eyes. Tell us with your eyes."

I can't lift my arms? I tried anyway—I had to try—and discovered it was true. I couldn't lift either arm. *Why wouldn't I be able to lift my arms?* I was normal and healthy, and normal, healthy people can lift their arms. I tried again, determined, but nothing happened. My arms didn't budge. I was wrapped from head to toe in bandages like a mummy. I was trapped. I couldn't speak. I couldn't move. Panic set in, and I blinked in frantic confusion. My heart raced, and I started to cry as I grasped just how seriously hurt I must be.

"It's OK, Steph, it's going to be OK," Page reassured me. "You're hurt, but you're going to get better. You have the best doctors here to help you. Show me which face feels right, and they'll get you some medicine. Just use your eyes." Page moved her finger along the row of faces. When she pointed to the frowny face with wrinkled eyebrows, I widened my eyes and nodded. Or tried to nod.

"This one?" Page asked. She looked over at a nurse I hadn't noticed until then. The nurse nodded and left the room.

Page put the sign down. "She'll be back to adjust your medication, and then you'll feel better."

"Oh, Stephy, we're so happy to see you," my mom said. She put her hand to her mouth, and tears that had been welling up in her eyes spilled onto her cheeks. "Those green eyes."

"Do you remember being in an airplane with Christian and Doug?" Page asked.

I felt lost, like a tourist in a foreign country—no language, no map. Page and my mom leaned forward, waiting, while I slowly processed every word again. *Being in an airplane with Christian and Doug.* If I concentrated, that did sound familiar.

I blinked.

"Do you remember when you crashed?"

The fog around my thoughts was too thick, and I felt like I was drowning in the sea of pain. I inched my head to the left.

"Your airplane crashed. In August. It caught on fire and you got burned. You have burns on your body, but everyone here in the burn center is taking such good care of you. You're going to get better."

It sounded horrible. *A fiery airplane crash? And I had been there?* Another wave of panic hit me as my thoughts again turned to Christian and our children. *Where were they? Were they all right? And when was I going home?* Then I was struck with the fear of what the answers might be. I pushed away the questions. I couldn't bear to know.

I didn't remember an airplane crash. It scared me to think that I didn't remember something I had apparently lived through. If only my mind could stretch a little further, maybe I could remember, understand. But I couldn't do it. The memory was past my reach.

"Christian's OK," Page said. "He was hurt, but he's doing much better. He's in another hospital now. He's been with you every minute that he could, Stephanie. He'll be thrilled you're awake."

"Your children are fine," my mom said.

My children. A sickening surge of anxiety, fear, and shame rushed through me. *My sweet children—how could I have done this to them?*

"They're in Provo. Courtney has Claire, Jane, and Oliver," my mom continued slowly. "And Lucy has Nicholas, and they're doing great. They are just fine. So many people are helping, Stephanie. People are giving so many things to your kids—you should see the gifts they get from complete strangers!"

I struggled to understand. My children were living with my sisters? I was thankful and heartbroken in the same instant. So grateful that my sisters were caring for my children, and unbearably sad to think that they were doing it because I couldn't. I pictured them at Courtney's house—I knew just where they would sleep, and I imagined Courtney sitting on their bed, the kids beaming at her with rapt attention at one of her clever stories. And Lucy, the germ-a-phobe, would diligently watch over Nicholas. Lucy's husband, Andrew, would take him riding around their farm on the tractors he loved so much.

I had been away from my children for *three* whole months. It was inconceivable. Knowing they were safe was a huge comfort, but it was too overwhelming to think beyond that. If I could have, I'd have asked my mother and Page to stop talking about the children. But, understandably, Mom and Page were eager to give me updates.

"We put the girls in school in Provo, Stephanie," my mom said.

Days before the accident Claire had started first grade and Jane had started kindergarten in Mesa. Now they were in Provo at my old elementary school.

"They really like it. Jane has Mrs. Whittaker."

Mrs. Whittaker was a family hero. She had been Lucy's teacher, but we all adored her—Mrs. Whittaker's smiling face was something I remembered clearly.

"And you would love Claire's teacher, Mrs. T. She is so sweet and really helping Claire deal with this." *Oh good, Claire has a great teacher, too.* It was a brief, bright thought.

"Ollie's doing good," my mom continued. "He's having so much fun with all the little boy cousins. And Nicholas just loves the chickens in Lucy's backyard."

"We all love you so much, Stephanie," Page said. "Everyone's going to be so excited you're awake."

I stared back at them silently.

"Do you remember being with Doug?" my mom asked, her voice cracking. "He didn't make it." She paused, as though to let the news settle. "Are you OK?"

Hot tears streamed down my cheeks. It was too much: I was lying broken in a hospital in Arizona; Christian was hurt; our children were in Utah; and our dear friend Doug had died. I stared at the ceiling, and she seemed to understand that I didn't want to hear any more. I closed my eyes tight against the pain but couldn't escape the confusion, the devastation.

Page left the room to tell Christian that I was awake. He had just left his rehab hospital for the afternoon to visit his parents at their home. The nurse returned, and I noticed her dark curly hair and kind blue eyes. This time she spoke to me. "Here you are!" She clasped her hands and smiled. "Oh my goodness, you're finally awake!"

My mom stood to hug her. "Stephanie, this is Kristin. She's taken such great care of you, all these months."

Months? The idea that I had been in a coma for months—that I was one of those people I'd only ever heard about—began to take shape. I looked again at the date on the white board. *November 5, 2008.*

"I'm so happy to see you, Stephanie," the nurse said. "You have such a cool family. I love being your nurse. Now, let's help you with your pain. You're here on the pain scale?" She pointed at the face second from the end again. "Do you need more medicine?"

I widened my eyes, and she turned to the bank of machines at my left to increase my dosage.

Another nurse walked in the room and stood next to Kristin. She squeezed my mom's shoulder. "This is Amber," my mom said, grabbing Amber's hand. "She's been with us through the hardest times, and she took such good care of Christian, too."

Amber smiled, and tears welled up in her eyes. "Well, hello, honey. Is that really you? Are those your beautiful eyes?" Kristin wrapped her arm around Amber's shoulder, and they looked down on me, smiling like I was their long-lost sister.

The fact that I was awake was the big news that day, and hospital staff streamed in to marvel over me. Within an hour of waking up, I met my physical therapists Deb, Connie, and Kevin for the first time, although they'd been working on me for weeks. Other nurses and staff came in throughout the day, too. All of them were complete strangers to me, but they seemed to care very much that I was awake. "Well, there you are!" they said, or "You're awake!" and "Look at those green eyes!"

My mom hugged them as they smiled at me. She seemed intimately connected to each of them, and Page had hushed, knowing conversations with the nurses and therapists. I sensed their investment in me, and the connection they had forged with my family over the months I'd been asleep. Even though they were strangers to me, I felt embraced by kindness as I woke up in a completely different world. All I could do to join the celebration was blink at them silently with my green eyes.

When she came back, Page assured me again that the children were OK. My parents and siblings, along with Christian's parents, had all discussed what was best for our children and had agreed that I would want my sisters to care for them.

"Jesse and Lindsay would want you to know they were willing to take the children, Steph. They said you had asked them, and they would have done it, but it made more sense for Courtney and Lucy to take them and they were more than happy to."

Courtney and her husband, Christopher, had one baby boy, and Lucy and her husband, Andrew, didn't have children yet, although they'd been trying. The week of the crash, Lindsay had been just a few days from having her fourth baby. Another wave of nausea hit as I realized all that I had missed. Little Maria would be three months old already and I hadn't even met her, and Courtney's son was six months old.

"Lindsay is still helping out where she can, and Lisa and Meg and Katy and Suze"—my other sisters-in-law—"all help, too. Don't worry, Steph." Page assured me, "All the kids are together as much as possible, and they eat dinner together every night." I didn't doubt they were in the best possible hands.

Christian had been in a coma for five weeks, Page explained. He had been in the burn unit in the room next to mine, but had made enough progress to move to a rehabilitation hospital during the day and stay at his parents' house at night. He had broken his back, and his face, arms, and legs had been burned.

"His room was right next door to yours. When he woke up he came to see you as often as he could."

I felt myself shutting down again. I couldn't think about Christian or the children, or the pain of being apart from them threatened to overwhelm me. Being awake was such a feat in itself that pushing away additional unwelcome details quickly became a matter of survival. It was hard for me to wrap my mind around even the basic facts of my situation:

I'd been in the Arizona Burn Center in a medically induced coma for eleven weeks, a chemical sleep to spare me from the literally unbearable pain of my injuries.

My baby Nicholas had turned two. Claire had turned seven. Halloween had come and gone. Barack Obama had been elected president.

My body was covered in bandages. My fingernails were black. My burned lips were so swollen that I could see them in my peripheral vision. My head had been shaved so my scalp could be used for grafting skin.

I hadn't seen my husband in almost four months.

I had been on the brink of death, flatlining twice in the helicopter on the way to the hospital and a few more times once I'd arrived. I'd been in such critical condition that the doctors had performed my first surgery in my own bed because moving me to the OR was too risky.

Apparently, I had been in surgery as often as my body would allow—every few days to harvest and graft new skin. Second- and third-degree burns covered most of my body, meaning that not only had the surface of my skin been burned, but the underlying connective tissue was also damaged. The burned skin was dead and would rot or harbor dangerous infection if it, and the damaged tissue underneath, weren't completely scraped away in a process called debridement. The doctors scraped away my skin to save my life. It was a moment's consolation to learn that they had paused before they took the knife to my face, before they carved away the tissue that had defined my facial features, before they scraped my beauty away.

I slept restlessly for the next few days, drifting in and out of consciousness at all hours. Each time I woke, silent and immobile in a hospital bed, I stared at the ceiling while urgent questions pressed at all sides: *How could this have happened to me? Will I ever be able to move again? What's going to happen to my family?* I couldn't speak to ask my questions, but I was so terrified of the answers I wouldn't have asked them anyway. I'd try to lift my arms again, and my best efforts continued to be utterly futile. I may as well have been trying to lift a car. Panic staked a claim in my heart and gained frightening momentum. I did my best to push it away, but I was in a sinking ship, and for every hole I plugged, a leak burst open somewhere else. The water kept rising. And terrifying memories of the crash began to surface. Scattered images and sounds flashed through my mind. A wall of orange flames. The pungent smell of burning skin mixed with jet fuel. People shouting above the dull roar of fire. Dark black smoke, and a leaf above me in the sky.

Thirteen

··

L ittle by little, I was able to put the pieces of memories together until a clear picture of that day emerged.

We'd had a great day at the ranch in Bluewater. Christian had
been eager to show Doug the ranch he'd talked so much about, and
proudly showed his instructor what the Nielsons had built over so
many years.

Sometimes in life we find a version of ourselves in someone a
few years ahead of us. We know they're cut from our cloth when we
see the path they've taken and the choices they've made that shape
their lives. Doug had become that sort of role model and mentor for
Christian. Doug was a good person in all the ways that were meaningful and admirable to Christian. He was a loving husband and
father, a faithful member of the Church, a responsible and honor-
able person. He became much more than a flight instructor over
the months they'd spent together. Doug helped Christian achieve
his lifelong dream of flying, but the greatest gift he gave us was his
friendship.

At the ranch we visited the incredible garden that Russ drove all
the way from Mesa to tend every week. Then we took Doug out on
the four-wheelers to show him more of the property. After a couple
of hours, Doug said we'd better go so he could get back to his late-
afternoon flight students.

We stopped at the trading post to pick up my sought-after moccasins. I'd written about them on my blog and joked about setting a
new trend. "I'm bringing moccasins back—were they ever in?"

Christian and Doug teased me about coming all the way to Bluewater to buy shoes.

"You just wait." I laughed. "Soon everyone will have a pair of these babies."

We stopped at Subway on our way back to the airport in Grants, New Mexico, a twenty-minute drive from Bluewater. Doug and I filled cups with water at the soda fountain. "Wasn't that fun? What a beautiful ranch," he said, with his amiable, easy smile.

I smiled, too. Bluewater never failed to impress. "We're so glad that you could see it. What a great day."

At the airport Christian pulled the front seat forward so I could climb into the backseat of the two-door airplane, then he got in directly in front of me. As soon as we boarded, I put on my moccasins and the smell of new leather filled the cockpit. I loved my new shoes and couldn't wait to post a picture of them on my blog. After we took off in Grants we flew back over Bluewater for an aerial view of the ranch. Golden, the caretaker who lives on the ranch, was standing near the barn. He looked up and waved. He was small, just a dot on the vast prairie. It struck me as eerie, the distance between us, how he waved at us silently from the ground, how we drifted away from him in the sky.

We flew over isolated stretches of high desert prairie for about an hour before we reached the tiny town of St. Johns, Arizona, where we planned to land and refuel.

"I wish we had time to stop and see David and Carol," Christian said of a favorite aunt and uncle who lived in St. Johns.

"I'd love that. We need to do that next time."

Doug stayed with the airplane for refueling while Christian and I went into the airport to use the bathroom. When I came out, Christian was on the phone with his mom.

"We'll be home in about an hour and a half. Thanks, Mom. Love you."

"Is she doing OK?" I asked.

"She's doing great. Sounds like they've had a fun day at Grand-Mary's."

I climbed into the backseat again, and Christian and Doug boarded and assumed the controls. Listening to their discussion, I was reminded again how amazing it was that Christian was a pilot. They started the engine, and we taxied down the runway. The asphalt sped by as our speed increased. Whenever we flew, I loved that second when the airplane lifted off the ground, when I could feel weight defy gravity. The ground dropped away below us. Seconds later, though, I sensed something was wrong. Christian and Doug's normal cockpit dialogue seemed strained. A wave of worry rippled through my body, but I talked myself out of it, sure they had everything under control. But suddenly they were talking about obstructions ahead. I tensed, truly afraid, especially when I heard the frantic edge in Christian's voice.

He and Doug checked the instruments and gripped the controls. Nothing could have made the situation more frightening for me than to see that Christian and Doug were alarmed.

We're not crashing, I thought. *He won't let anything bad happen. We're not really going to crash.* But as I looked out the window at the houses that bordered the airport below us, we came closer and closer to their trim lawns and tidy flower beds. A split-second avalanche of fear buried me.

"No!" Christian shouted. Doug was flying the airplane, and Christian lifted out of his seat, as though he was trying to see what was ahead.

Suddenly, we were going down. I put my head between my legs and saw our four children, running and laughing around me, in bright sunshine, on green grass. I thought of Nicholas, and how he'd cried for me that morning. I felt sick to my stomach. *What have I done?*

And then we slammed into the ground. The airplane lurched like a roller coaster that had fallen off the rails. I heard the loud crack and scrape of metal against the ground and then a dull thud. Everything went dark.

I woke up surrounded by blinding flames. I squinted against the red and orange blaze. There was fire everywhere. The heat licked at my face, and I put my hands up to protect myself from the pain. The heat surged against my hands. I pulled them away to look for Christian and Doug. I couldn't see them, just a wall of flames and smoke.

My head throbbed. I reached for my seat belt but couldn't find it. Instinctively, I covered my face again with my hands. When I moved them to search for the buckle, the blistering heat scorched my face, blinding me. I couldn't find the seat belt. I didn't know where Christian and Doug were. In the smothering inferno, I smelled acrid, burning flesh. Terrified, I realized it was mine. I was burning alive. I screamed for help, louder than I had ever screamed before.

I don't want to die like this, I thought. *I don't want my family to remember me burning. I cannot die this way.*

I screamed and screamed. I couldn't get out. I couldn't find the seat belt and I didn't know how I would get to the door anyway. No one could hear my screams, and I knew it. I let go of the panic, the urgency. If I just relaxed, I realized, it would be over soon. It would hurt—terribly—and then it would be over. Just a couple of minutes and I'd be gone.

As soon as I gave myself up to that thought, someone arrived to help me. I knew it was my grandmother, but not by sight. I just knew, the way you recognize someone in a dream. It was my nana Aurora. I could tell she wasn't alone; I felt suddenly surrounded by people, but I didn't know them like I knew her. She guided my hand to the seat belt buckle and helped me unfasten it. Then she led my hand to the handle of the airplane door, and together we opened it. Somehow, I stumbled out.

"Roll," my nana whispered.

I fell to the ground and rolled. When the flames on my body were smothered, I became aware of people all around me, shouting above the roar of the fire. Nana was gone.

A man rushed to me and knelt. He cradled my head in both of his hands and put it in his lap. Above him the branches of a tree spread out over me, and I noticed the green leaves flutter against the blue sky.

"You're going to be all right," the man said.

The fire thundered in my ears. Scattered shouts of rescue and panic pierced the dull roar.

"It's going to blow!" someone yelled. "Get the hose!" The burning airplane popped and crackled dangerously near a propane tank and neighbors-turned-rescue-workers yelled back and forth above the noise. I braced myself for another explosion, but the roar of the fire held steady.

"My husband was in the airplane, too," I said to the stranger. "Can you see my husband?"

"There are two other men, one over here and one across the road."

"The other man is our friend. Are they OK? Are they . . ." My voice trailed off. I couldn't ask if they were dead.

"They're both alive. They're hurt, but they're both alive."

Thank you. My relief and gratitude were suddenly overtaken by unbearable pain that tore through my thoughts and for a second drowned out the deafening roar of the fire. I gasped for breath. Suddenly, my body stung as if hot irons had been pressed against my bare arms and neck. My face felt tight, as if my skin had shrunk two sizes in the last few minutes. My body was still smoldering, radiating prickly heat, and my jeans trapped the heat against my legs with searing pressure.

I tried to pull my pants off, but my hands were useless. In confusion, I held them up to my face to see why they weren't working.

Hand-shaped flaps of skin hung from my wrists. I could see the bones of my fingers. I stared in disbelief. *Those couldn't be my hands.*

"You're going to be all right," the man who held my head repeated. But I saw the panic in his eyes.

I quickly put my hands back at my sides. My heart raced, and I cried out over his reassuring words. "No," I sobbed. "What happened to me? What is the matter with me?" I cried to the leaves in the tree. "What happened to me?"

"Look at me," the stranger said, pulling my focus away from the horrible truth. "What's your name?"

"Stephanie." I stared at a leaf above me. It was so removed from the chaos. I wished I were the leaf, gently waving in the faint breeze, serene and calm on a Saturday afternoon.

"I don't want to be here," I whimpered. "I don't want to be here. I want to go home and make dinner for my children." How could I make this go away? *Go away*, I thought, *go away. Heavenly Father, please make this go away.*

"My mom is going to kill me," I said. "She didn't want me to fly. She hated flying. This is going to break her heart."

"Stephanie"—he looked at me intently—"how many kids do you have? How old are they?"

"I have four children." Even as I answered, I realized he was trying to distract me. *This is what they do in movies, and I'm falling for it.* But answering was harder than I expected. "Four children. Um, Claire is . . . is six, and Jane is five. Jane is five . . . and Oliver, um, he's . . . three. And Nicholas." I started to cry again as I pictured Nicholas clinging to me that morning, begging me not to leave. "My baby Nicholas," I sobbed, "is almost two. He's so little, and he asked me not to leave this morning. He asked me not to leave."

I shut my eyes tight against all of it, willing every horrendous part of this away from me, and from Christian and our children, but the pain and the noise crowded into my thoughts. When I opened my eyes, the leaf was still there, waving gently in the breeze.

"You're going to be OK," the stranger said again, this time with more conviction. I stared at the leaf, and a flutter of hope beat in my heart. I took a breath. Maybe it was true.

"Thank you for being here," I said to the man who held my head. "You don't have to stay."

"I'm going to stay," he said. "I'm going to be right here."

More and more people gathered around. I felt guilty we'd ruined their day like this. A woman came over to me with a blanket. "It's only been a few minutes, and half the town must be here," she said. She kindly held up the blanket between me and the growing crowd.

Another man hurried over. "Are you LDS?" the man asked. "Would you like me to give you a blessing?"

"Yes," I said. "Yes, please." This was the kind of story I'd heard about all my life, a tense and hurried priesthood blessing in the midst of an emergency. It struck me that this was real, and that I was the emergency. He called over someone else who must have also been a member of the Church, and they knelt beside me.

"My name is Stephanie Nielson," I said, knowing they would use my name for the blessing. I felt comforted before they even put their hands on my head. Of all the ways I needed help, I needed God more than anything. I needed reassurance that the glimmer of hope I had felt was real. I was so thankful that a stranger in a strange town could offer me something so familiar and hopeful. It's what my dad and Christian would have done, I realized, and I thought how grateful they would be for this man's willingness to help me.

"Stephanie Nielson," the man began the blessing, "with the power of the priesthood which we hold, we lay our hands upon your head and give you a blessing . . ."

A rush of peace consoled me while he spoke. My heart quieted and my mind relaxed in the familiar security of faith in a loving God. The men closed the blessing, "In the name of Jesus Christ, amen."

"Thank you," I whispered. "Thank you so much."

The men stood to leave, and suddenly a woman had taken their place, kneeling next to the man who held my head.

"Stephanie, I'm here," she said. I instantly recognized her as Christian's aunt Carol, but I would have just as easily believed she was an angel. Her familiar, loving face seemed to glow in contrast to the confusion and noise around me. "Christian asked someone to call us, and we came right over. David is with Christian and Christian's OK—he's just across the street. You're going to be OK, too. All right? You're going to be OK, Stephanie. I'm going to go tell Christian that I talked to you, and I'll be right back."

"OK. Please come back." Her familiar face was such a comfort.

"I'll be back," she called as she ran off to Christian.

I looked at the man holding my head again. The pain I felt obliterated my inhibitions. "Will you please help me take off my pants?" I asked him. "They hurt so bad. Please help me take them off."

"We just have to wait for the ambulance to get here," he said. "We shouldn't move you at all, and they'll be here soon. Just a few more minutes, OK? I can hear the sirens. They're coming."

The thought of an ambulance arriving brought me comfort. "OK," I agreed, "but can I please have a drink? Can someone just get me a drink?" I started to cry again and caught the eye of the woman holding the blanket. "Couldn't someone please just get me a drink?" I pleaded.

She looked at the man who held my head, as if to nudge him to answer. He apologized again. "I'm so sorry, but we just need to wait for the ambulance."

Carol rushed back over and knelt beside me. "Christian was so worried about you, honey, but I told him you're here and you're going to be OK. He's in some pain. I think he hurt his back, but he's going to be OK."

"Thank you, Carol," I said through tears. "I'm so sorry. I'm sorry you had to come, I'm sorry we're here like this," I bawled.

"Oh, honey, no, no, no," Carol said. "Don't you worry about us. We're here to help you. We love you so much."

The pain was so unbearable, drowning out just about everything else. I stared up at the leaf again as the sirens approached. In just minutes, it had become an anchor, a symbol of my hope. But as the sirens wailed closer and closer, a breeze stirred the jet-black smoke that poured from the wreckage. A cloud of smoke blew over the tree. My leaf was gone.

"I don't want to be here," I cried again. "I don't want to be here."

Sirens wailed and medics swarmed around me. Carol helped the woman with the blanket shield me as they cut off my shirt to see my wounds. They covered me with a sheet and lifted me onto the stretcher. The stranger kept his hands under my head all the way to the ambulance.

"Thank you so much," I said. "Thank you for being here. Thank you."

"You're welcome. It's OK," he said. "You're going to be OK." He stepped back while I was loaded into the ambulance, and I never saw or heard from him again.

"Christian will go in the other ambulance," Carol called. "He'll be right behind you, sweetheart."

A minute later, the EMTs loaded Doug in next to me and closed the ambulance doors, muffling the commotion outside. I was shocked to see Doug's skin. It was charred—ashen and black like charcoal. It was frightening to look at and all the more surprising when he said, "Stephanie, we did it. We made it!" just as positive and upbeat as he had ever been.

The ambulance lurched forward, siren wailing, as the EMTs hovered around us, prepping us for sedation. "We need to get you on some pain medication. We'll put an IV in right now."

"It really hurts," I moaned to Doug.

He was triumphant. "But we made it. We're going home." Then he asked, "Can someone call my afternoon students and let them know I've got to cancel for today?" One EMT tried to make Doug comfortable while the other searched my body for a viable vein for an IV.

I saw a worried look pass between the EMTs as they continued to look for a vein that could support an IV. One of them shook his head. The driver spoke quickly into a CB radio, a string of medical language I don't remember, except for "We've got a fifty percent and an eighty percent." I didn't know what it meant, but I knew he was referring to Doug and me. It didn't sound good.

"Try her feet," the EMT working on Doug said, and my EMT slipped off my moccasins.

"Perfect," he said. "Her feet are in perfect shape."

I tensed at the piercing stab in my left foot, and then seconds later everything was dark.

Fourteen

I woke up almost three months later to a new life that felt as empty and restless as a fitful dream. I remember distinctly that first day of consciousness—November 5, 2008—but the next few days are a blur. I slept and woke erratically as medication wore off and then was adjusted to manage my constant pain. I had no sense of day or time. As far as I knew, I had been asleep for twenty minutes or two hours. It may have been 2008 or 2020. I had no capacity to tell the difference. And it didn't seem to matter anyway. My life was dictated by the mandates of doctors and nurses, who attended to me constantly, whether I wanted them to or not, whether I was awake or asleep.

Sleep was a blessed escape, not just at night but anytime. It was often medically induced and therefore unavoidable, but I also often willed myself to sleep as a way to cope. If reality was too much, if the waters were too deep, I could just close my eyes and drift away. Often I woke in the middle of the night—alone, after visiting hours. The hospital was eerily quiet, and the stillness around me bred absolute terror. I could avoid it in daylight, surrounded by visitors and the bustle of the hospital. But at night, images would flash through my head, endlessly cycling like the ticker at the bottom of the news screen. I saw the wall of flames I'd woken up to in the airplane. I saw Doug's charred skin and the thick dark smoke layer the sky. I felt the helplessness of screaming and knowing no one heard me. I smelled my own flesh burning.

Those unwanted memories were a springboard for other dark thoughts. I imagined a fire raging through the hospital, or a terrible flood sweeping through the halls. Trapped in bed, I would never be able to escape. The burn center was in downtown Phoenix, and I pictured a crime spree right there in the hospital, dangerous gunmen coming to take my life.

Outside my window the blades of the Life Flight helicopter would whir as it touched down and took off. They sounded dangerously close, and I imagined the helicopter crashing through my wall, bursting into flames. I wouldn't even be able to cover my head against the debris.

Sometimes I dreamed I was in a video game. The halls of the

hospital were complicated levels to navigate, the doctors and nurses enemies to defeat. I was trapped in the same maze of halls and obstacles again and again. I could never finish the level. I could never find a way to escape.

I was half dreaming and in the firm grip of narcotics, but to me these thoughts were as real as any memory I had of walking or dancing or being held in Christian's arms. They all seemed appallingly possible and ended with a question so horrifying it took my breath away: *What would I do?* The answer was always the same: *nothing.* I could do nothing. I was powerless. Eventually, as these scenarios played in my head, my heart would race, and the beeping monitors would get the nurses' attention. Someone would rush in to increase my dosage, and I'd slip away into darkness again.

But though sleep brought great relief, I always paid a price when I woke up. The entire time I was conscious in the Arizona Burn Center, I never once remembered where I was when I woke up. Over and over again, I would jar awake, and the same confusing questions surfaced. I knew I should know where I was, but I didn't. I stared at the ceiling, praying, *Please, Heavenly Father, help me remember where I am.*

And then all at once, the leaks burst and I was sinking, drowning in the awful reality, wishing I could forget again.

There had been an accident.

I almost died.

I was burned over 80 percent of my body.

I couldn't move.

Our children were far away, and Christian was hurt, too.

I wondered how badly he'd been hurt. Page had told me he'd been in a coma, too, so I knew his injuries must have been serious. He was better now, but I didn't know how to gauge what "better" meant. He still needed medical help, and he wasn't well enough to be at home with our children. I thought about how dramatically our lives had changed. I thought of sitting with him on our back porch swing after dinner, watching the children play in the yard. As I stared at the hospital ceiling, I knew that part of our life was over forever.

When Christian came to see me for the first time after I'd woken up, it was during those early days when I drifted in and out of consciousness. I don't recall seeing him as much as *knowing* he was there, like the kind of dream you only half-remember, more sure of the feelings than the circumstances. He sat by my bed. I sensed that he was stronger than I was, that he could move and walk on his own. Hearing his voice had made me feel comfortable and safe. I loved feeling him near. But when I woke up, he was gone.

My mom was sitting next to me. "Christian was here, Stephy," she said. "He said to tell you he loves you. He's really looking forward to seeing you again."

To know he'd just been there was comforting. The memory of his voice was peaceful, but I was nervous to have him come back. Our lives were ruined. How would we ever manage to be happy again? I was afraid to know the truth about his injuries—maybe they would be even worse than I imagined. I didn't know what we'd say to each other. The accident created such a multitude of consequences for me and for the people I loved. There were a million unbearable fears about Christian, my children, my own injured body. For the time being it was easier for me to trust in the care of my parents and siblings and push thoughts of Christian away.

My mom had put her busy life in Provo on hold to be with me as much as she could. She was on the Provo City Council at the time of my accident, and she rearranged her full schedule and responsibilities so that she could be with me in the hospital. It was as if I were a child again, under her watchful care, and I basked in her constant, unwavering attention. Like she always had, she believed in me and blazed a trail of faith that I tried to follow.

Page had also been with me as much as possible ever since the accident. She was a registered nurse, and although she hadn't been working as a nurse at the time of my accident, my doctors had allowed her to be involved in my care. She made arrangements for her family of eight to be taken care of for weeks at a time as she stayed by my side. At one point she even brought all of them to Arizona with her so she could be near them but still help me. Page translated and shared what the doctors said in terms our family could understand and cling to. She filled in the gaps and softened the blows. She lobbied for my comfort and did everything she could to help me.

All my siblings and their spouses had visited me while I was in a coma. Knowing they had all been at my side, whispering in my ear, blessing me, probably teasing me, too, was incredibly comforting.

"Stevie left something for you, sweetie. He wanted to be sure you got it." My mom pulled a pack of Big Red gum from the bedside table drawer. It was the kind he'd always had in his college backpack when I was a little girl.

"He sat with you," she said, "and talked to you about how you used to watch *Family Ties* together. He said you would remember."

I did.

When he came down from Utah to see me, Stevie had slept at our house with our dog Jimmy, even though he's allergic to animals.

"He didn't mind Jimmy at all, he just wanted to be where you had been. He loves you so much," my mother said. She paused and caught her breath. "We all do."

I had always been grateful for my large family, but more so now than ever. My brothers and sisters believed in me, and loved me, and that nudged me forward when I faced the first painful steps of this journey.

"Steph," Page said, "we wanted to talk to you about moving to the University of Utah Hospital." It was in Salt Lake, just forty-five minutes north of Provo. It was another excellent burn unit, where the chief surgeon, Dr. Saffle, was known as "the father of burns" because he had developed so many of the techniques used in burn care. At the U of U Hospital, I would be closer to our children and the hub of my siblings—my parents and all but one of my siblings and their families still lived in Provo. "What do you think, Steph? Do you want to go to Utah?"

I widened my eyes. *Utah. Home.* An unrealistic hope was born almost instantly: in Utah everything would be better.

While I lay in a coma, Page and her husband, Vance, had even bought a house in Provo for Christian and me to live in once we were well enough to go home.

"It's a white brick house in Mom and Dad's neighborhood, Steph, and it has an apple tree next to the bedroom window and a great backyard. The mountains are so close—it's an amazing view. It needs a lot of work, but we're going to fix it up for you."

I was immediately thankful for the idea of a new home and Page and Vance's generosity. I thought about our lovely home in Arizona—the orange trees and our darling backyard tree house. It felt like a distant memory, and I realized I could never go back there, back to that house, crammed with reminders of the beautiful life that had slipped through our fingers.

Page continued, "You'll be right by Mom and Dad and Courtney, and so close to the rest of us. And it's three houses from Old Willow Lane. I knew you would love that."

I did. I had played on Old Willow, a wooded lane fenced off from cars, as a little girl. It was sacred childhood ground. Living near it would be nice. I pictured myself, strong and healthy, taking the children there. Old Willow, and an apple tree. The mountains and a great backyard. I forgot about being nervous to see Christian. By the time we got to Provo, all this would be behind us. We'd have a fresh start together. I pictured a healthy, happy life in Provo, since that's what life in Provo had always been for me.

Yet any sense of hope was fleeting in the face of the grim reality of hospital life, easily chased away by things like the excruciating daily torture of physical therapy.

Every afternoon the same physical therapist came to my room to work on me, flexing my emaciated muscles and stretching my skin. He did his job, and did it well. To me, it felt like my skin was being pulled within an inch of tearing, like my limbs were being ripped right off. I associated him with unbearable pain and therefore came to see this very nice man as dangerously menacing.

One afternoon he arrived when I was alone with my dad, who was visiting for the first time since I'd been awake. When the physical therapist came in for my daily torture, my dad was telling me about the BYU football season and how the snow had stuck in the valley for the first time that year. My dad stood to leave the room. I still couldn't speak but wanted so desperately to plead, "Daddy! Please don't leave me! Don't leave me with this strange man!"

The physical therapist spoke to me kindly. I know he did. But his intentions twisted in my head, and the agony made me irrational. "Stephanie, I'm going to lift your arm and slide this foam block underneath. We'll attach it with Velcro, like this." He talked while he looped the Velcro around my arm. "We'll do it on your other arm, too. It's called the butterfly, and we'll keep it on for a while. It will stretch the muscles in your arms."

This man is touching me. He should not be touching me, I screamed in my head. When he was finished, my arms rested on the blocks, extended just inches from where they had lain at my sides, but it felt like they were being sliced by knives at the shoulder.

He then went to work bending and straightening each of my fingers. It felt like he was using unreasonable force, but when I looked, each finger was being moved the tiniest fraction of an inch. "You've been asleep for a long time," he said. "I wonder about where you've been, Stephanie. You know, I read a lot about near-death experiences, and people who say they've been to heaven." I cringed as he bent each stiff finger. "I think you've been there, too." He looked at me curiously. "Is that where you've been? Have you been in heaven?"

His words stirred something inside me. I thought carefully about what he asked. *Had I been somewhere else while I slept?* A faint memory emerged, and grew stronger. I did remember being somewhere else. He was right. The thought was peaceful at first, as serene as a sunrise. I had been with Nana Aurora, not only at the crash but somewhere else, too. Somewhere far away, somewhere beautiful.

Heaven. Was that where I'd been? I had seen Christian there, and Doug. I had talked for ages with Nana. I felt warm and light remembering it. I wanted to tell the therapist what I remembered, but I couldn't speak. And then suddenly the thought frightened me. *I had almost died.* I knew what heaven was like because I had almost died; because I had almost lost the life I wanted so much to live. I had expected the physical discomfort he brought, but I didn't expect he would unearth such upsetting memories and feelings. I had a desperate urge to push the therapist away, to scream at him if only I were able to speak. *LEAVE ME ALONE! Get out of here with your blocks and straps and stretchers. I'll get better without you.*

I kept thinking about how close Christian and I had come to dying. Because Christian and I had wanted an exciting day-trip in an airplane, because we'd chased this dream of flying, I had almost left my children without a mother. As it was, they barely had one anyway. I was certainly of no use to them now. So while the memory of heaven was perfectly peaceful, it was tangled in stubborn knots with the fact that I had ruined my life and deeply hurt my children. Alone with my thoughts, I had come to many bleak conclusions, but none was more certain than this: I had done something awful—unforgivable—to my sweet and innocent children.

I desperately missed each of them, and it was painful to think about them. I had let them down immeasurably, unfathomably. I had told them I'd be back for dinner, and I hadn't come home. I was so thankful that my sisters were caring for my children, but I couldn't control the flood of anguish at not being able to hold them or feed them myself. It wasn't my sisters' responsibility. It was my responsibility, and I couldn't live up to it.

I ached to think how Nicholas had clung to me when I left him with Mary, how I'd impatiently put him down and hurried away. Oh, if only I'd known what I was hurrying into. I pictured him crying in his crib, alone, at night. Did he wonder where I was and why I didn't come?

And what about Ollie? Who would know about our make-believe games, where I was the captured prisoner? Would they know the game could change at any moment, and I became the princess he would save? I couldn't think of our boys without crying.

Of course I worried over our girls, too, and ached for them, but I somehow knew they would be OK. I remembered watching them from across the parking lot on their first day of school in Mesa just days before the crash. Claire had grabbed Jane's hand and led her to her new teacher. I knew they'd be all right as long as they kept holding hands, even if school was in Utah now.

I thought back to our school shopping trip the week before the crash. The girls loved trying on clothes. Claire was excited by whatever she saw, smartly matching bold colors, plaids, and patterned tights. Jane was more particular in her choices and sought out the exact pair of appliqué jeans she had in mind, and then searched for the perfect headband to match. I had smiled at how their choices matched their personalities, how their individual tastes were developing. Now I ached to picture them twirling in the dressing room mirrors, beaming with excitement over their new clothes.

Would they remember me? Would they remember school shopping or making our paper doll houses or chalk painting on the sidewalk? Would they remember that once their mother was lively and beautiful? And what about the other children we had planned to have? Would I be able to have more children? We had been planning to try again this fall; instead I'd spent it lying in a hospital bed.

I'd been awake, and silent, for four long days before the doctors were able to remove the breathing tube from my throat. When my trach came out, my vocal cords were weak. My throat felt rough and raw. I could only manage a hoarse whisper.

Page asked, "What was that word you were saying the other day? The one we couldn't guess?"

I had mouthed it over and over. "Thirsty?" they wondered. "Fill me?" "Will me?" In frustration, I had given up.

"Guilty," I whispered. "I feel guilty."

T*he next day, I woke up from a nap and was surprised to see a strange man in the corner of my room.* My first thought was to wonder if anyone else could see him. Was he real? He was painfully skinny, and his head was shaved. He had a white plastic shell around his torso. The right side of his face was red and raw. Bloody scabs covered his cheeks. He scared me, and I couldn't understand why he would be in my room. I panicked as he started toward me with slow, labored steps. *What is happening?*

As the man got closer I realized it was Christian. My chest tightened. He wore the pajamas bottoms I'd given him for Christmas the previous year, but he'd lost so much weight they hung loose on his skinny frame. With his bloody face and shaved head, he looked like he belonged in a horror movie.

"Hi, darling. How are you today?" He gently touched my arm.

I looked away, stunned by his appearance. "I'm awful," I whispered, my vocal cords still weak. "How are you?"

"So happy to see you, so happy you're awake." Christian's voice cracked and tears welled in his eyes.

I couldn't say anything. His face scared me, not just because it was frightening—although it was. I was more shaken and sickened to realize that I must look worse, so much worse. Of course I had known my face was burned, but I hadn't had a sense of how horribly disfigured it would be until I saw him. If I could barely look at my husband, how would I ever face looking at myself? Distress and agony pressed hard around me. If I shared even a hint of what I was feeling, I knew the floodgates would come crashing down and I would certainly drown.

Christian gently touched my head and then my arms, but I didn't look at him.

"Stephanie, I'm sorry for what has happened to us. I can't express how sorry I am."

I stared at the white board.

"I thought you were right behind me when I got out of the airplane. I thought you were right there. I'm so sorry. I wanted to save you."

I shook my head. "It's OK. This isn't your fault." I didn't blame Christian, I didn't want him to feel sorry. I wasn't angry with him.

Mainly, I didn't want to talk about it.

"Nice pajamas," I said.

He looked down at the floor. "Thanks."

I shut my eyes tight. In spite of myself, tears seeped out. I felt the world get smaller again. I willed it all away—the ache in my heart, the wounds on his face, any memory that we had once been so happy.

I kept my eyes closed and fell asleep.

I couldn't bear to see Christian again, and I asked Page to keep him out of my room. His scars, and all that they meant, scared me. Being near him shook my already unsteady footing in this new world. He was a physical reminder of the accident. He was proof of what I had been trying to avoid with everything I had: we had in fact crashed in a blazing inferno and Doug had died, and we were hurt and scarred, and our children were in Utah . . . and the painful cycle of thoughts launched again.

The next day I heard Page's muffled voice out in the hall and then, louder, I heard Christian's agitated response. "What do you mean I can't go in? She's my wife, Page. I want to see her."

On some level I realized how selfish it was to keep him out of my room. I knew I was ignoring his needs and his emotional pain. I was sorry for that, but not sorry enough to change my mind.

Fifteen

Seeing Christian's wounds—and considering the reality of my own—had left me reeling, devastated to my core. The emotional weight of it was crushing, but I chose not to share it with anyone. I didn't know where I'd even begin, but more than that, I didn't want to share how vulnerable I felt. I had already been stripped of any physical independence; I wanted to prove that I could handle the emotional challenges on my own. It was a lonely choice, and the beginning of a lonely road.

Since my burned skin had been scraped off, new skin was being grafted on in sections, like a gruesome patchwork quilt. Temporary grafts used pig skin or cadaver skin, but permanent grafts require the patient's own skin, so the surgeons harvested my healthy skin where they could. My abdomen, chest, upper legs, and back had miraculously not been burned, and they'd also used skin from my scalp. But I still had so little healthy skin, the doctors had to manufacture more. They would harvest tiny samples of healthy skin and send them to a lab in Boston, which then grew a genetic match. It took three weeks to grow a rectangle five centimeters by ten centimeters, at which point it was flown back to Phoenix, where it was stapled on. Once the new skin had taken and begun to grow on its own on my body, the staples were removed. It was a delicate, painstaking process, and even the smallest infection could compromise the weeks of progress the doctors had made with my new skin, so keeping the wounds clean was vital.

After each grafting surgery my wounds were wrapped in white gauze bandages. Because of the potential for a disastrous infection, the bandages had to be changed twice a day and the fresh wounds scrubbed clean with an agonizing solution of saline and peroxide. If the new skin hadn't attached, the unsuccessful grafts had to be scrubbed off, the wounds kept open and clean until the next time in the operating room.

The process was excruciating—one of the major downsides of being conscious—and the pain started the moment they bent my limbs and joints to move my body. But, then again, I learned that I was lucky to even have limbs. During my first days in the hospital, most of the skin on my body had been scraped raw and was thus dangerously susceptible to infection. The doctors had warned my family that amputation of my arms and legs was likely, if enough new skin didn't arrive from the lab fast enough. They lived with this grim possibility for several days until it was clear that the new skin had taken and was infection free. Sometimes, when I thought things couldn't get any worse for me, I would remember the blessing of having arms and legs. They were in terrible shape, but I was grateful I had them. My future and prognosis would be infinitely more devastating if I'd lost my arms and legs. I tried to keep this in mind as the nurses worked.

A team of burn techs who specialized in dressing changes worked quickly, but the process still took almost two hours. Sometimes my dressing changes took place in my own bed or often in a special room down the hall, with a tub where the bandages could soak before they were removed and where my whole body could be submerged and scrubbed. I always closed my eyes against the onslaught of pain or stared intently at the ceiling tiles, breathing deeply through the agony. When the nurses were done, I was essentially raw—but clean—and then dressed in sterile bandages. Until next time. Which always came sooner than I wanted.

Page was occasionally allowed to stay with me for dressing changes. Because they were so painful, she brought along anything she could think of to help me relax, including a CD player with my favorite Mindy Gledhill CD and essential oils to rub on my temples. She sat near my head and did her best to soothe me while the nurses worked.

When they pulled off the bandages, it was like having duct tape ripped off my raw wounds, taking my thin layer of skin with it. I writhed and moaned. Page stroked my forehead and rubbed my temples. "I know it hurts, Steph, I know."

They pulled another bandage off. Searing, white-hot pain rocketed through my body, taking my breath away. "I'm dying," I cried. "I'm dying now."

"No, honey, you're not going to die." The nurses reassured

me, but their voices sounded far away. The pain was so intense I passed out. When I came to a few minutes later, Page and the nurses had stepped aside. I was alone on the table, naked.

I looked at my arms and discovered why it had been so difficult to lift them. They were emaciated—nothing but skin and bone. I also noticed they were covered in what must be some kind of burn netting, a strange medical-grade fabric with an uneven texture and a bizarre pattern of purple and pink swirls. I looked down at my legs and noticed they were also wrapped in the strange fabric. Page came back to soothe me, and the nurses returned and continued the dressing change. I watched them pour water over my legs and I noticed I could feel it, even though they hadn't removed the tights. In shock, I realized those drastic purple spirals laced with bright pink weren't tights at all. They were the scars on my skin. I was overcome with horror—the shock sucked the air out of my body. I tried to catch my breath. Devastated, I looked again. *That is my skin.* I had feared how grotesquely scarred I would look, especially after seeing Christian. But the reality surpassed my worst fears. I took fast, shallow breaths to combat the rise of nausea. Everything hurt worse than it had the second before. I wished the nurses would stop touching me, and that I could slip back into the darkness forever.

I was still trying to grasp the repulsive idea that my skin was a mess of bright swirled scars, uneven and discolored—horribly ugly— when Christian came to visit me that afternoon.

Again, I asked Page to not let him in. I heard him shout at her from the hall, "Page, don't do this. Please don't keep me out!"

My nurse Kristin was in the room with me, and we listened anxiously. I couldn't make out Page's response, but Christian was loud and clear. "I'm her husband, Page," he yelled. "I want to see her."

I prayed that Page could keep him out. I just couldn't bear to see him, now that I knew what I looked like.

"This is hard, isn't it?" Kristin said.

I nodded.

"You and Christian have a beautiful family."

"Thanks."

All the nurses knew about our family, not just because we had both been patients, but also because Christian's youngest sister, Elizabeth, had covered the walls of my room with photographs of our family and excerpts from my blog. The nurses had all talked about how cute our children were, and how they could see we had a beautiful life together. But before I woke up, the fire marshal saw the room plastered with papers and photographs, and he insisted that they be removed. It was, quite ironically, a fire hazard. Thank heavens. I wouldn't have wanted to wake up to all those images of the life I used to have.

Kristin looked toward the hall, where Christian and Page were talking. "He loved to come and visit you. He just wanted to be near you. And I could tell you liked being near him, too." She smiled. "Do you want to know how we knew?"

Kristin told me about the first time Christian had visited me. I was still deep in a coma, and he had been awake for just a few days. We were in rooms 1 and 2, the most critical rooms in the Burn Center. He was barely able to move, but the nurses helped him into a wheelchair and brought him to my room, where I lay sleeping, covered in white bandages. They had wheeled him in and then left us alone.

Outside the room, doctors, nurses, and our families watched as he lifted his burned hand to mine. He spoke to me and gave me a blessing. My heart rate spiked, enough that the nurses had to come in and ask Christian not to touch me.

He pulled his hand away and just talked to me, but my heart raced again, so fast and so hard that the nurses returned and asked Christian to say his good-byes for the day.

"We'd never seen anything like that, nothing even close," Kristin said. "*That* is true love."

I'd always known that Christian and I had something special, and this story reminded me of what we shared. I realized how difficult it must be for him to be shut out of my room, so when he tried to visit again a few hours later I let him in, although my heart was racing.

"I know you didn't want to see me earlier," Christian said. "But I'm here for you. I want to help, Stephanie. I love you."

I didn't look at him. "Everything has changed." I wanted to speak forcefully, but all I could manage was a fierce whisper. It would be weeks before my vocal cords would heal completely.

"Some things haven't. I love you. That hasn't changed." Christian was firm. "That is not going to change. And we're in this together. We're going to get better."

Even though the alternative to getting better was languishing in the hospital for the rest of my life, it seemed more realistic to me than getting better. And on some level, I still had trouble believing that Christian could still love this weak, ugly, fragile version of myself. I tried to change the subject.

"The nurses are nice, huh?"

"Yeah, they're really great, Stephanie, but I don't want to talk about the nurses. I want you to know that I love you, and we're going to get through this."

"OK," I said. I just couldn't share his optimism though. "You don't have to stay. Maybe you should go take care of our children instead of staying here with me."

"Stephanie, I'm not going anywhere. Our kids are OK. I am here to help you."

With characteristic persistence, Christian was back the next day and the next and the next with the same message of hope and commitment each time. As he hobbled into my room day after day, wearing another pair of baggy pajama bottoms and his turtle shell back brace, assuring me again and again that he loved me and that he would always love me, it began to dawn on me that we were bound by more than a plane crash. It was the eight years we had spent together before the crash that mattered.

"Stephanie, you're the first thing I thought of when I woke up. I wanted to jump out of bed and see you."

I forced a smile. "Thanks. Not much to see, though, huh?"

"You're exactly what I need to see, Steph. *You.*"

He leaned closer, and with his eyes just inches from mine, the certainty of his words struck me with full force. Inexplicably it was as if a switch had flipped, and I suddenly believed him. Feeling our bond again, and remembering I could trust and rely on him, and how good we were together, was like taking my first deep breath in weeks.

"You really think we can do it?" I asked. I knew he could, but I was worried I couldn't.

"Yes, I really think so. I know we can."

For now, that overall conviction was enough. I was still too nervous to delve any deeper into specifics about our children, the accident, Doug, my injuries. There was something I was curious about though.

"Christian, do you remember being somewhere together . . . when we were asleep?" I asked tentatively.

"What do you mean?"

"Well, I remember seeing you, being with you—not in the hospital. Other places. Once we were in a field, walking and holding hands and you said you had to go. I didn't want you to. I begged you not to leave me, but you said you had to go to get ready for when I came back. I didn't understand what you meant, but you seemed to get it. I think you had to come back to your body because it was time for you to wake up. I was so sad you had to leave. I waved good-bye and then you were gone."

"I don't remember, Steph, but I'm glad we were together. That sounds nice."

Christian reached over and rubbed the back of my neck where I wasn't burned.

I shivered as his touch sent a jolt of memory through me—how much I'd loved feeling his skin against mine.

"Sorry, did I hurt you, Steph?"

"No, it feels good." I closed my eyes, not to shut out the pain, but to savor the moment.

"Ever since I woke up, nights have been the worst," he said after a moment.

"For me, too," I agreed. "Actually, everything's been the worst, but nights are really bad."

Christian laughed drily. "Yeah, skin grafts, a catheter, dressing changes, a ventilator, feeding tubes, a broken back. Those were pretty bad."

"Don't forget physical therapy," I added.

"But nights were so awful. I was having these terrible dreams. I'd wake up screaming and sweating. I've never had a dream feel so real. At the rehab hospital they let my mom come and stay with me. She slept next to my bed, and the nightmares went away."

"That's sweet," I said. "I'm so glad she was there for you." I meant it, but fear snaked its way into my heart. My husband, once the strong and capable provider for our family with his great job and pilot's license, was so rocked by our crash that he needed his mother to sleep with him.

"Even when I started sleeping at my parents' house, she stayed with me. The nightmares totally went away when she was close. And then when Ollie came to visit, he slept with me. He kept them away, too."

I was struck by the complete role reversal. Our three-year-old son was protecting his father from nightmares.

E*motionally and physically, we had such a long way to go.* I was getting stronger every day, but the progress was slow. About a week after I woke up, the nurses and physical therapists helped me sit up in bed. It was a painful milestone. Everything about it hurt—my stiff joints resisted motion, my raw skin stung at every movement, and my shriveled muscles strained. The nurses slowly pulled me to a sitting position and kept me propped up with their arms, calling out encouraging words.

Dr. Caruso, the chief burn surgeon who had worked on me from the very day of the accident, was walking down the hall. He noticed the commotion in my room and stopped by. His big frame filled the doorway, and he stood there, staring at me with his hands in the pockets of his white lab coat. He didn't say a word, just watched, and then shook his head a little and smiled before he walked away.

"Did you see that?" a nurse asked, and the therapists chuckled. "He can't believe it. He can't believe you're sitting up, Stephanie. Oh, you've come such a long way!"

The staff cheered for me, but I was in so much pain I only had room for a fleeting, triumphant thought: *I did it.*

Aside from sitting up, my other big accomplishment after seven days of being awake, and many grueling hours of physical therapy, was being able to move my fingers and raise my arms. But there was always another hurdle just ahead. My next goal was to lift both arms and touch my index fingers together in front of me. The physical therapist asked my mother to work on that with me. It sounded laughably simple.

As if they were made of lead, I lifted both arms with tremendous effort and brought them together in front of me. I expected my fingers to touch, tip to tip, just like I had imagined they would when the therapist described it. But my fingers didn't touch, and in fact missed each other by several inches. I watched it happen but still questioned it. *Why can't I do this?* I had a body that obeyed my wishes, a body that ran miles at a time and taught yoga, that carried children, folded laundry, made dinner. *At least I used to.*

My mom smiled at me and nodded, as if she'd known that would happen. "Don't worry," she said. "We'll get that figured out." And just like that, there was hope. I couldn't do it now, but we'd get it figured out. It became one more skill to add to the list. Someday, I would: feed myself, walk, go to the bathroom, bend my arms, sing, pick up my children, take a shower, and touch my index fingers together. Sometimes the enormity of the list got the better of me. Those were moments I sobbed inconsolably. But when my mother looked at me and nodded like that, I could handle the list. I could face item after item, as long as she was there to say, "Don't worry. We'll get that figured out."

Sixteen

I had been in and out of skin graft surgery several times in the week I'd been awake. Before each surgery the doctors would come into my room and explain the next procedure. I didn't listen very carefully. I trusted them, and knew it wouldn't matter anyway if I objected. They were the doctors, in charge of this shell of my body in a way I simply wasn't. I had no sense of how this or that surgery would benefit me in the long run. I continued to have a very limited belief in the future anyway. Everything was right here, right now. What I did understand was that, whatever they did, it would hurt. That was the bottom line for me—when I woke up, it would hurt just the same, whether I knew what was coming or not.

So I hadn't really been paying attention when the chief plastic surgeon, Dr. Lettieri, whom I liked and trusted, had talked about fixing the skin around my eyes, which was so tight it was causing my eyes to droop. What I do remember is that when I woke up, I couldn't see. At first I was panicked, but that quickly settled into an unusual sense of resignation. In this awful new life I was living, the disabilities were piling up. I wasn't sure I would even be able to walk again, and not being able to see felt like just one more thing to deal with. My greatest concern was how Page and my parents would react. They'd already been through so much because of me. If I were stoic, maybe they would take this development a little easier. As gently as I could, I explained that something must have happened to my eyes during the surgery. I was blind.

"Oh, sweetie, they sewed your eyes shut," my mom said. "Don't you remember Dr. Lettieri telling you that?"

"They're sewn shut? Why? For how long?" I started to cry. So much for being stoic.

"Stephy, Dr. Lettieri had to sew them shut, so they could heal. I know it's hard, but he had to do it so your eyes can get better. The stitches will come out in a week or so."

I'd felt claustrophobic because I couldn't move, but that was nothing compared to when I couldn't see. As my world had gone dark, so did my heart. This seemed to be beyond what my mom could "figure out." The belief in Christian's conviction that we had a happy future ahead all but disappeared. I couldn't keep watch on the clock to mark the slowly passing hours, let alone anchor myself in Christian's eyes.

All I could do was lie there in the darkness hour after hour. I couldn't help but drift to the past, thinking back to my previous life. I walked through our home in my mind, remembering the weight of a basket of folded laundry in my capable hands as I walked past my bright yellow guest room where my desk and computer sat waiting for me. I wandered through our kitchen and living room, smiling at the silhouettes I'd made of our family hanging on the wall above the fireplace, looking carefully at my favorite prints on the pale blue walls.

A ritual I had always loved was walking through our quiet house after the children were asleep and before Christian and I went to bed, to lock the front door. The house was still, the kitchen was clean, the toys were put away.

With a click of the dead bolt, the dangers of the world were locked out. I felt safe and our children were protected. I passed their bedrooms on the way back to mine. They were each sleeping deeply. Sometimes I'd call Christian in from our bedroom to see the funny position Jane had gotten herself into in her sleep before I straightened her body and covered her with her blanket again.

And then I'd crawl in bed with Christian, complete. Nothing could threaten our comfort and happiness when we were safe in our home, our children sleeping soundly at the end of a good day.

But how could I protect my children now from the outside world when they were in another state and I was for all intents and purposes the living dead? There was no dead bolt big enough to protect us from this, nowhere I could snuggle up and forget about the world around me. That reality weighed in urgently, ugly and unrelenting.

My once happy memories became oh so painful as I lay there. Christian tried to comfort me with thoughts of home. "Soon we'll be home, darling," he said, "sleeping in our own bed. I know it's going to be a while, but I can't wait to ride the motorcycle around the block, sit next to you on our porch swing, take the family on a bike ride."

I was surprised he'd even suggested it and told him that I had no intention of returning to Mesa. "Christian, that's never going to happen. I can't ever go back to that house. This is going to be a new life for us, and it's not going to happen here. Once we move to Utah, I don't want to come back."

Christian took a deep breath. "You mean, after you get better, you want to stay in the house that Page and Vance bought? You want to live there permanently?"

I could hear the disappointment in his voice.

"Yes, I just can't go back to Mesa. It will hurt too much. That life is over."

He was quiet for a few seconds before he said, "OK. We'll do what you need to do."

I knew he'd be sad to leave Arizona—the home we loved and the future he'd been building. I knew he wanted to go back to the job he loved, so full of possibilities. But he never mentioned staying in Arizona again.

One of the hardest parts about being blind was not knowing what to expect when I heard the door open. A steady stream of people came to my room—nurses monitoring my medications every few minutes, checking on my electrolytes or blood count, tending to my feeding tube or adjusting the physical therapy butterfly. Whenever I heard the door handle turn, I took a breath and prayed for help before whoever it was did whatever they had come to do.

The burn techs who did my dressing changes were almost always attentive and kind, but they were also human. Maybe they thought I was too medicated to be conscious, but one night they came in to do a dressing change when my eyes were sewn shut and they didn't say a word to me the entire time. They spoke over me while they worked, unwrapping me and scrubbing my wounds raw, then cleaning and dressing them again. They took pictures to measure my progress and chatted casually about one of their toddlers, who was being potty trained. I felt like I didn't exist. I was just a thing, to be lifted, carried, scrubbed, and medicated. They finished their work on me and continued their conversation as they walked out of the room. I melted into tears. I felt like I was nothing.

So it was all the more touching when, a few days later, in the very same circumstances—blind, during a nighttime dressing change—a new burn tech named John spoke to me the whole time.

"We're working on your arms now, Stephanie. . . . I'm going to adjust the bandages on your legs. . . . We're going to take your picture now."

"Thank you for talking to me. Thank you for telling me what you're doing to me," I said, crying tears of gratitude. "You make me feel like a person."

"You're welcome," he said. "That is exactly who you are. You're a beautiful person, Stephanie."

I lay in bed the next morning, wondering if I really was a person anymore, blind, disfigured, and immobile as I was, when my sister Courtney came to visit. It was the first time she'd been to see me since I'd been awake.

"I feel so stupid." It was the first thing I said to her. "I feel so dumb about what happened."

"Steph, there's nothing to feel stupid about. It was an accident."

"I know it was an accident, but we never should have gotten in that airplane together. It was stupid. Think about the mess I've made—for my children, and Christian, and Mom, and you and Page and Lucy. I feel so stupid."

"Steph, please, no. Don't. We love you so much. We're happy to help. We *want* to help."

"I'm going to find a way to pay you back," I said.

"How about you move to Utah, be my neighbor, and we'll help each other raise our children?" Courtney suggested.

I turned my head toward her voice and nodded. "OK, deal." It sounded equal parts wonderful and impossible. My hope faded again as I thought about the miserable road ahead. I cut her off before she could bring up the children again. "I don't want to talk anymore, OK?"

There was a long pause. "OK." She touched my hand. "I love you, Steph."

A few minutes later the door clicked closed.

Although I trusted Courtney enough to tell her everything about how I was feeling, it seemed too exhausting to explain the complicated emotions I was wrestling with. Grief, gratitude, faith, and despair fought for my attention. During this time of darkness, especially because I felt incredibly alone, I was more grateful than ever that I'd always had a relationship with God, my Heavenly Father. I had always believed that Jesus Christ not only suffered for my sins but could heal my heartaches, too. When I poured out my heart to God, I knew He understood exactly how I felt without the justifications and explanations I would have to make to others.

The foundation of my faith in God had been laid when I was a little girl going to church. I remember even then being moved to tears by music or the words of a talk. As I'd gotten older, my faith had grown deeper. For some people, there is a pivotal moment when their belief is crystallized, but for me, my belief in God has never wavered but instead has continually grown stronger. At each stage in my life I seemed to find more beauty and solace in my connection to my Heavenly Father. Marrying Christian in the temple had strengthened my faith in God's plan for me, and bearing children had brought me closer to Him. Now I needed God more than I'd ever imagined I would, and I was so thankful for the gift of faith that seemed to have blessed me throughout my life. I'd always prayed, but I'd never had this much to ask for.

Dear Heavenly Father, I am so afraid. Please help me to feel safe. I am worried. Please help me feel peace. I feel so alone. Please comfort me.

A saying I heard often at church was to get on your knees and pray, and then get on your feet and go to work. I wanted nothing more, but I could not bend my knees or get on my feet, and I was lost. I'd always asked God for help with the things I was doing—mothering our children, remodeling our house, writing blog posts, navigating my lonely days in New Jersey, going through labor, reaching out to neighbors. The answers to my prayers had almost always come as inspiration that involved the work of my own hands, strengthened by God. The work I longed to do now was to get out of bed, to make dinner for our children, to be a mother again, but I knew I couldn't. A different kind of work was required now. The work of lying down, of letting my body heal, of exercising faith without moving a muscle.

Being without sight humbled me. I let go of my fear—some of it at least—about my appearance. *I'll deal with the changes in how I look, Heavenly Father, but please let me see my children again.*

Christian and I had chosen a phrase from a hymn as our family theme during the time we lived in New Jersey. *Courage to accept thy will, to listen and obey.* These words compelled me now. I needed courage more than I ever had, and as I prayed, I felt my own assurance that I would be all right, that everything would be all right. I didn't know how, but I believed it. The weight of worry that had lain heavy on me lifted. The knots of anxiety in my stomach loosened. The clouded thoughts in my head cleared. *It will pass,* I was told. *This time will pass.*

As I lay thinking about my recovery, the image of a tree came to mind. It was small and spindly now, easily toppled by the wind. But there was potential in the tree, to grow deep roots and blossoming branches. I pictured each stage in my recovery as a new branch—moving my fingers, lifting my arms, sitting up, someday standing on my own. The branches also represented my many blessings—my relationship with Christian, my loving parents and siblings, my own sweet children. Yes, it was frail now but could grow into something marvelous, with full branches and beautiful leaves, sturdy enough to withstand wind and weather, strong enough to protect our family in the days and years to come.

These feelings of hope were a blessing to me—such a welcome comfort—and I did my best to hold on to them. It wasn't easy—I found that many times the seeds of hope were often swept from my grasp by fierce waves of doubt and depression, but I always prayed that my hope would return. And one way or another, sooner or later, it would.

*C*lick. *The door opened. As usual, I wondered who would* walk through and prayed for strength to accept whoever it might be and whatever their errand was.

"Good morning, Ms. Nielson," said Dr. Lettieri's familiar deep voice. "How are you today?"

"I'm OK. I really hate having my eyes sewn shut, though. It's really awful."

"Well, let's take care of that then, shall we?"

It was the last thing I had expected to hear. Had it been a week already? "Really?"

"Yes. Let's take out the stitches right now." He removed the bandages and the cold steel of the scissors brushed my eyelids as he clipped the stitches. Just like that I could see again. He was the first thing I saw, and I loved him more than ever.

I could see! I know it wasn't the first miracle in my recovery, but it was glorious. I still couldn't move, and I couldn't feed myself, and I couldn't walk or stand up—and the list went on—*but I could see.*

Seeing again was a "tender mercy." In the Book of Mormon, the prophet Nephi says, "But behold, I, Nephi, will show unto you that the tender mercies of the Lord are over all those whom he hath chosen, because of their faith, to make them mighty even unto the power of deliverance." In General Conference a few years earlier, one of the Twelve Apostles, Elder David Bednar, had given a talk about tender mercies. He taught that tender mercies are moments when you feel personally recognized and assisted by Heavenly Father, and ever since then, Christian and I had used that phrase to describe those moments in our lives. When Dr. Lettieri unexpectedly removed the stitches from my eyes, it was definitely a tender mercy that redefined my hope in recovering. I was so deeply thankful that the darkness was over. That day, the hospital ceiling was as beautiful to me as any sunset or mountain view. I lay there thinking about other tender mercies, the times I knew my Father in Heaven had been involved in my recovery.

My mom had told me about a time in October when I was in critical condition. The doctors had told my parents how a severe infection in my liver had taken a turn for the worse, and they didn't believe I could overcome it. They had stopped short of saying I would die, but my mom, who always worried an extra measure, understood that the doctors were telling her it was time to say goodbye. My brothers Matt and Jesse happened to be visiting at the time, and both my parents were there as well.

My father asked Jesse to give me a priesthood blessing. The rest of the family bowed their heads and listened as Jesse put his hands on me. As he spoke, sure that my spirit could hear, he felt impressed to offer me a choice, essentially between heaven and earth. It was time to decide, he said, if I was going to go or stay. If I chose to stay in my body, he blessed me with a full recovery, a rich and happy life, and strength and patience as I healed. If I wanted to, though, he knew I could leave my mortal life behind.

The next day, my vital signs were up and the infection was almost gone—a tender mercy indeed.

As my mother told me about Jesse's blessing, a whisper of memory fluttered inside me. Now as I lay looking at the ceiling, thinking about that story, I felt something familiar. A memory emerged. I had made a choice. I was away from my body, in that beautiful place where I spent time with Nana, and I was asked to choose. I could stay there if I wanted, and be released from my physical body, or I could go back to Earth. In either case, I had work to do, and it could be accomplished in heaven or on Earth. If I chose to return to my body, the road would be long and hard. I would experience pain and embarrassment for the rest of my life, but I would know the joy of having a mortal body. I missed my body in that moment and suddenly understood the gift a physical body is—even an injured body. My spirit longed to be in my body again. It was my choice. I didn't worry about Christian or my children because I knew more than ever what it meant to be bound by the promises we'd made when we were married in the temple. I somehow knew they would all be cared for. I thought about watching my girls get married and my boys go on missions, and I realized I could experience it from afar, but it wouldn't be the same. I wanted to experience it with Christian. I wanted to come home. I wanted to be a wife and mother again on Earth. I was told that if I went back to Earth, my life would have meaning and purpose beyond what I could comprehend, but I was reminded again that it would be difficult. I asked what I could do to make it easier. *Let the light of your faith inspire other people*, I was told. *Share your hope.*

Seventeen

....

*S*hare your hope. *The thought comforted me—maybe I could inspire others.* I was already eager to give something back. I was so grateful for the extraordinary efforts of my family and friends; their generosity was astounding. And I soon learned that so many others—complete strangers—also had rallied around me and my family over the last four months. One morning I suddenly remembered my weekly yoga classes. "Oh, Mom," I moaned. "I was supposed to teach yoga. What happened to my yoga classes?"

"The studio did the nicest fund-raiser for you," my mom said. "They put together a huge carnival. Stevie and Suze took their kids, and they had such a good time. The studio organized it, but so many people helped. They raised a lot of money for your family."

She told me about the white balloons they'd made with Christian's and my silhouettes, the iced silhouette cookies, and how the volunteers all wore handmade aprons and bright red lipstick in my honor. There had been face painting, magic shows, and balloons for the kids, she told me, as well as a silent auction at the studio and craft booths, too.

"They did all that for me?" I asked. I couldn't imagine how much work it must have been to organize an event like that.

"They did. They love you, Steph, and they wanted to help."

I was filled with gratitude, and humbled, too.

"You know," my mom continued, "they're not the only ones. People all over the world have made donations and organized events for you."

That was unbelievable news. "How did they hear about me?" I asked.

"I wondered the same thing at first. Do you know we had newspaper reporters and TV cameras show up at your door in Mesa? And then they came to my house in Provo." She told me how they had wanted on-camera interviews and news about my condition. That's when she began to realize the scope of our story. "The *Today* show came to the house and connected to Matt Lauer by satellite. He said the nicest things about your family. And Lucy wore one of your shirts on the show, and so many of your readers recognized it and gave her a hard time for stealing your clothes!"

I laughed and rolled my eyes. "I guess people are really watching out for me."

The story of our accident was bigger than anyone in our family imagined it would be, she told me, and she realized it was because of my blog. Courtney had kept it alive and also updated people about our story on her own blog.

"You've touched so many lives. There's a whole room of cards for you at home. Stacks and stacks of notes from people who love you."

An entire room? I will never be able to write that many thank-you notes.

She told me people had sent things for our children—deeply personal and thoughtful gifts like handmade blankets, hand-sewn dolls made to resemble our family, wooden blocks that looked like our favorite brands of food, clothes and games and pictures for our children.

I had seen tragic stories—sometimes even cried for a family's heart-wrenching loss featured on the news—but I'd never done anything like this for someone else. This flood of kindness was astounding, and I couldn't grasp why people would reach out like that to *our* family. With all the heartache in the world, why us? It was heartening to learn about every thoughtful gift, and deeply humbling to be the recipient. My problems felt so personal, contained in our little family, and yet complete strangers had reached out to help us in such significant ways. I couldn't understand why people were so drawn to our story and worried that I was undeserving, but this outpouring of support became an incredible source of strength for me.

Just then, Christian came to visit, and my mom left the room to give us some time alone. When I told Christian how astounded I was at the support we'd received, he told me about a balloon launch that had been held in our honor.

"About a week after the accident," Christian said, "someone had the idea to have a balloon launch for you in Provo, and Courtney spread the word on her blog. She knew how much you would love it."

She was right, of course. Ever since I was little, my mom had taken the birthday boy or girl in our family to the Y Mountain to let off balloons with birthday wishes inside. Over the years, I had written about the tradition, which Christian and I were carrying on with our children, and posted pictures of many birthday balloon launches. There was something magical about sending a wish into the sky and watching it float away.

"At the same time in every time zone, people gathered and released their balloons. All around the world . . . Provo, Mesa, North Carolina, Hawaii. Balloon launches happened in twenty-three states, Steph. There were even balloon launches in Australia and Germany and England."

"Christian, I can't believe it. I can't believe people would do this for us."

Christian went on to tell me how my friend Mindy Gledhill had held a benefit concert for us in Mesa, and Claire and Jane had gone onstage and sung with Mindy during the concert.

"I heard there wasn't a dry eye in the house," he said.

I was so proud of my little girls and could just imagine how much they had loved performing for an audience. Earlier in the summer, a lifetime ago, they had stood out on our sidewalk, singing for money. They were outside for at least an hour, earnestly singing their little hearts out until a couple of benevolent neighbors had given them two quarters. I smiled to picture them onstage at a real concert, in front of a real audience. I smiled until I remembered why they were there, and then the image of my two little motherless girls, holding hands and singing, broke my heart.

"Steph," Christian said after a pause, "it's been almost two weeks. I think it would be good if you could call the kids, just talk to them and let them hear your voice."

"Page thinks so, too," I said. "But I don't want to do it." Even the thought of speaking to them brought tears to my eyes. I could only think about what I had done to them, how I had disappointed them. I didn't believe a phone call could even begin to make it better. They were in the capable hands of my sisters. *Let the children enjoy their lives in Provo,* I thought, *and move on without me.*

"Well, think about it, OK?"

His question was unnecessary. As painful as it was, I couldn't think about anything else. I longed to hear their little voices, to listen to their laughter and stories. I wanted to ask them about their Halloween costumes and their new friends. I wanted to feel their boundless energy and soak up their natural wonder for life. I wanted nothing more than to speak to my children, but it was as impossible for me as getting out of bed. I was sure I did not have the strength to do it. My identity and confidence as a mother had been stripped away. I felt worthless and so terribly incapable.

My mom came back in the room, holding a stack of envelopes. "I had these notes in the car. I wanted to read them to you. This is just a taste of what people have been sending."

She sat down next to Christian and put on her glasses.

"'*Stephanie,*'" she read, "'*my family has been so touched by your story. Thank you for giving me hope as a mother. Thank you for not giving up. You are so strong and we are praying for you every day!*' That's from Ani in Virginia."

She opened another. "'*Nie!*'" she read enthusiastically. "'*Thank you for your blog. It helped me so much before the accident, and now you have helped me more than you could ever know. I want my family to be close like yours. Thank you for that insight.*' And that was from Mary in California," my mom said.

"This one is all the way from Germany, Steph, from Marta. '*I pray for you every day. Your story has inspired me so much, and I find peace and solace in your journey, that I can overcome anything. If Nie can do it, I can do it!! You are amazing! Thank you. I will pray for you!*'

"And then listen to this one: '*Because of you and your story, my husband and I want children and a family like yours. Thanks for that! Chloe, North Carolina.*'"

These strangers were praying for me, they believed in me, they remembered me as a happy, dedicated mother. I was heartened—maybe there was still some part of that left.

I turned to Christian. "OK, I'll do it. I'll talk to the children."

I said it quickly, before I could change my mind.

The next day Page dialed Courtney's number and Christian held the phone to my ear.

Claire answered, bright and direct, as spunky as ever. "Hello?"

"Hi, Claire, it's Mom."

"Hi, Mom, you sound so different," Claire said.

"My voice isn't the same yet." I explained how the doctors had just taken a breathing tube out of my throat. "My throat isn't all the way better yet, so my voice sounds funny." I paused. "But it's still me." I said it for myself as much as for her.

"I miss you, Mom. When can we come see you?"

It was the question I had dreaded. "I don't know, Claire. I hope it will be soon. I miss you, too, sweetie, so much. How's school in Utah? Do you like it?"

"It's really good. My teacher is so nice and Seth is in my class and we're having a party on Friday and . . ."

I sobbed silently while my adorable, grown-up six-year-old described her class and her teacher, her new friends and her favorite game at recess.

When Claire handed the phone to Jane, I heard her say, "Mom's voice sounds funny, but it's really her. Oh, and she's crying."

I tried to stay in one piece while I asked Jane about kindergarten, but I couldn't. I cried while she told me about how much she liked school and how much fun she was having with her Utah cousins.

When it was his turn, Ollie was as sweet as ever. "I love you, Mommy. I miss you," he said. I shook with quiet sobs. My little Ollie.

"Mommy. Love you," Nicholas said, and then ran off to play.

Courtney put them all on speakerphone to say good-bye. It was a chorus of, "Bye, Mom. I love you," from the sweetest children in the world.

"I love you, too. I love you all so much."

Christian hung the phone up, and I felt like my heart, so recently stitched back together, broke into a million tiny pieces again. I sobbed openly. The children sounded so good, which was of course what I hoped for. But it stung, too, to think that they were doing fine without me.

"I never want to do that again," I said fiercely to Page and Christian, to myself, to the hospital walls. *Never again*, I thought. I couldn't bear the pain of loving them so much, and being so incapable of giving them what they needed. It would be easier when I was better, I decided. I would talk to them when I got better.

If that ever happened.

T*hat night I woke up in the middle of the night to the eerily* quiet hospital. The now familiar anxiety settled over me. I was alone. I couldn't move. I began replaying the accident over and over, hoping for a place to stop the tape and find a way out of this hell. What if Christian had never taken flying lessons? What if I had stayed with our children that morning? What if I had just held Nicholas as he clung to me? *What if, what if, what if* . . . It was endless.

Images from the accident flooded me. The airplane in flames, the heat burning my throat, the crackle and roar of the fire, holding up my hands to see that the skin had fallen right off them. Now I was alone in this dark hospital. I was trapped—*trapped*—in a hospital bed so far away from my children. My heart started racing. My breath came in short bursts. *I have to get out of here,* I thought. *I can't stay here.*

I sat up in bed. My determination to escape this hell overcame my inability to move. The bed alarm—designed to sound when there's a change in pressure—went off. Machines around me beeped a frantic warning, and the night nurses rushed in.

"What are you doing?"

I crumpled back against the bed as they called out instructions to one another.

"I've got her oxygen. You check her drain."

"It's OK. What about her central line?"

"It's back in. Her catheter's okay. Give her more morphine."

The nurse pumped medicine into my central line, and in a few minutes I was sleeping heavily.

The next night the nurses fastened my arms to the sides of the bed with Velcro straps. I'd already felt restricted before, but now I truly couldn't move at night. To make matters worse, they brought in a babysitter, an Arizona State University student who sat in the corner of my room and studied all night. My family wasn't allowed to stay past nine, and so this babysitter sat with me overnight to intervene if I tried to get up again. Now instead of lying awake in the middle of the night worrying about the accident or the future, I lay awake fearing the person who sat in the corner. I felt like a scolded, naughty child who'd earned herself a rotten punishment.

The morning after my failed escape, Kristin came in.

"Sounds like you had a pretty wild night, huh?" She smiled.

"I guess. I just wanted to get out of here so bad."

"Well, that's dangerous, Stephy. You could hurt yourself. We want to help you get out of here, too. It just takes time."

When she left the room, I thought about what she had said. They wanted to help me get out, too. I had proven that I wouldn't be leaving on my own terms. I would have to leave on theirs. I was tired of the constant pressure to work harder, to try again, to submit my weakened body to the torture of getting stronger. But they weren't going to quit, and so I made a decision. I dumped all my frustration and heartache into a resolve to do whatever they wanted so that I could get out of the hospital as quickly as possible.

Noticing my new efforts, the therapists would sometimes use my children as motivation. "Pretend you're making dinner for your family. Reach for the spaghetti sauce high up in the cupboard," they said. Or, "Reach high, like you're practicing ballet with your girls."

"Try that one more time," they encouraged. "Think of your kids."

"I'll try it again," I'd say, "but please don't mention my children. Please don't talk about them."

I was willing to work harder, but it was too painful when it was tied to my children. Besides, on some level the real motivation came from my personal pride. *I'm not a quitter,* I reminded myself. *I don't want them to think I'm too weak to do this.* So I worked harder in therapy and asked for breaks less often. I had occasionally flat out refused to do something that was too challenging for my baby muscles or too painful for my tight, sore skin. But I didn't refuse anymore, not after I decided that the only thing I could control was how hard I worked, how determined I was. If that was all I had—and I was quite sure that was it—I would give it everything.

Eighteen

My new commitment to working harder came with a desire to really see each of the people who made up the huge team of professionals who were caring for me every day. I had grown so used to a constant parade of strangers coming in and out of my room, monitoring every last detail about my health. These people were involved in the matters of my survival, but I didn't know anything about most of them. They had lives, too, I realized. When nurses and therapists came in, I tried to stop thinking about myself and get to know them.

"How are you?" I'd ask. "How's your day? What's your family like? Do you have children? What do you love to do when you're not at work?" Soon I knew about their families—their children or their parents, the things that brought them joy and the things that they cried about at night. In the smallest way, I was joining the real world again, connecting with others. I found comfort in the familiar feeling of being able to give to someone again, even if it was only a word of encouragement or a listening ear. I loved to tell them that I knew God was hearing their prayers, to share my belief that He understood them and loved all of us more than we could know.

Besides, if I didn't think of them as friends, I'd be too embarrassed about all they'd seen and heard. These nurses had seen me in every possible circumstance, at my most vulnerable and under the influence of all kinds of medication.

One day I lay in my bed, sedated, giggling, and my nurse Kelly asked me what I was laughing about.

"Oh, I was just thinking about having sex with Christian," I admitted dreamily. I was immediately embarrassed. *Had I just said that out loud?*

Kelly laughed. "That is the best news I've heard all day. I don't want to hear about it, but you just keeping thinking about it, honey."

My mom had a three-month head start on forming bonds with the medical team, and she had approached it with her characteristic affability. She brought them treats and lavished them with praise and gratitude. She remembered their names and asked about their families. But mainly she was so openly and unabashedly grateful for their excellent care of her daughter, and I think the staff appreciated her for truly appreciating them.

Kristin would come in my room and say, "Mommy Cindy just called. She'll be over in five minutes."

I usually needed the notice to pull myself together. I wanted to be calm whenever she came to see me. Our accident had been my mother's worst fear. She had warned us of the danger of flying and even begged me not to get in a small airplane. I knew I had broken her heart on that day in August. When she came to visit, I dried my tears and took a deep breath so I could smile when she walked in the room. It was worth the effort to see her shoulders relax and the crease in her forehead disappear. It was a small gift I could give for the hundreds of hours she had spent by my bedside, for the never-ending prayers she offered and the countless tears she had cried.

"Hi, Mom!" I smiled as brightly as I could.

"Good morning, sweetie! How's your pain today?"

"It's OK. How are you?"

"Oh, I'm doing good. I had a visit with your mailman this morning. He asked how you were doing."

I loved my mailman. We chatted on my porch every day and the children often brought him popsicles while we visited.

"You know, he came to the prayer meeting your ward held for you and Christian at the church."

"He did?" I had no idea he'd care that much.

"He did. Someone in your ward let him know they were holding a special prayer meeting. They were all so concerned about you, and they've been so good to us while we've been at your house. Last night some of the ladies brought over a delicious dinner. They're so thoughtful."

They were so very thoughtful. I wished I could make dinner for someone who needed it.

"And, Steph, your sweet neighbor, Rhonda, she's walking Jimmy every night. She knew he'd be alone after the accident, so she came over to feed him, and she's come back every evening to take him on a walk."

I hadn't thought much about poor Jimmy, who must be so confused to have his family suddenly disappear. I was glad to hear that he, too, was in good hands. Rhonda and I weren't close; mostly we'd just waved to each other as we passed in the neighborhood when she was walking her dog. I wondered if these stories of thoughtfulness and care would ever end.

"Reachel came by last night." She had been my close friend for years, ever since she'd married Christian's best friend from high school, Andrew. "You won't remember this, but she came to see you while you were asleep. She taught you French lessons. She joked that you might wake up fluent."

My mom told me how Reachel had set up a Web site as a central place for online donations and was dedicated to raising money for us. I was amazed at such an enormous gift, and then smiled to think that was just like Reachel to be so hardworking and well organized. I missed her.

My mom continued, "We put Vance in charge of the fund until you and Christian are ready to use it." Page's husband had always been good with money. "Some of the donations paid for your brothers and sisters to come and see you. They all wanted to be here, and we knew you would want them here."

I loved knowing my siblings and their spouses had been to see me and felt so grateful for that gift. How would I ever thank Reachel?

"Lindsay Jones came to see you, too, while you were in the coma." Lindsay and I had just begun running together earlier that year, but she had quickly become my best friend. "She read to you from the *Ensign*." It was the Church's monthly magazine. "And she had a big yard sale for you, too. It was really successful."

"Mom, this is amazing. Everyone's so kind. Please tell her thanks for me. I miss her."

"You know, they'd love to see you." It was more a question than a statement.

"I can't, Mom. I'm just not ready. Tell them I'm sorry."

Even among my family and Christian's there were few people I wanted to see. I wasn't ready to venture beyond family yet, although visitors had tried to come. The nurses had told me that strangers had come to the Burn Center looking for me, and they'd had to establish a password for visitors—Sundance, after the beloved ski resort where

I'd worked as an instructor—to keep well-meaning, but unwelcome, people from dropping by.

Even having the visitors I dearly loved was sometimes difficult. They had to suit up—sterile hospital robes, gloves, hats, masks, and booties. And then, after they'd gone to all that trouble, sometimes the visit overwhelmed me, and I would just fall asleep. Part of me wanted very much to welcome them, to entertain them. I was thankful for their love and support, but at the same time, I didn't have anything to give. They naturally wanted to ask about the accident; they'd been wondering what my perspective was for weeks. But it was never simple. "The airplane crashed," I would say, and it was like the epicenter of an emotional earthquake. It was too hard to articulate my feelings and too painful to relive what happened.

But for my mom, after all she'd been through, I really tried to be good company. I hadn't spoken to anyone about how my nana had helped me, but I wanted to tell my mother. It had taken me several days to gather my courage. I couldn't separate the beautiful memory of Nana from the frightening fact that I had almost died. But I knew my mom would love to know that I had been with her mother. She'd told me my whole life how much I reminded her of her mother—the same looks, and tastes, and even mannerisms.

"Mom, I want to tell you something about the accident."

I had her full attention. She hadn't pressed for details about the accident, understanding that I would talk about it when I was ready, but I know she was eager to hear anything I would tell her.

"When I woke up in the airplane, and there was fire all around me, I screamed and screamed for help, but no one could hear me and I realized that was it. I was going to die. It was inevitable."

My mom wiped a tear from her cheek.

"I was terrified, but I gave up trying to get help. I just accepted I was going to die. As soon as I did, someone came to help me. Mom, it was Nana."

She drew in quiet breath. "Oh, Stephanie," she whispered.

"There were other people there, too, but I didn't know them like I knew Nana. When I got out of the plane she told me to roll. And then it got so noisy and people were running everywhere and shouting and she was gone.

"But she's come to me while I've been lying here. At first, I just felt her—I just knew she was there, and I know we spoke. She taught me about how things work in that space between life and death. She was very busy in Heaven, and happy, and full of purpose."

"Oh, Stephanie, I'm so relieved you were with my mother. Elder Holland met with the family in September," she said. Elder Holland was a distinguished Church leader, an Apostle, and a friend of my parents. "He talked to us about angels, and I wondered if you might be with Mother."

"Elder Holland met with the family?" I was surprised someone hadn't told me about that sooner. He was one of my favorites to listen to in General Conference. His messages always left me full of hope and inspired to be a better person.

"He prayed with us, and we all felt this power, like he spoke to God as though He were in the room with us. He prayed for you and Christian. It gave me such hope, Cubby, that you were going to be OK." She paused. "He talked about angels, and said he was preparing a message for General Conference about angels and that he specifically had you and Christian in mind as he was writing it."

She patted my hand. "Thank you for telling me about Mother," she said through her tears. "You'll never know how much it means to me."

Just as I was aching for my babies, wondering who would pick up my sweet Nicholas when he cried in his crib at night, I saw that my mother had wondered who cared for me as I slept. She must have hoped I wasn't suffering. And I think it was equally comforting for her to hear that her beloved mother was happily doing her part on the other side.

"Mom, I saw Katie, too." My mom had just told me the day before that my cousin Katie had passed away while I was in the coma. I hadn't wanted to share the fact that I had already known she was on the other side, but I realized now that this knowledge could comfort my mom, and Katie's family. "Sometimes Nana and I would visit Katie." My mom's eyes widened, and she leaned in closer.

"She's doing good. She doesn't want her family to worry." Katie had struggled through the last years of her young life. "She's going to be OK."

My mom wiped tears from her eyes. "Aunt Jani will be so relieved to hear that," she said. "What a gift."

*My siblings were all gathered at my parents' house for Sun*day dinner and were eager to talk to me. Christian held the phone for me while everyone in Provo gathered around the speakerphone. Hearing them together like that felt so warm and familiar. Like I was there—almost.

"Hi, everyone," I said in my hoarse whisper.

"Steph, it doesn't sound like you. Is this really our Baboon? We don't believe it. You'll have to prove it," Matt teased.

I whistled a little tune I'd always whistled as a little girl.

The phone vibrated with their explosive laughter. I had surprised them. Ever the eager little sister, I was so proud to make them laugh.

They passed the phone around, and I talked to everyone. I could see them in my parents' living room, spread out on the couches and the floor. Some people would be in the kitchen, cleaning up or serving dessert. I could hear the children running around, shouts and muffled laughter. I could imagine the conversations that were unfolding, my brothers' deep voices consumed in a recap of the last BYU football game. I heard my sister-in-law Lisa say something that made everyone laugh.

Oh how I loved and missed this great big mass of Clarks. These were people who knew everything about me, and I couldn't hold back the tears as they each told me how much they loved me, how hard they prayed for me, how certain they were that I would get better. Talking to them was difficult, because it reminded me again of how far removed I was from that normal life they were all living, but I was so grateful for their support.

My brother Matt and his wife, Katy, came down to visit just two days later. They were cheerful and brightened my day with stories of driving the Mini Cooper that Lindsay Jones's husband, Spencer, had lent them, and visiting Trader Joe's, which I had raved about. Matt had also driven to St. Johns to see the site of the crash, hoping for his own understanding of what had happened.

Katy looked at me with tears in her eyes. "Stephanie, I know you can do this," she said. "I know there will be hard times ahead, but I believe in you. Stephanie, you are so strong." We both cried, and she repeated it. "We'll get you home to Utah and you're going to get stronger and stronger. I know you can do this."

Katy's father had passed away when she was young, and that challenge seemed to give her a perspective and determination that made her the family cheerleader, always upbeat and hopeful. I'd heard her give pep talks to family members before, but I'd never heard her speak so forcefully to me. Because she believed in me so completely, her words fueled me to believe in myself. Katy's pep talk gave me a boost of encouragement I relished.

There was no question that I wanted to go to Utah. On some level I continued to believe that things would automatically be easier there, as though the altitude would miraculously heal my broken body. The doctors had told me that I could be transferred very soon, but the specific date was up in the air. In the meantime, my parents were scheduled to return to Utah that day.

The idea of being without them left me feeling vulnerable and worried. My anxiety, always ready to spring into action, had done just that, and I cried as my parents said good-bye.

My dad sat down to comfort me. "You'll be home soon. We'll get you to U of U hospital for a few weeks and they'll fix you right up. You could be home by Christmas, Cubby, just think of it. We'll sit you by the fireplace, and the Christmas tree will be up and you can listen to Johnny Mathis's Christmas CD. We'll get out the train, and I'll make you steamed cauliflower with cheese."

My dad had always worked so hard to create great Christmas memories for us as we were growing up and even as adults. He made his famous vinegar and beets and turned up the holiday music to full blast and decorated our Christmas tree in so many lights it glowed like it was on fire. I thought of all the Christmases I'd spent at home, and how badly I wanted everything to go back to the way it was. I sobbed while he spoke.

"We're going to get you home, and we're going to get you better," he said fiercely, with tears in his eyes.

Just a few days later, it was all arranged. After four months at the Arizona Burn Center, I was on my way to University of Utah Burn Center, on a chartered medical jet, with Christian at my side.

The hospital staff wondered if I would be afraid to fly and asked if I wanted a sedative. I didn't. I was surprisingly relaxed. Christian was by my side, and Page was flying with us, too, and I knew we'd be fine. I watched Christian glance nervously at the pilot every so often, but I was calm as we left Arizona behind and flew north to Utah. On our way to Salt Lake we flew over Provo and the snowy heights of my beloved mountains. "Are you in pain?" Christian asked, noticing the tears sliding down my cheeks.

I shook my head. "I'm OK." I looked out over the mountains that had always seemed to nourish my soul. I'd grown up in the shadow of those peaks and canyons. I'd become a mother there. The mountains had been a source of strength for me, a place of revelation and also grounds for personal triumph as I proved myself on their trails. I silently resolved that I would climb them again. I would be back on those mountains. My feet would hike every trail I had ever loved. I didn't tell Page or Christian, but I kept the promise close to my heart.

Nineteen

The U of U Hospital is on Salt Lake's east bench, tucked against the foothills of the Wasatch Mountains. The Burn Center is on the fourth floor, and as a nurse pushed me through the halls, I noticed the sweeping view of the valley. My parents had met us at the airport and joined Christian and me and the rest of the medical team from our flight as we made our way to the hospital.

"Look how close the mountains are, Cubby!" my dad said.

"You're back in Utah, Stephanie!" Christian said, echoing my dad's enthusiasm. "There's even supposed to be a snowstorm tonight. Won't that be great?"

My mom chimed in, too. "Isn't it wonderful? You're home. It will be so nice to watch the snow out the window."

"That will be nice," I said. "I'm happy I'm here."

Christian and my parents beamed. Snow was nice, and I had missed it, but it didn't mean as much to me as they thought it would. What made me happy was how pleased Christian and my parents were.

We approached a room with my name on the door, and I was jarred to see it had been decorated with snapshots of Christian and my children and me, smiling happily in another life. It was the first time since the accident that I'd seen a picture of my former self. I knew the photographs were a gesture of kindness, but it was a sobering reminder of all I had lost. I closed my eyes as we passed by them.

Some of the staff was waiting to greet us, including one of the surgeons, Dr. Cochran. She was tall and slender, with professional warmth I was immediately drawn to. "You have four children, right?" she asked kindly. She told me she was a mother, too. Then she explained they'd be doing surgery in the next few days. "We'll start with some work on your face. You'll really be happy with the results," she said. The plan was to release the tight skin around my eyes to make it easier for me to see.

From the moment I arrived, I felt welcome and cared for. The hope that things would be easier here burned a little brighter.

The windows in my room looked out over the entire Salt Lake Valley to the west and the gentle snow-covered foothills to the north. Christian and my parents and I watched the sun sink behind the mountains across the valley. A million city lights twinkled on below us. Everything looked so small from my windows, except for the mountains and the sky. Something about that perspective comforted me, and I liked that the view was familiar. It wasn't Provo, but it was awfully close to home, and for now that was enough.

I hoped the most miserable days of my recovery were past, left far behind in Phoenix. I was grateful to have closed that chapter in my life, and I felt the hope of a fresh start in new surroundings. I thought of my children, just forty-five minutes away, and although I was still nervous about seeing them, I let myself look forward to it. The thought of being their mother again seemed one step closer. For a while, everything did. Transferring to Utah had been a big goal, and I had made it. Other milestones still seemed far off, but being in Utah was an encouraging step forward.

The next morning, most of my siblings and Christian and my parents gathered in a conference room in the burn unit with the chief burn surgeon, Dr. Saffle. He swept into the room with a purposeful stride.

"Good morning. Welcome to Utah. Everything all right so far? Good." He had gray hair and a salt-and-pepper beard. His eyes were small and intense behind thick glasses. He was five feet six inches of pure business. "I believe Dr. Cochran has already told you about your first surgery here, but we need to discuss the weeks ahead."

I sat in the corner in a wheelchair, feeling very much like a little girl, not only overlooked but incapable of making my own decisions, as he addressed his comments to those around me.

He continued brusquely with a storm of information. "After surgery we'll continue her physical therapy in her room, and also take her down the hall to the physical therapy room to work on standing, walking, and fine motor skills. We'll get her standing by Thanksgiving, and walking by early December. We've got to get her off that feeding tube, so we'll work on getting more calories in her. And we need to get her kids up here for a visit, but she's got to see herself before they do, so she'll need to start thinking about that." He looked directly at me. "And then we'll get you home."

I was stunned, not just by his message but also by the way he delivered it. Everyone else had questions and ideas, and they mapped out a time line for my recovery. I sat there silently, feeling overwhelmed and relieved not to have to participate. The goal was to have me home by Christmas.

I would go to Page's house first, it was decided, so she could take care of me there, then I would slowly transition into our new house and live first with Christian for a few weeks before our children came home. My family seemed pleased with the discussion, but I was nervous.

Dr. Saffle emphasized how hard the coming weeks would be. "You each play a role in Stephanie's recovery," he said to my family. "Please support our efforts to help her. It's not going to be easy, and we can't have you undermining the work we're doing." He paused and said it again. "This is not going to be easy."

Of course it wouldn't be easy. I was daunted, but I summoned my courage. Everyone seemed so sure I would get so much better at home, so I set my sights on Provo. *Let's get going, then,* I thought. *Let's get this over with.*

But as the nurses wheeled me back to my room, I noticed the other burn patients lying in their beds. They looked helpless, wrapped in bandages and lying so still. I was one of them, I realized, and the reality of the painful work ahead washed over me, weakening my resolve. I tried to hold back the tears as the nurses put me back in bed. Being touched and moved and bent hurt terribly, but that pain was overshadowed by the thought of the daunting list Dr. Saffle had just introduced.

"You can do this, Steph," Christian reminded me.

I looked blankly out the window and nodded. "I know," I said for his sake, but without much conviction.

Here I was in Utah, and everything was as bleak as it had been in Arizona. Although the set had changed, the plot remained exactly the same—a broken girl travels an endless road of pain, distress, and grief. With Dr. Saffle in charge, it may have even gotten worse. I was overwhelmed by the physical expectations, but even more so by the emotional hurdles. No one in Arizona had ever mentioned looking at myself, but it was practically the first thing Dr. Saffle had said to me. The reality of my disfigurement sunk a level deeper. This wasn't going away. *This is my life now, and it isn't going away.* That night, as the sun went below the horizon, my incredibly fragile sense of hope in the future sank with it.

As it turned out, I was behind schedule from almost the first moment. My surgery the next day didn't go well—the grafts hadn't taken, and my bleeding had been out of control. I was in such severe condition that I'd been sedated again. I woke up several days later in a more critical room—one right next to the nurses' station so I could be more easily monitored.

I wanted to get to know the new nurses, this new crew of people who were so essential to my survival. It didn't feel right to me to have nurses come in to take care of my physical needs without knowing something about them. They were always courteous, but I needed more than courtesy. As with my team in Arizona, if a person was going to be changing my diaper, I needed a personal connection.

One nurse was planning a wedding, and so we talked about her wedding dress and the plans she was making. Another was expecting a baby, and I asked about her doctor's appointments. I genuinely liked to hear about their lives outside the hospital. I don't know if it made a difference for the nurses when I knew something about them or we could talk about something that was happening in their real lives, but for me, it felt different when I said thank you if they knew I cared about them.

However, when it was time for their shift to end, I had to adjust to the miserable realization that they actually were going to lead the lives we'd talked about. They were off to enjoy their evenings, running to the locker room to change, walking to the bus, stopping to pick something up for dinner. I remembered driving to Trader Joe's and getting out of my car effortlessly. I thought of pushing a cart through the aisles, planning dinners I would make for my family. I'd been so innocently living my life, and though I'd made every effort to appreciate my many blessings, it struck me now just how much I had taken for granted.

I looked out my window at the hikers and joggers on the snow-covered foothills and I remembered how invigorating it was to exercise in cold weather, the chilly sting on my cheeks, and the heat my body generated as my heart pumped. Was I grateful enough to have a body that could run before I lost it? Did these hikers even comprehend the incredible freedom they enjoyed, how lucky they were to put one foot in front of the other?

By far the most ordinary thing I'd taken for granted in my healthy life was the ability to go to the bathroom without assistance. I certainly missed that. My catheter was pretty low maintenance from my point of view, but it didn't take care of everything that needed to come out of my body. Sitting on the toilet was torture. It was excruciating to bend my knees, and I didn't have the strength to hold the bars on the wall to support myself. Pooping while a nurse or even Christian held me was unthinkable, and so I had been having bowel movements in diapers, though rarely, since I was also terribly constipated.

Claire had a terrible go with constipation when she was three. She screamed and shook, trying to hold it in. Christian sat on the bathroom floor and said encouraging things like, "OK, Claire, let's have a whopper today! I know you can do it!" We never figured out why she was so horrified, but we felt like real champions, or sometimes survivors, when she finally went.

I thought of her while I lay in bed in a diaper, pushing for all I was worth. Without a shred of pride left, I went to the bathroom in my diaper and then asked my nurse, Shawn, to come in and clean me up. He was always encouraging, and if anyone had to change my diaper, I was grateful it was Shawn. But of all the low points in my hospital stay, this was the most humiliating. As I told him how much I hated it, he kindly pointed out that I wouldn't have to do it anymore when I could get up and go to the bathroom by myself. Like everything else, it sounded so simple, but there were a thousand steps leading up to it.

Months earlier I had been changing diapers, and now I was wearing them. This confirmed everything I'd felt about my lost abilities. I wasn't fit to care for my children, as I was nothing more than a child myself. The sense of independence I considered part of my character was gone. I wasn't just asking these people for help here and there because I was worn out from a long day; I was completely dependent on them for not just my comfort but my survival. The thought that I could do nothing for myself, not even go to the bathroom, haunted me, and I swore I'd get strong enough to do it on my own.

Lucy came to visit me the first weekend I was in Utah with big news. She was pregnant. I was happy for her, genuinely happy that the baby she and Andrew had hoped for would bless their home. I wished I could jump out of bed and hug her, then go somewhere to celebrate. *We should be going out to lunch*, I thought, *not worrying about me in the hospital.*

"I was hesitant to tell you," Lucy confided. "I knew you'd be happy, but I knew it would be hard for you, too."

She was right. I was happy for her, but as much as I wanted it to, my happiness for her could not outweigh my sadness for myself. I wanted a baby, too, but for now—and maybe forever—it was impossible. I'd been too afraid to ask if the doctors thought I'd be able to have more children.

"Steph, I brought you some food," Lucy said. "I thought you might like something from Café Rio." It had always been my favorite. I'd even written blog posts about it when we lived in New Jersey.

The hospital staff had suggested my siblings bring my favorite takeout, hoping that something would sound good to me. True to Dr. Saffle's word, the staff had done their best to help me begin eating solid foods. But nothing sounded good, not even Café Rio. The only thing I really wanted was water—I longed to feel cool water down my throat, but I couldn't have any, because it didn't have any calories. In the burn unit, it's all about the calories. They offered me Sprite and lots of Gatorade, but that sounded awful to me. They started bringing in trays loaded with a variety of food, more than I could possibly eat, hoping that something would interest me. But nothing did. Page's husband, Vance, and Lucy's husband, Andrew, brought me a small refrigerator for my room, and Page optimistically stocked it with yogurt, string cheese, and fruit. I could manage to eat a little of the protein shake the nurses brought, an ice cream–protein concoction called a burn shake. They weren't delicious, but I could down a few spoonfuls, and in time I didn't throw them up again. I could bend my arms a little by this time, but not enough to get a spoon in my mouth, so I'd been given a white plastic extender that a spoon fit into so a regular spoon became a spoon with a twelve-inch handle. With the help of the "white weenie," as we lovingly referred to it, I could get a spoon to my mouth. Even with the white weenie, though, eating was clumsy and challenging, and my mom often fed me one bite at a time, as she was doing that afternoon when Dr. Saffle came by.

"If she's ready to eat," he said gruffly, "she needs to use her own fingers and her own hands. Don't feed her."

He left us in a state of shock. Had Dr. Saffle just scolded my mother? Were we in trouble, like a couple of naughty kids? She had fed me because I'd asked her to. I couldn't believe that he had spoken to my mother like that. We were furious at his insufferable bedside manner, and I started to cry.

"He's doing this for your own good," my mom said, "but his way of going about it is just mean. Don't you worry, though, Steph. There's nothing to be sad about."

But once I'd gotten started crying, I couldn't stop. He was right, I *should* be able to feed myself, and get out of bed, and walk and take care of my children. The sting of Dr. Saffle's reprimand was overshadowed by my sadness for so many other things. At the top of the list that particular day was the fact that my sister was having a baby, and I wasn't.

Twenty

I woke up, blinking and in a groggy haze. I turned to see Christian next to my bed.

"Hey, honey, you're awake."

"Did I die again? Did I almost die?"

He leaned in close to me. "No, darling. The surgery went fine. You're doing great."

It was a few days after Thanksgiving, and I had just had surgery to repair the skin around my elbows. A familiar feeling lingered in my memory, like the last remnant of a dream. It was a pleasant feeling, and I thought carefully backward. What had I been dreaming about? *Nana.* But it wasn't a dream; I had been with Nana again. The beautiful feeling evaporated. Had she come to take me away? Despite the confusion and pain that I lived with, death was still a terrifying thought, and a strong possibility, considering how close I'd come to dying over the last weeks and months.

I put my hand on Christian's. "I don't want to die, Christian. I'm so afraid to die."

"You are not going to die," Christian told me calmly. "Let's grow old together and die at the same time. Remember?" It was something Christian loved to say, even before the accident. "That's the way it's going to happen, and it won't happen for a long, long time."

I looked in his big brown eyes and felt calmer. I could see how exhausted he was. He had moved in with Courtney and Christopher and was doing his best to reengage as a father to Claire, Jane, and Oliver. Nicholas was still at Lucy and Andrew's. Every morning he would help get the children off to school, and then a home health nurse arrived to do his dressing changes at Courtney's. In the afternoons, he would go to his physical therapy and then get a ride to the hospital to visit me. But as soon as he could drive (probably sooner than he should have), he drove himself to the hospital to see me. He was with me almost every day. It was always easier to manage the fear when he was near, but still, I carried a particular feeling of unease after this surgery, which even Christian couldn't shake.

The next day when Page visited, I told her how scared I was of dying, and then how scared I was of living. The familiar waves of anxiety I'd felt throughout my recovery crashed against me, but now with a different twist. Remembering the accident always sent me into a panic, but now I was beginning to think more concretely about the future. *How will I manage day-to-day tasks, like brushing my teeth?*

How will I face going out in public? Could I ever be home alone again? I worried that once the reality of the situation really sunk in, Christian wouldn't want me anymore, that he would find someone else who deserved his love. I was afraid of being treated like an invalid all my life. I saw months and years of emotional and physical anguish ahead, and worried that the caregivers in my family would run out of patience with me before I was healed.

Page did her best to comfort me with encouraging words about our faith in God and the progress I'd already made. Her company kept the fear at bay, but she saw the desperate look in my eyes when it was time for her to leave. When I was alone the worry would take over, an unrelenting cycle of anxiety.

"Stephanie, would you like someone in the family to stay here with you every night?" Page asked. "There are certainly enough of us, I think we could do it."

I was hesitant at first because I didn't want to inconvenience anyone, but the thought of having my siblings come and stay with me was instantly comforting. Page sent out what we now call "the babysitting e-mail" to ask for help. She included a calendar where everyone could sign up for a night, and they did. They agreed to come and sleep with me on the reclining hospital chair next to my bed, a guaranteed awful night's sleep, but they each came anyway on their scheduled night and brought indescribable relief with them.

Courtney was the first to visit. I was so happy to spend time with her and thanked her again for taking care of my children. "I don't know how I'll ever repay you and Lucy."

"We made a deal, Steph. You'll be my neighbor. That's how."

"Court, I'm really sorry I didn't want to talk to you when you came to Arizona."

From Courtney's smile I understood she had been hurt, but had already forgiven me. "It's OK. I understand. Today Claire—"

I interrupted her. "Tell me about something else, Court." I wanted to know the children were doing well, but right then it was too painful to hear more than that.

So she told me about the times she'd been to visit when I was in a coma. She had talked to me a lot, but then she also sang, just to mix things up a little.

"Steph, one day I sang Nelly Furtado in your ear, and you shook your head like you wanted me to stop. We laughed so hard!" Courtney said. "It was such a good sign."

I couldn't remember this, but I smiled to think of my shaking my head. I had *loved* Nelly Furtado, and listened to her throughout my first pregnancy. But then her music reminded me of being so sick and I could never listen to her again. Apparently not even when I was unconscious.

A few days later I was cheered again by an impromptu slumber party. Both Jesse and Lucy showed up at the same time to stay for the night. They each thought it was their night to stay with me. We are the three youngest, and we'd spent more consecutive years living under the same roof with one another than with any of our other siblings. It quickly became a sleepover, with Lucy in the chair and Jesse on a makeshift bed of layered blankets on the hospital floor. Talk about brotherly love.

Somehow we got started talking about *Saved by the Bell,* the after-school TV show we'd taken so seriously as kids. Jesse had us rolling with his versions of Kelly Kapowski and Zach Morris.

I had forgotten how good it felt to laugh. We went back and forth remembering our favorite, and the most ridiculous, episodes.

Lucy admitted her big crush on Slater, and then said, "Jesse, I think in junior high, you totally wanted to be Zach when you grew up."

Jesse tried to deny it, but we teased him all night.

Staying up laughing with Jesse and Lucy that night was easily the most fun I'd had since the accident. *Saved by the Bell* was the goofiest thing we could have talked about, but it reminded me that life had been funny. If *Saved by the Bell* could still make me laugh, there were so many other things to rediscover.

Matt was next up on the overnight rotation. He arrived just in time for my last heparin shot of the day. My blood had been clotting, so I received two shots of the blood thinner each day. Heparin shots are supposed to be injected in fatty tissue, not muscle, and can usually be given in your stomach, but I was so emaciated the nurses had to go looking elsewhere. They had settled on my inner thigh, where they grabbed a handful of skin to avoid injecting into muscle tissue. I dreaded those twice-a-day ten seconds when the injection had to be administered with slow, even pressure. It stung the whole time, like a vicious, drawn-out bee sting.

After the heparin, the nurse gave me all of my night meds—to treat anxiety, depression, insomnia, and pain, plus a couple of other shots for good measure.

When the nurse left, I said, "Just so you know, Matt, I usually throw up in the morning." He deserved fair warning.

"Is that normal? I mean, is that OK?" he asked.

"I guess. I don't know why, but I wake up sick every morning and I'll need you to help me take my burn mask off before I throw up."

"OK, good to know. I can do that. I've seen lots of throw-up in my life, you know."

The nurse came in to put my burn mask on for the evening. It was a clear plastic mask fitted to the exact contours of my face, attached by elastic Velcro straps that kept it in place. It was supposed to soften and compress scars as they developed, to keep my skin smooth and preserve the shape of my face as much as possible. The mask fit snugly around every contour of my face, just like it was designed to. I couldn't move my face when I wore it. I felt so claustrophobic I could barely breathe, and it hurt my sensitive skin. I hated that mask.

Matt smiled. "Lookin' good, Baboon." He settled into the recliner and grabbed the TV remote. "Can we watch this hunting show?" he asked.

I would have watched anything he wanted, I was just grateful to have my big brother there with me. Matt flipped between hunting channels and the local sports show as I drifted in and out of sleep.

A few minutes later he asked, "Baboon, are you awake?"

The agreement was that you didn't go to sleep before I did. I had asked Page to make that clear in the e-mail. I wanted my siblings there to protect me from my anxious thoughts until I fell asleep.

"Babbs?" he asked again.

I didn't answer. I could tell he was exhausted. He flipped off the TV, and I watched out of the corner of my eye as he turned over in the recliner with two hospital blankets over him. Soon he was snoring.

I was alone, but not afraid. I listened to the sound of his breathing next to me and pictured him with a sword and shield, stabbing my horrible dreams of crashing airplanes and blinding fire. I dozed off, feeling protected by my brother.

A few hours later, when the night nurse came in to check on me, Matt sprang up with bloodshot eyes, his hair a mess. He was ready for action, but it was just a routine check. He lay back down in the recliner and went to sleep.

Around six-fifteen I woke up coughing, just like every morning, and just like every morning, I knew how the coughing would end. Matt came over and took off my burn mask and rubbed my back while I threw up. I expected to feel embarrassed throwing up in front of my brother—especially those awful sounds—but I didn't. Between heaves, I said, "Turn on the news, so you . . . don't . . . have . . . to . . . watch me . . . throw . . . up."

But he stayed right where he was with his hand on my back, rubbing the peach fuzz on my neck, just like he did when I was a little girl.

The nurse came in to clean me up, and Matt went out to the hall to take a phone call. The nurse reminded me that it had been about five days since I'd sat on the toilet.

"Stephanie, you're constipated," he said, "and you'll need to try today."

Matt came back just as my breakfast buffet on a tray was being served. I insisted that he eat the food, since I wouldn't be touching it. This had two advantages: I liked feeding my siblings, and if the nurses saw an empty tray, I hoped they'd be fooled into thinking I was eating more than I actually was. While Matt ate, he asked if he could do anything else before he left for work. I knew the nurse would be back to see if I was going to use the toilet, and I thought maybe I could do it if Matt stood guard outside my room.

He looked at me and laughed. "I guess I owe you that one, don't I?" He reminded me of the many times when he was sixteen and I was five that he would tell me he'd just caught a rat in the kitchen and was about to flush it down the toilet, but was pretty sure I'd want to see it first. Fascinated, I'd run to the bathroom to find something altogether different had been left in the toilet. As we laughed, Matt shook his head and apologized. "Sorry about that, Steph. Good luck."

"Promise me you won't let anyone in—no one, not even a doctor."

"I promise. No one comes in this door until you say the word."

He and the nurse carried me the short distance to the toilet, which was thankfully right in my room, and helped me get situated. Matt pulled the curtains and glass doors to my room closed, and in the gap between the curtains and the floor, I watched his red Crocs pacing back and forth in the hall.

I had always believed my siblings would do anything for me, but now they were proving it in a thousand ways. The list went on and on—they made sacrifices to spend the night with me, to care for our children, to provide a place for us to live. They made me laugh and cheered me up when no one could. They prayed for me and protected me, and above all, surrounded me with the love that enabled me to heal. My brothers and sisters loved me like they always had, and despite all the upheavals in my physical and emotional life, they reminded me of the one thing that had always mattered most in my life: what it means to belong to a family.

Twenty-one

One day in late November, with a nurse at each arm and a physical therapist to hold my clumsy, swollen feet, I finally stood. Helping me stand required firm pressure on both arms—another notch on the pain scale. The nurses helped me rock back and forth on the edge of the bed and eventually got me on my feet, which were wrapped in bandages and so swollen I had to wear Page's teenage son's shoes. I looked like a clown. My feet seemed like they weren't even attached to my body, as if a wire had been disconnected and the signal had been lost. No matter how hard I concentrated, I could not get them to obey.

But there I was, standing—for the first time in almost four months. The nurses then helped me into a wheelchair to take me on my first trip to the physical therapy room. By the time they'd gotten me sitting up in bed, then on my feet, then sitting in the wheelchair, forty-five minutes had passed. Every joint screamed. When I complained about the wheelchair, the nurse gently pointed out that if I learned to walk I wouldn't have to ride in a wheelchair.

I nodded and smiled, but seethed inside. *Oh, really? Would that be easier?* I wanted to pull her hair.

As we made our way down the hall, she warned me that there was a mirror on the wall in the physical therapy room, and for that I was very thankful. Dr. Saffle had told the staff to encourage me to look at myself, but she knew I wasn't ready. I avoided looking at the mirror for all I was worth. I had no desire to see my reflection—I wasn't even tempted to look. The next time I went to physical therapy, the therapists offered to cover it with a sheet when I came in, until one day Dr. Saffle walked in during my session. He tore the sheet off the mirror and yelled, "What are you thinking? She needs to see herself! We're trying to *help* her, not just give her what she wants." He stormed out of the room.

The nurses had been scolded, and I felt the sting of it, too. But my eyes did not find their way to that mirror. Sheet or no sheet, I did not plan to look until I was ready.

Meanwhile, I had to focus on physical therapy, which felt a little like preschool. First, I sorted shapes from one box into another or attached similar objects to each other. There was a board with colored pegs, and my job was to place the appropriate doughnut-shaped ring on the peg of the same color. How hard could that be? And then I tried it. My fingers grasped and fumbled for the shapes. When I finally got one, I usually dropped it. At first, self-conscious around the therapists, I tried to be cute and pleasantly say things like, "Oh, wow, I can't do that. This is really weird." But the longer I tried, the more frustrated I got. No one helped pick up the shapes I dropped, and that seemed rude. I stopped thinking about being cute. This was hard, and I was annoyed. "Just keep trying until you get it," they said. I couldn't see how that was ever going to happen. As hard as I had tried to push away thoughts of the accident and how damaged I really was, in physical therapy the evidence was unavoidable. I couldn't pick up wooden shapes and put them on a peg. *How could I possibly function outside the hospital?*

I despaired when I compared my body's capacity now to what it had been just months ago, and when I measured my own pitiful abilities against the demands of motherhood. My children were stronger than I was. I had been stronger myself when I was a child. Often I would daydream, thinking about running and the rhythm of my breath and my even steps. Or I'd space out, thinking about doing pigeon pose in my yoga class. What if I just jumped up and showed the physical therapists what my body could do? *Watch this!* I'd cry, and wrap my arms and legs around each other in eagle pose. *See, I don't need to be here, I'm perfectly healthy.*

I reached over to pick up a block just as Zack reached for it, too. Adorable little Zack was just eighteen months old and had been badly burned in a house fire. "Here, Zackie, you do this one." I handed him a shape to sort, and he put it in the right pile. My mother heart rejoiced. "You did it! Good job!"

When he cried and fussed, I wanted to comfort him. "Oh, Zackie, it's OK." I wished I could pick him up and make it all better. My mothering instincts came on in a rush. Yet when the physical therapists suggested that I bring my own children in, I resisted. I didn't want them to see how upset I was that I couldn't do something a two-year-old could do. I didn't want them to see how incapable I was. Besides, the other burn patients looked scary, and I didn't want my children to see them.

There was a teenage girl named Anna who'd fallen into a bonfire.

She seemed so despondent she was almost lifeless. Even I wasn't as hopeless as she was. And there were two middle-aged men who were burned in a work accident. They weren't as severely hurt and they often joked with the other patients and each other. But Zack was my favorite. Loving little Zack gave me hope for motherhood again.

M*y dad was serving in the state legislature, and it was in* a special session during my stay at the University of Utah, so he was in Salt Lake at the Capitol Building almost every day. He came to the hospital for lunch as often as he could and shared stories about his work in the legislature and the people at the Capitol who had asked about me. They opened every session with a prayer, and one day they'd prayed for me. My parents and Page, Lucy, and Courtney had all been invited to the floor for the prayer—a great honor and acknowledgment for us all.

At the beginning of December, my dad brought my laptop along when he came to the hospital for lunch. He encouraged me to blog again. He wanted to see me sharing this new world I found myself in and reconnecting with my blogging community, but I wasn't ready yet. The answer was no, adamantly *no*. The part of my life that I shared on my blog had been real and beautiful, but now it was over. Besides, when I thought about my posts all summer, I was embarrassed. I'd written about my perfect life and my husband the pilot and a stupid pair of moccasins, and then we crashed. Despite my many well-wishers, I was afraid there would be people who would think that I deserved this for bragging like I had. And what could I possibly share about my depressing and miserable life? Being funny was out of the question—there was nothing funny about it. And I surely would not be posting any pictures. I didn't even want to look at my once-beloved laptop.

I was afraid of catching a glimpse of myself in the reflection of my computer screen. I remembered a silly e-mail prank I'd received once, with a link that directed me to a beautiful picture of a field, where I was told to look closely for some detail in the picture, and then the image flashed to a screaming monster, and I'd practically jumped out of my chair. I was afraid I would be the scary monster on the computer screen.

Probably because I resisted efforts like my dad's attempt to get me blogging again, and because I stubbornly refused to look at myself, the hospital sent a psychologist to talk to me. She wanted to discuss the accident, my children, my relationship with Christian, the worry and guilt I felt. Always my mother's daughter, I didn't want to be rude, but I was not going to talk to a stranger about any of it. I trusted God with the thoughts that cycled through my mind, but I wasn't going to unearth them for someone else, just because they wanted me to. I would continue to heal my heart in my own time, on my own terms, with God's help. I answered some questions placidly and then resorted to my only escape: sleep. The psychologist was gone by the time I woke up. I made it clear to my doctors that I didn't want her to come anymore, but they insisted. Somehow she always seemed to come right around the time I needed a nap.

The therapy that actually helped me heal came from talking to Christian. He had been through all of it, too, the terror of the crash and the physical and emotional pain I was experiencing now. No one could possibly understand what we had been through, how frightening it had been to go down in a panic and then wake up surrounded by flames. I didn't know how to explain the feelings of panic I had felt every time someone had yelled, "It's gonna blow!" when they thought the propane tank near the fire would explode. No one could imagine the smell of our burning flesh, the fear and worry about each other, the loss and guilt we felt that our dear friend Doug had not survived.

Christian had always been my rock, my anchor, and now more than ever before I needed his support and understanding to face life again. He calmly and gently and with unwavering optimism led me toward the future, one day at a time. I looked forward to his visit each night. He arrived in time for dinner, and we talked about the day. It was surprisingly like our old life, only now he was the one who had stories about our children.

"The kids went sledding with Jesse today," he told me. "They can't get over the snow here." I pictured them coming back to Courtney's house, pink-cheeked and clamoring for hot chocolate. "Claire and Jane are happy in school, but they're already looking forward to Christmas break. They're thinking about gifts for you." They had also been busy making lists of their own, Christian told me. "Jane and Claire want berets for Christmas," he said.

"Berets?" I asked. They loved the Madeline books, and I was sure that's what had inspired them, but it sounded so grown up.

It seemed every day the Christmas lists were a little different. The girls wanted American Girl dolls, boots, and *Ivy + Bean* books. Claire wanted a kimono—she was on a Japanese kick, Courtney said—and Jane wanted a kitchen set to play with. Ollie wanted a racetrack, and all the supplies to look like Indiana Jones, a BB gun, and a backpack. Nicholas was too young to have much of a list, but I had a feeling Lucy and Andrew would be buying him anything and everything his little heart desired.

Oh, our sweet baby Nicholas. Would he be all right? Would any of our children be all right? Could they possibly grow up and live happy lives after what I felt I had done to them? Christian assured me that they would. I didn't have the eyes, or the heart, to see beyond the four walls of my hospital room, but he saw that our children would come away like us, hurt, but stronger. Every night, he assured me that we were *all* going to be OK.

"This is not our life forever, darling. Think about where we'll be a year from now. In just a year, everything will be different."

I truly appreciated his optimism, but I still had a lot of trouble when it came to actually visualizing what this new life would look like. He set ambitious goals for when I would come home. Maybe I could be home by our anniversary, on the sixteenth. If not then, by Christmas for sure. He was so hopeful about going home.

Christian talked about how great the house was going to look, and told me about all the people who were working on it. "Do you remember Heidi from high school? She got a big group of people to come and help. Our neighborhood friends and ward members are all pitching in."

My fifth-grade teacher had planted a tree in the front yard. A friend painted my basement. My sister-in-law Lisa chose paint colors and light fixtures and furniture that she knew I would like. Lucy's husband, Andrew, was putting in cement countertops for us.

I felt genuinely incredulous that people would give this much to us, and that feeling of amazement never wore off. I was always shaking my head at yet another outpouring of generosity and because now, I was certain: I would *never* be able to write enough thank-you notes.

I cried tears of genuine gratitude as Christian told me about how neighbors, strangers, family, and friends were working together to make a comfortable home for us. But I also cried tears of regret and sorrow. They were helping because I was so sick, and I hated that reality. They were helping because I was too weak to do anything for myself.

"Who will make dinner, Christian?" I worried. "Who will do the laundry and make lunches for the children?"

"I'll do it, Stephanie. I can do all of that stuff. I can cook, and clean, and give baths, and fold clothes." He smiled. "You might even learn a thing or two from me."

No amount of worrying on my part could sway him in the least. Every night he went through the whole speech again and combated every fear and doubt I had with his optimism and unwavering faith. But I could see how tired he was, trying to reengage as a father, trying to get better himself, and giving everything he had to keep me afloat. I was always asking him to stay with me just a little longer, constantly unleashing my darkest fears on him. I didn't want him to have to take care of me like this for the rest of our lives. I realized always being the strong one must be taking its toll on Christian. His endless optimism and pep talks, his boundless commitment to me and the children, must have required depths of energy and stamina that I couldn't have imagined possessing at the time. I wished I didn't need him so much—I felt like such a burden. It was another layer of guilt that kept me awake at night.

Twenty-two

My new home, room 9, had an entire wall of glass, with big glass doors that slid open. I preferred the curtains closed, but when Dr. Saffle walked into my room, he always swept them back dramatically. "Let's show you the world!" he boomed. "It's good for you to see the living!"

Dr. Saffle came for brief, intimidating visits. "You doing all right? Have any questions?" Then he looked at my wounds and set up a schedule. "We're going to fix that one on Thursday and that one on Tuesday." And then he walked out, leaving the curtains open.

After they'd made their rounds to all the patients, Dr. Saffle and the rest of the medical team gathered next to the nurses' station right by my room, and I could hear every word of their conversations through the glass. And if for some reason I had trouble hearing, I could read their lips. I didn't seem to be meeting their expectations, and hearing them talk about what I hadn't done made me feel like a child who'd disappointed her teachers. I would have plugged my ears if I could have bent my arms, but instead I hummed loudly to block out their conversations. But this phrase began to filter through anyway: "Has she looked at her face yet? Work on that again today."

When the nurses brought it up, I told them I wasn't ready and hoped that they would listen. I just needed a few more days, I'd tell them, mostly to get them to leave me alone. Things had been getting better for me, and I didn't want to ruin it by looking at my face.

Christian was supportive and knew I would do it in my own time, but he also knew the hospital staff wasn't going to give up. "They're not going to leave you alone, Steph. Wouldn't you rather do it on your own?"

In theory, yes. In real life, no. I changed the subject and asked about Christmas. Christian said he wanted me to help buy gifts for the children. "That's always kind of been your territory, hon. I'd love it if you would help with the shopping this year." It was a pretty thinly veiled tactic to get me to engage in my former life, but I was willing to go along with it. It wouldn't be much, but at least I could say I had picked *something* out for my children this year. Christian brought my laptop to the hospital, and we agreed I'd get online and buy berets for the girls and a backpack for Oliver.

The nurses helped me after he left, and I asked them to start the computer and get me online. If I didn't look at the screen when it was dark, I wouldn't see my reflection. My fingers were clumsy on the keys, and I slowly typed each letter. It had never taken so long to get to Google, but once I was there, I felt a shift in my mind. *I know how to do this*. I knew just where to get a backpack for Ollie and exactly where to look for berets for the girls. Doing it so slowly was frustrating, but I remembered how fun it was to pick out things for our children. I wondered what I could get for Christian and decided on a Vitamix blender so he could make protein smoothies to help him gain weight. *I used to like this*, I remembered. *This used to be fun.* As it turned out, it was still fun, and after a few more clicks, the Christmas gifts were on their way. I grinned as I closed the laptop. I was glad to have done something for my family, and especially proud that I had done it on my own.

I thought about what Christian had said. He was right. Though I did not want to look at my face, I worried about how long I could resist the hospital staff. I had such little say in what went on in my life. Through the weeks of surgeries, dressing changes, physical therapy, and constant medical supervision, I had come to think of myself as the property of the hospital, a *thing* that they managed. How long could I tell them I wasn't ready to see myself before they forced me to? And was I even capable of making that decision on my own?

But I wasn't ready to make big decisions for myself. When the nurses did start to ask me what *I* wanted, pushing me to become more independent, I was at a complete loss to respond. When they presented me with an option, I would look at my mom, as if to say, *I don't know, is that what I want?*

About three weeks into my stay in Utah, a nurse asked me about my antidepressant meds, a routine prescription for all burn survivors. He wondered if I wanted to stay on such a high dosage. Thankfully, Christian and my mom were there to discuss it.

The nurse ignored them. "How do *you* feel, Stephanie?" he asked.

I just looked at him, bewildered. "I don't know."

"How would you feel if you didn't have as high a dosage?" he pressed. "Do you think you're feeling well enough to lower it?"

"I don't know."

My mom came to the rescue. "I think she needs to stay where she is for now," she said.

The nurse shot my mom a patronizing look. "I appreciate what you're saying, Mrs. Clark, but we really need to hear what Stephanie has to say. Thank you."

Although I knew he was trying to help me, I just wanted to disappear. Didn't he know I was sick? I wasn't ready to make these decisions—I wasn't sure I would ever be ready. That's why I had my family around me. I couldn't do it on my own.

Later that day the doctors consulted Christian and me about my upcoming skin graft surgeries and changes in medications. As usual I gladly let Christian take the lead in these discussions. They mapped out a plan, and I was thankful I could rely on Christian for help.

When Christian came back the next afternoon, my parents had been to visit and had made changes to the plan that Christian and the doctors had agreed on. I was like a neutral third party, willing to do whatever the people I trusted thought was best. No one ever intended to undermine Christian, but I sensed he felt slighted.

Christian asked the nurse why the plan had been changed. "Mr. and Mrs. Clark were here today. They felt a different course would be in order."

"Oh." Christian was silent as the nurse left the room.

I sensed the strain he felt, although he didn't say much about it, I'm sure to spare my feelings. He was doing his best to become a father again while loving and supportive me, but he was navigating both of those roles with heavy input from the Clark family. When they had different opinions about my care, Christian always lost. His role as provider and father was essential to his identity, just as being a wife and mother had been essential to mine. I knew how it must hurt him to have that role overlooked. When my family told Christian that they were worried that he wasn't in the best shape to make decisions on my behalf because he himself was still injured and medicated, he began to wean himself off his pain medication and antidepressants so he could prove he was qualified to take care of me. He didn't talk about how hurt he was, but I imagined the lonely drives back and forth from the hospital every day and the heartache that he kept to himself.

B*y the beginning of December, just as Dr. Saffle had pre-*dicted, I was taking my first steps. The physical therapists got me to the edge of my bed, and we rocked back and forth until I had the momentum to stand. I still wore my nephew's giant shoes, and my feet looked and felt terribly clumsy, but with a physical therapist at each arm and someone behind me to help move one foot in front of the other, I took three steps. More accurately, I went through the motions of walking while the therapists did all the work, but it was a start.

The next day we did it again, and the day after that we added a few more steps. Finally the circuits were reconnecting, and I was able to lift my own feet. My muscles were working! A week later, I was walking fifteen feet to the door of my room and back to my bed. I felt like I'd run a marathon. My muscles got stronger every day, and soon walking only required two helpers, and a few weeks later, only one.

On the one hand, it did feel good to be able to walk. But that didn't mean I liked it. It was intense physical work that left me frustrated and exhausted. The staff, consistent with their effort to give me more ownership over my recovery, encouraged me to initiate the daily walks. "You need to start asking for this. You need to be the one saying you're going to get up now." I politely agreed but never did volunteer for the pain that came with getting out of bed.

Dr. Saffle didn't let up on his insistence that I join the land of the living. He instructed the staff—I heard him outside my door—to get me out of my room as much as possible. I could go on short walks, or a wheelchair ride through the burn unit, or even better, have my parents take me and Christian out on a date. I could just picture us in the backseat of my parents' car, like a couple of nervous teenagers. I was definitely not ready to be in a car. To my anxious mind, any moving vehicle was a potential disaster, and I imagined a grisly car wreck. It was much safer to be pushed through the halls of the burn unit.

To satisfy Dr. Saffle, Page and Christian took me "out," to a waiting room just outside the burn unit where families could gather while their patient was having a dressing change or in surgery. Page looked at a row of pamphlets on the wall while Christian and I talked. Then she called Christian over and handed him a pamphlet. I heard her whisper, "You might want to have a look at this." I could see the title, *Intimacy and Burns*.

I trusted Christian completely and I needed him desperately, but my heart was still too raw to think about our physical relationship. Sex belonged in our other life, the one we had lost forever. I hated my body now, and the thought of Christian looking at me or touching me with the kind of attraction we used to share made me sick to my stomach. The thought of being intimate was as ridiculous to me as doing the long jump in the next Olympics. I shook my head. *No need for that brochure*, I thought. *We will never be doing that again.*

Twenty-three

O ne of the nurses, Thayne, was particularly insistent about the issue of looking at myself. On a Tuesday in December, he brought in a mirror and laid it facedown on the rolling table next to my bed. I didn't have the strength to do it, but I wanted to swipe my arm across the table and send that mirror shattering to the floor.

"My next shift is on Friday. I'm going to leave the mirror here. Will you do it by Friday?" His full beard made him look even sterner, but his eyes were kind. I knew he was trying to be helpful.

Agreeing to look at myself was easy, because I knew it meant Thayne would leave me alone. "Yes, by Friday," I agreed, even though actually going through with it was the furthest thing from my mind.

I understood that Thayne, and Dr. Saffle, and everyone who wanted me to look at myself cared about my healing. But I still resented their pressure. Why couldn't they just leave me alone? I wanted to look when *I* was ready.

The next day, on another assignment from Dr. Saffle, Christian and my parents took me on a wheelchair ride to the hospital restaurant. Christian loved the garden burger and fries there. My mom and dad had eaten at the restaurant, too, and they'd told me about the oversize photos of world destinations that lined the hallway. When they came back to my room, Dad said they had gone all the way to Paris for dinner. "We took a left at Zimbabwe and then straight on past Germany." He'd say anything to make me smile.

The nurses dressed me in a sweatshirt and hat, put two pairs of thick socks on my feet—but thankfully left off the giant shoes—and tucked me into a wheelchair with at least three heating blankets. Dad pushed me down the hall and out of the burn unit. I listened to the door close behind us and felt my stomach tighten as we approached the outside world. In all these months, my closest family and the burn team were the only people I'd seen. More importantly, they were the only people who had seen me.

The foyer was busy. People were getting on and off the elevators, coming in and out of hospital doors. For the first time, I saw how strangers looked at me. I detected horror, disgust, pity. Maybe it was sympathy, or compassion, or kindness, but it didn't matter to me. What mattered was that there was a reaction at all. I was not just another person in the elevator—I demanded attention, even though it was the last thing I wanted.

Months earlier, I'd loved being recognized in Target as Nie Nie, the fun, creative mom who loved skirts and red lipstick. That was exciting, because it was who I wanted to be. But now I was fragile and ugly, and I wanted to be invisible.

As my dad pushed me down the hall, Christian took my hand and limped faithfully alongside me the whole time in his awkward turtle-shell back brace, which made him walk funny. He still had his gruesome scars. This was a far cry from the countless times we had walked hand in hand through the neighborhood. I imagine we must have made a truly pathetic sight.

Adults reacted, yes, but then they quickly looked away, or at least pretended to. But kids were the worst, because they stared. Kids gaped without apology. And thoughts of my own sweet children filled my head. *Would they be just as horrified?*

My mom bent down. "It's all right, sweetie, it's going to be OK," she said in her most soothing voice. We rode the elevator to the top floor of the hospital. My dad pushed me past the posters of Germany, Zimbabwe, and Paris I'd heard so much about. They were beautiful, faraway places, but the hallways of the hospital felt foreign enough for me. My family wanted to show me the view of the city from the enclosed glass bridge that connected two buildings of the hospital. From the top floor, you could look out over the entire Salt Lake valley. The city lights glittered golden as far as I could see, and the Salt Lake temple, tiny from up here, glowed white. It was surrounded by the colorful Christmas lights on Temple Square. It was a beautiful view; everything sparkled. Christian stood next to me, holding my hand, while my parents and Page stood together on the other side. We were quiet, looking out over the city.

Then my focus shifted. Instead of looking *out* the window, I looked *at* the window. And for the first time, I saw my reflection after the accident. It was dim and blurry, but there I was. I couldn't make out details, just general, horrible shapes. I sucked in a breath and collapsed against the chair. It was worse than I'd expected.

"Are you getting tired, honey?" my dad asked. I nodded. "We better get you to bed."

Just as we turned to go back to the burn unit, a woman in her thirties approached us. She ignored my parents, Page, and Christian, and headed straight for me with shattering enthusiasm.

"Hey, I know who you are," she blurted. "I've been praying for you." She put one arm around me and gave me an awkward wheelchair squeeze, oblivious to the needles of pain she sent blazing through my body. This stranger violated one after another of my invisible barriers. First she looked at me, then recognized me, talked to me, and then she touched me. I felt sick, and cried some more.

As we left the bridge, I saw the woman texting furiously. I could only imagine the subject. "Christian, did she have a camera phone?" I asked, gripped with fear. "Did she take a picture of me? What if she has a picture of me, and sends it out to everyone?"

"No," he assured me. "She didn't take a picture of you, Steph. I promise. I watched her the whole time. I wouldn't have let her do that."

We made it back to the cocoon of the burn unit about forty-five exhausting minutes after we'd left. It was the first time I'd felt happy to be there. As the door closed behind us, I was tired to my bones. I don't even remember getting into bed, and I even slept through my heparin shot that night. I had just enough energy to feel angry that being pushed around in a wheelchair could wear me out.

When Thayne came in on Friday, the mirror was still in a drawer. I didn't tell him about seeing my reflection in the glass upstairs. It wouldn't have satisfied him anyway.

"You can't go the rest of your life without looking at yourself," he said to me, like a school principal might talk to a naughty child.

I'm not going to go the rest of my life without looking at myself. I'm just not going to do it right now. I resented the fact that he acted like he had some right to insert himself into my life and demand that I do the hardest thing I'd ever done.

I knew I couldn't hold out forever and I knew I was being stubborn. I just couldn't let go of the hope that something would click, and one day this horrible idea of looking at myself wouldn't seem so horrible anymore. I wanted to wait until that happened, but the hospital staff had other plans.

That Saturday night, after another long day of therapy and tears, my nurse helped me settle in with a classic movie. If Bing Crosby couldn't make me forget about my life for a few hours, I didn't know who could. When he visited, my brother Christopher had brought *White Christmas* and a host of other classics that we watched together. He'd left the movies for me, which I so appreciated. *White Christmas* had been a favorite since I was little, and I was happily swept into the world of the Columbia Inn in Pine Tree. As soon as it was over, I wanted to watch it again, even though it was 2:00 A.M. I waited for the screen to brighten, and the movie to start over. It didn't. A few seconds stretch long when you're desperate for distraction. I pushed the call button on my bed. I closed my eyes and waited. But no one came.

I pushed the button again. No one came. I pushed it again, and my desperation was multiplied. I knew the danger of being alone with my thoughts. I pushed the button again.

My nurse didn't come, but Dr. Saffle appeared in my doorway. He was wearing a suit.

I'd never seen him at night. I'd never seen him in anything but scrubs. I'd never seen him not hurry. "Wow, you look nice," I blurted out, shocked to see him standing in my doorway. He sauntered in like he had all the time in the world.

"I was just on my way home from the burn team Christmas party. Thought I'd stop by and see some of my patients," he said. "I saw your call light on. What do you need?"

"I just want my movie to work," I said.

I was afraid he would reprimand me for being up so late, but he just pulled the chair over to the TV and stood on it to adjust the DVD player. The screen lit up. "*White Christmas*," he said. "This is one of my favorites."

Dr. Saffle put the chair next to my bed and sat down. I had never seen him sit. I was sure he was not here just to watch a movie with me. I waited for him to say something.

A few minutes later he turned to me. "Stephanie, it's been almost five months since your accident. That's a long time to be away from your kids. You've got to look in the mirror. Your kids need to see you, but they can't come up here until you've seen yourself. You need to take this step."

For Dr. Saffle, this was gentle. I felt encouraged.

When Christian stood in my hospital doorway the next night, he held a hand mirror he'd brought from home.

"Stephanie, it's time," he said. "They're not going to give up about this. I know you don't want to, but they're going to make you miserable until you do."

I looked at him and cried. I knew he was right. It had been almost five months since I had looked at my own face.

Christian sat on the edge of my bed and laid the mirror facedown on my lap. "I know you can do it. It won't be as bad as you think. This will be good for us, Stephanie, good for our family." He smiled. "And then Dr. Saffle and Thayne can stop bugging you about it."

"OK, I'll do it," I said. "I'll do it. Let's count to three and turn it over together."

Christian started. "One . . . t—"

"Wait. Stop." I shook my head. "I need to do it alone. Come back in fifteen minutes."

Christian agreed, and I asked him to pray with me before he left. Christian prayed that God would bless me with strength, courage, and comfort. He prayed that my heart would find peace, and feel my worth.

"I love you so much, and you are beautiful to me. You'll always be beautiful to me, no matter what, OK?" He briefly described my scars as the same bright pink and purple swirls I'd seen on my legs, with some dried blood and scabs. "But all of that will go away. It's going to get much better. And, Stephanie, your eyes are as beautiful as they always have been."

I stared at Christian and tried to trust. His facial scars had improved, and I hoped mine would, too.

"Oh, I almost forgot," he said. "Your ear looks a lot like mine." He pointed to his right ear, which had been badly burned and misshapen. "We have matching ears to go with our accident."

I smiled up at my husband, so thankful for his strength.

He gave me the world's gentlest hug and then stood to go. "Promise you'll do it?"

"Yes, I promise." I put my hands around the mirror.

When he left, I prayed again. *Please, Heavenly Father, help me. Help me like what I see. Help me be brave. Please bless me to find the old me, somewhere.* That prayer went straight to heaven. In an immediate response, my heart felt calm, comforted. I could do this.

I took a deep breath and turned the mirror over. I started at my bandaged chest and worked my way up. My neck looked a lot like the skin on my arms, scarred and blotchy. I kept going. I looked at my chin, then my lips. Could those be my lips? They were huge. When I got to my nose, I cried out and put the mirror down. My nose was completely different, smaller and misshapen. I was unrecognizable. *Unrecognizable.* The weight of that word settled heavy on my chest.

I took another deep breath. *Maybe it wasn't so bad*, I thought. *I'm overreacting. It wasn't so bad.* Determined, I picked up the mirror again. It was bad. My cheeks were blotched with bloody scabs. My lips were swollen, my nose was all wrong. Half of my left ear was burned completely off.

My face was frightening. It scared me; it would scare anyone. I felt like I was wearing a Halloween mask. Panic pulsed through my entire body. I could never let my children see this. How could they ever love me? My sisters would have to keep our children forever. I would need to be put away somewhere, away from human contact for the rest of my life. I knew the world didn't accept people like me. People who looked like I looked were treated differently. It was a fact absolutely no one could argue with. Others were relentlessly critical and rude, or sickeningly condescending. Christian, my parents, and siblings— they'd been looking at me for all these months. How could I have let that happen? I never wanted to be seen again. These thoughts were gaining dangerous momentum when I tipped the mirror up to my eyes.

My green eyes looked back at me, and hope rippled through my soul. These were the green eyes I had inherited from my father, with golden flecks that Christian loved. I caught my breath. I saw God in my eyes. I saw reassurance. I even saw a glimpse of triumph. I was still me. Those eyes were *mine*. The life I saw in them came from God, and that gave me hope for the life of my body. I put the mirror facedown on the bed again. I had done it. And maybe I had seen what Dr. Saffle hoped I would.

Twenty-four

I was still in the hospital on December 16, our eighth wedding anniversary. The hope of spending it at home had come and gone. I still didn't eat like the doctors hoped I would, couldn't walk as much as they thought I should, and I hadn't seen my children yet.

I remembered the busy preparations the morning before our wedding, waking up and running over to my neighbor Vanessa's house for the final fitting of my wedding dress, and then getting ready to go to lunch with Lucy, our last time as single sisters. My flowers were delivered, and Page's family arrived from California, where they lived at the time. The night before, Christian and I had spent all night moving my things into our home in downtown Provo.

I laughed remembering how Christian had said that in just thirteen hours we'd be married, and he could touch my boobs. And then we'd woken up the next morning to the most beautiful snowstorm and gone to the temple to make promises to God and each other about our marriage and our eternal commitment to one another. Those promises were being tested in ways we never even fathomed, and they were holding stronger than ever. If there was anything to celebrate on our anniversary it was that.

Unwilling to let the day pass without a celebration, Christian planned to spend the night at the hospital. The nurses made a DO NOT DISTURB sign for our door, trying to encourage a romantic evening. The chef made a special meal for us—black beans and salmon—and even put a flower on the tray of food that was delivered to our room.

"These have been eight wonderful years, darling. You're the light of my life. I don't know what I'd do without you." His voice trailed off, and he put his head in his hands. "Stephanie, I thought I'd lost you. I'm so thankful you're here. I love you so much."

I wanted to wrap my arms around him, to soothe the memory of those awful feelings. Tears stung my eyes. All I could say was "I love you, too."

"I have a gift for you." He pulled out a little jewelry box, and inside was a pair of beautiful gold earrings with a gold inlay of Christian's silhouette on one and my silhouette—or what used to be my silhouette—on the other. Christian had asked Lucy's husband, Andrew, a marvelous jeweler, to make them for me. "Christian, thank you. I love them." I asked him to put them on for me.

"I'm so sorry for what's happened to us," Christian said as he put them in my ears. "I wish we could trade places, and I could be doing the hard things you're doing. I wish I could do them instead of you."

"Christian, I never wish for that. I never blame you. What happened to us wasn't your fault. I never think that, OK?"

"I just wish I could take it from you, Steph, that you didn't have to go through all this. But I know you're going to get better. Life isn't like it used to be, but it's still going to be wonderful, Stephanie. It's still a beautiful life."

He touched my hand gently. Ever the optimist, he believed the pieces of our life would come together again, while I could only focus on how bleak it was that we were spending our eighth anniversary in a hospital room.

"Remember this one?" Christian said. " 'If there is any honor in you, promise me never to do that again.' " It was Guinevere from *First Knight*, one of our classics.

Christian answered himself with Lancelot's lines: " 'I don't know about honor. But I promise you. I won't kiss you again till you ask me to.' " He waited. "OK, so ask me to."

I smiled. It was such a comfort to return to our old rituals. "Christian, will you kiss me?"

"Gladly." He leaned over me and kissed my forehead.

"How about on the lips?" I suggested. We hadn't kissed each other's lips since the accident. My lips were so burned and swollen, and I hadn't been ready anyway, to even consider our physical connection. I needed Christian in so many ways, but was still too raw emotionally to need him that way.

Christian raised his eyebrows. "Really? I thought you'd never ask."

But as he leaned down I shook my head. "No, never mind. I'm sorry. Let's do that later."

He didn't hide his disappointment.

"OK, OK. Kiss me," I said. "Let's kiss."

He came close again and I stopped him. "No . . . wait."

"Stephanie," Christian groaned. "Come on."

I took a deep breath. "OK, let's kiss."

Our lips touched awkwardly, Christian leaning over my hospital bed in his back brace. It was not unlike the goofy first kiss of a couple of young teenagers, but I loved feeling the warmth of Christian's face next to mine. I missed the comfort of his physical touch, and my stomach fluttered a little, remembering.

He helped me put on my burn mask and then put on his.

"I hope we don't scare the nurses," I joked. It was funny until I thought of our children. *What if our burn masks scare our children?* I wondered.

"Good night, darling. I love you. Thank you for eight wonderful years."

Christian settled into the recliner in his stiff back brace and face mask. I noticed his misshapen right ear, and the scars on his cheeks. My faithful husband.

"I love you, too."

The next day I woke up buoyed by the memories of a sweet evening with Christian. Going home and rebuilding my life as a wife and mother was becoming a very real possibility, but I still had a paralyzing fear of seeing my children. I was afraid they wouldn't recognize me, or even worse that they would be scared of me. What would I do if my own children rejected me? The hospital staff saw it as the next necessary step, but I wasn't ready. If I took just a little more time, I thought, maybe I could somehow resolve the guilt I felt and seeing them would be less painful. The truth is, I probably never would have felt prepared, but I kept hoping that a few more days would somehow make a difference. Because I kept insisting I wasn't ready yet, the hospital staff had suggested to Christian and my sisters that a surprise visit might be best.

Page and Christian were in my room a few hours later when Page announced that they had brought the children to see me.

I panicked. "I can't do this. I can't see the children now. I'm not ready for this. We've got to do it another time." My heart raced. This was too much, too soon, too unfair.

"They're here, Steph," Page said firmly. "They're on their way up. You have to do this."

I started to cry. "No, I'm not ready. I don't want to see them yet. I'm not ready for this. Please don't let them in."

Christian understood my fear. "Steph," he said, "it won't be as bad as you think. I'll be here. We can do this together."

Then suddenly Courtney and Oliver wandered in. After all these months, my little Ollie was right there in my room.

I couldn't help myself. "Get out!" I cried. "Get out of my room! He can't come in here! GET HIM OUT!"

Courtney hurried Ollie out, and Page descended on me. "Stephanie," she scolded, "you are their mother. If you don't do this now, you'll keep putting it off. These are your children. They're your responsibility." She was fierce. "It's time to be strong for your kids. They are here, so you'd better pull yourself together."

Her words stung as if she had slapped me. "I can't do this," I said. "I can't see the children now. I'm not ready for this." I started to cry.

"They're here, Steph," Page said firmly. "You have to do this."

Christian leaned down and got close to my face. He spoke kindly. "Don't hurt their feelings; they're so excited to see you. This is just the first step, OK? It really is going to be all right."

Courtney had closed the curtain behind her, but I could hear Ollie out in the hall, asking for me. Page was right. They were my children, and they were here to see me. I didn't have a choice.

Page went out to the hall to tell Ollie he could come back, and Ollie rushed through the door. Christian held out his arms. "Hey, buddy, come see Mom!"

Oliver climbed on the foot of my bed and smiled up at me. "Hi, Mom," he said, like we'd seen each other earlier that day. He drove his Matchbox car on my bandaged leg. I was still so sensitive to the lightest touch but would have let Ollie climb all over me if he wanted to. He didn't want to stay very long, but at least he stayed for a minute. I wanted him to hear my voice, to realize I was the same mother I'd been before. I was so surprised that he didn't seem to mind how different I looked that I didn't even think about how different *he* looked, how much he'd grown, until he'd left.

Ollie slid off my bed and opened the little fridge in my room. He was fascinated by its contents.

"Ollie, do you want to take a drink?" I asked.

"Yeah!" He grabbed a Gatorade and ran out of the room to show his sisters.

Christian smiled. "You're doing great, Steph." He nodded encouragingly, and then went to the door to bring Jane in. She was so excited she let go of his hand and ran in the room. She took one horrified look at me and then stared at the floor.

I couldn't hold back the tears. "Janie, you're so grown up! Look how short your hair is. I love it!"

Her eyes were glued to the floor.

"I'm sorry I'm different, Jane," I said. "I know I don't look the same, but I promise I'm still your mom. I'll get better, I'm going to look better. And I still love you so much. I really miss you, Jane."

She didn't look up.

"Jane, will you look at me?"

I looked at the top of her red head and watched the rapid rise and fall of her little chest. She was on the brink of tears, too.

"Janie, will you look at Mommy?"

Finally she looked up, but she looked at Christian. "Can I go now?" she said.

Christian nodded and hugged her. "I love you, Jane." He turned to me as she walked out of the room. "I love you, Steph," he whispered.

Out in the hall, we overheard Jane say, "Claire, don't go in there."

I gasped. It was that bad. I pleaded with God that I could keep from dissolving into convulsing sobs. *Please help me make it until they're gone*, I prayed.

Christian went out in the hall to bring Claire in, but she refused to come.

I called to her through the curtain, "Hi, Claire. I'd love to have you come in. Will you come and say hi? I really miss you, sweetheart."

"I miss you, too, Mom," she said through the curtain. "But I don't want to come in."

"OK. Maybe we can just talk for a minute?"

Claire agreed and told me about making decorations for the school Christmas tree.

Nicholas had fallen asleep outside in the hall, so he didn't come in that day. In a way it was a relief to not be rejected by him, too.

Courtney and Page came in for just a minute before my sisters gathered our children and took them back to Provo.

"You did it," Page said. "This was a great step."

"I love you, Steph," Courtney said. "It will be better next time."

I pleaded with Page. "I can't do that again. Please don't have them come back. Please let's wait until I get home to do this again."

Tears rolled down my cheeks. "That was awful," I moaned. "So awful." Christian stayed with me as my tears turned into deep sobs. I had trusted everyone else with so many decisions, but this had backfired. Horribly. I felt like I had been ambushed. Seeing my children had gone as terribly as I had feared it would. I had never hoped it would be perfect—I knew better than that. Like looking in the mirror, I had just hoped if we could give it enough time, it would somehow be easier on the children.

When my nurse came back to check on me she brought drawings that my sisters had left for me. They were colored-pencil pictures Claire and Jane had drawn. In one, Jane and I were holding hands. In another, Claire and I played in a garden of yellow daisies. The nurse hung them on my wall, sure they would brighten my spirits. I stared at those happy pictures of my children and me, but they broke my heart. I called the nurse back in and asked her to take them down.

She was reluctant. "Are you sure?"

I was sure.

Being a mother was my purpose in life, the source of my fulfillment, and my children were afraid of me, they had rejected me. That fact leveled me. I was inconsolable. I wanted to die. Why had I chosen to stay in this awful body full of problems I couldn't fix? *There is no reason to be here. My children don't even love me.*

Those precious, beautiful children didn't deserve a disfigured, incapable mother. They needed someone strong, who could take care of them no matter what. Seeing them, and the way they looked at me, destroyed any hope I'd harbored that I could take care of them again. I was inadequate in every way, and they didn't even want to look at me.

Twenty-five

I *woke up the next morning with a deep ache in my heart. I* wanted to wipe away the memory of the night before. The nurses knew the children had come and they wanted to hear how it went, but I couldn't talk about it. "It was awful. Please don't ask me," I said. "Tell the other nurses, too. It was awful."

I turned to God again in prayer. *Please help me through this. Please help our children.*

A song from church came to mind, a song I had learned as a child and was teaching my children called "A Child's Prayer."

> *Heavenly Father, are you really there?*
> *And do you hear and answer every child's prayer?*
> *Some say that heaven is far away,*
> *But I feel it close around me as I pray.*

I sang the first lines over and over out loud. "Heavenly Father, are you really there? And do you hear and answer every child's prayer?" I needed Him so desperately. But the next verse, a parent's answer to the child's questions, comforted me, too.

> *Pray, He is there*
> *Speak, He is listening.*
> *You are His child.*
> *His love now surrounds you.*

I prayed for hours that morning, pleading with God for understanding and assistance. I had prayed on my own every day, with Christian and with my parents and siblings. I was certain our prayers were being heard by our loving Heavenly Father. At times, I had distinctly felt embraced by God's love and the sweet assurance washed over me that I—and everything—would be all right. But now I began to wonder when He would miraculously swoop in and make it all better. I had been faithful—when was He going to solve this mess for me?

In the Arizona Burn Center, and even when I first got to Utah, my part was to lie still and let my body heal. The only thing I could do was exercise faith. But now, I realized, the time had come to put myself back into the equation. I had reached a point where God could only help me if I was working, too. He would help me walk again, but not by snapping a finger while I lay in bed, feeling sorry for myself. He could bless my relationship with my children, but I would have to try, too. If I did my part, He would do His.

I also prayed for help in forgiving Page for scolding me, and soon my anger toward her cooled, and I felt guilty for being so mad at her. I knew she was only trying to help and had done what she thought was best. And maybe she was right. I was too heartbroken to sort out blame and responsibility. It had happened—my children had seen me—and now I had to deal with it.

During my dressing change later that day my mom went to Pottery Barn and bought me a gift, a little Christmas village house. It was all white with a peaked roof and perfect little paned windows. It lit up when she plugged it in near my TV, and I stared at it for hours, wishing I could escape to that little house and shut the door. I'd hide from everyone and everything inside its perfect tiny walls. The longer I stared at it, the more I believed it would be possible—someday—to have a life-size house that could be the same kind of haven. That house became a gift I cherished, my little house of hope.

I didn't really know where to start with my children after that first time they visited, but the psychologist suggested that I call them every day so they could hear my voice and remember me as their mother without having to process the changes in my appearance. It was still painful to think of them living their happy and playful lives without me, but I tried to follow the advice I'd been given, and I called them almost every day. My children had never been very interested in talking on the phone to long-distance relatives, and now, for every phone call, the stakes were so high. I did my best not to cry while they were on the phone.

I asked them about their school Christmas parties and how much snow was on the ground. Had they been sledding? Which cousins had they been playing with? I told them to ask Courtney to take them to get chocolate doughnuts and hot chocolate and drive around to see the Christmas lights. It's the kind of outing I would have planned and relished when I was well.

Above all, when we talked on the phone, I wanted them to hear my voice and understand that I was the same woman who loved them more than anything. I had taken care of them before, and somehow, I would take care of them again. And I wanted them to know that I loved and trusted God. I always reminded them to say their own prayers.

After talking on the phone each night for a week, I was much more prepared for their next visit. I did my best to make sure it went better than the first. I asked one of the nurses to help me put on the earrings that Christian had given me for our anniversary, and another nurse put her own lip gloss on my lips. I asked if we could get a tray of cookies from the hospital cafeteria, and we stocked my little refrigerator with root beer. All I could do now was hope and pray. I waited nervously for them to arrive.

Ollie rushed in ahead of everyone else. "Hi, Mom," he said and headed straight for the fridge. Just as I had hoped, his eyes lit up when he saw the root beer.

"You can have one, Ollie," I said. "Go ahead."

"Yay!"

So far, so good.

Lucy came in holding Nicholas. I couldn't believe how much he had grown. I'd missed months of my children's lives, and I could see it most in Nicholas. He was taller and had a big boy haircut. I was flooded with memories of folding his little onesies, feeding him breakfast in his high chair. He had just reached the stage of knocking over the tower of blocks I would build, and in my mind I could feel the touch of his chubby hands on my skin—he had a habit of putting his hand down my shirt when I held him.

"Hi, Nicholas. It's me, your mommy! Can I hold you?" I held out my arms.

He buried his head in Lucy's neck and wrapped his arms around her. One choked sob escaped, but I held others back. He looked up again but kept his head close to Lucy's. He pointed at the lights on the machines and all the tubes around my bed. Then he put his hand to his cheek. "Ow," he said. "Bite."

"Mommy got hurt, didn't she, Gigs?" Lucy said, looking at me sympathetically.

"Bite," he repeated, raising his hand to his cheek again.

Claire and Jane had stayed out in the hall. They didn't want to come in.

"Claire," I called, "Jane, I'd love to see you. Come and say hi, girls."

"I don't want to, Mom. Can I just stay here?" Claire said.

"I'm not going to come in this time," said Jane.

Courtney walked out to the hall and picked Claire up. "Come show her your tooth." She called in to me, "Steph, Claire lost a tooth on the way here."

"Oh, Claire! That's so exciting! Come show me."

She hesitated. "OK."

Courtney carried her in, and Claire pulled her lip down to show me her missing tooth. "Look." She smiled timidly, but I thought she could see I was still her mother—different body, but same heart. I doted on her for as long as she would let me, asking about the tooth fairy and if she had any other loose teeth.

Ollie kept opening drinks, about ten of them, and I would have let him open more if it kept him happy while he was near me.

"I miss you, Mom. I love you," Claire said. Then she looked up at Courtney. "Can we go?"

Courtney looked at me. "What do you think, Steph? Anything else you want to say to Claire?"

"Keep coloring pictures for me, OK? Thanks for coming. I love you so much."

Claire walked out to the hall and we heard her say to Jane, "It wasn't that bad."

I hoped it might change Jane's mind, but it didn't. She still wouldn't come. I was sad, but in a way, it was easier to have her stay in the hall than to have her come in and look like she'd seen a ghost.

"Janie," I called out to the hall. "I love you!"

Claire stuck her head in the door. "We're ready to go. Can we go now?" she asked again. She smiled at me, like she didn't want to hurt my feelings.

"I think they're just tired," Lucy said. "And I know they're hungry."

I was their mother. That was my line.

Courtney and Lucy gathered Oliver and one or two of the drinks he'd opened.

"Say bye-bye to Mommy, Gigs," Lucy said.

He waved obediently. "Bye-bye."

I fell apart before they'd gotten to the end of the hall and was sobbing when Lucy appeared in the doorway again, still holding Nicholas.

"He wanted to see you again, Steph. We got down the hall and he said, 'Mommy room' and pointed to come back." She carried him in. "Here's Mommy, Gigs. Do you want to say hi to Mommy again?"

She brought him to the end of my bed, and he leaned over and reached for my feet. My toes weren't bandaged, and my toenails were painted bright red. He touched my toes and said, "Mommy."

"Yes, Gigs, it's Mommy," I said. "I love you, Gigsy."

"Bye, Mommy," he said, and Lucy wiped tears from her eyes as she carried him out. "Love you, Steph. You can do this," she said.

I wasn't so sure. Yes, this visit was less dramatic because the children and I both had a better idea of what to expect, but for me, the emotional toll was the same. I cried myself to sleep that night, feeling frustrated that all the little bricks I kept laying in my feeble attempt to rebuild a life kept crumbling down around me.

I *t was hard to celebrate my physical progress with such pain-ful* emotional setbacks, but I was making considerable physical improvements. I had progressed enough to walk, with just one person at my side, all the way to the nurses' station outside my door. By the day after my children visited, I was able to walk all the way around the nurses' station, making a complete circle back to my own room again. I began to feel the freedom that walking would offer me, and I worked even harder. Within another week, I was solo, walking all the way around the burn unit, teetering forward slowly with small, but independent, steps. I couldn't wait to show Christian and Page and my mom and dad. I felt like a child with a new trick, and you can bet I wanted everyone who loved me to be so proud.

As I made my way around the burn unit, my stiff arms and legs and slow, jerky movements reminded me of somebody, but I couldn't quite put my finger on it. A couple of days later, a lightbulb went off. "It's the robot from *Star Wars*," I told Christian.

"C-3PO?"

It was true. I walked just like C-3PO. I told the nurses, and we laughed about that for days, and I not only enjoyed the joke—it was so true—but I enjoyed being able to make people laugh. My days in the burn unit were dark, and I still cried every day I was there, but I loved that I had found a way to make a few minutes of our day easier.

Soon it was time to try stairs. Page joined my nurse Rhonda and me as we slowly made our way to the staircase. As I walked down the hall some of the other patients congratulated me. The two middle-aged men I knew from therapy called out, "Way to go! Good for you!" One of them came to the door of his room and clapped as I walked by. "Oh, you're doing a great job. Look at you go!" Their words of encouragement were just what I needed. I *was* doing a great job, and I appreciated their cheers. I felt a dormlike camaraderie in the burn unit, since each of us knew the challenges we were facing like no one else could, and therefore how meaningful each triumph was.

We made it to the cool, damp staircase at the end of the corridor on the fourth floor, and I looked down at what I thought must be the longest set of stairs I had ever seen. It was ugly and stale in the stairwell, and I battled a constant fear of falling down. It seemed like my body would just break on impact if I fell on those awful steps. I wondered what would happen if there was an earthquake. Certainly Page and Rhonda would let go of me and I would fall. I was so afraid, and blood seeped through the bandages on my knees as I walked, but they cheered me on. And once I got down three flights of stairs, I had no choice but to go back up. After three flights, I was exhausted but satisfied. I did it. I would walk out of the burn unit on my own two feet.

As we made our way back to my room, exhausted but proud, we passed Anna's room, the teenager who'd been burned in a bonfire. She lay listlessly on her bed. Unhappiness seemed to radiate from her room. I had once been where she was—immobile, hopeless, and deeply depressed. Thankfully, I was beyond that early misery, and I never wanted to be there again. My heart went out to her every time I passed her, but I also felt grateful for the progress I'd made. I had been where Anna was, but now I was doing laps around the burn unit and climbing stairs. Being able to walk again opened doors of hope for me. "Look at her go!" I heard the echo of my burn-neighbor's encouraging words. *Look at me go.*

Twenty-six

From my room I could hear the door of the burn unit shut every time someone left. I still needed help in every way and was overwhelmed at the idea of life outside the hospital. And yet I began to feel more and more desperate to be the one walking out that door. I wasn't going to make it home for Christmas like everyone had hoped, but I would get well enough to leave the burn unit soon. And every time I heard the *swoosh* of the door as it opened and shut, I would picture myself walking through it, and back into the world.

Many of my wounds were healing to the point that during dressing changes, the burn techs were pulling off thin layers of skin in large pieces, which meant my skin was healing just like it was supposed to. With my wounds healing so nicely, the doctors were ready for me to switch from white gauze bandages to tight-fitting compression garments, made of stretchy fabric that would allow me to move but keep the scars that were forming on my body from getting too bulky. Only some of my wounds were ready for compression garments, so the others still had to be dressed with bandages before I was squeezed into the tight-fitting clothing.

Christian had been wearing his for weeks, and he loved them. But the first time I wore them, it felt as if I were having the life sucked out of me, like a blood pressure cuff was being pumped around my whole body.

"Take them off, take them off, take them off!"

Dr. Saffle was firm. "I know you don't like this, but I know you want to go home."

So I put my compression garments on every day and eventually got used to it. They even began to feel like protective armor, and I could see why Christian liked wearing them.

Dr. Saffle emphasized how important it was for me to wear my compression garments and my face mask if I wanted to go home, how I had to eat well and do daily physical therapy. "If you don't," he said, "you'll be right back here in no time. Can you do those things?"

It was time for me to own responsibility for my healing. I knew it was serious. I assured him I could.

On Christmas Day, our children would visit again and I had asked Christian to bring some things from home to make it feel cozier in my hospital room. I wanted blankets to cover the chairs and drape over the side table. Maybe things would go better if it didn't look so much like a hospital room. I also had him bring a stack of children's books and movies, hoping I could read to the children and that maybe, just maybe, they'd want to stay and sit next to me and watch a movie.

Christian came in first to give me a kiss. "Merry Christmas, darling," he said. Courtney and Lucy walked in with Claire, Oliver, and Nicholas. Jane stayed outside again.

"Merry Christmas, guys!" I said, doing my best to look as bright and happy as any mother would be on Christmas morning.

Claire and Ollie smiled. "Merry Christmas," they said.

Nicholas was still very concerned about the "bites" on my face, and brought his fingers up to his own face again. "Ow," he said, speaking for both of us. He touched my toes again.

"Hi, Mom," Ollie said and went straight for the refrigerator, as I had hoped he would. It was stocked with root beer again, and he started opening cans right away.

Claire handed me a package with framed drawings the children had made. Thankfully, this time I wasn't in the drawings, just bees and butterflies and Christmas scenes.

"These are beautiful! Thank you so much!" I said.

Then Christian and I gave the girls the berets I'd ordered for them, and Ollie his backpack. We had a twenty-pack of Matchbox cars for Nicholas. He clutched handfuls of cars in his chubby hands, and Ollie strapped on his backpack. Claire put on her beret; Jane had opened hers in the hall. "Thanks for the beret," she said. "I love it!"

"Merry Christmas, Janie," I called. "I love you, sweetheart!"

Despite the fact that Jane was still too afraid to be in the room with me, and I was lying in a hospital bed, and I'd barely seen my children in the last several months, watching them open their gifts actually felt a little like Christmas morning.

Christian helped the children tell me about Christmas morning at Courtney's, reminding them to share the best parts so I could hear a complete report. When they were done telling me about the excitement of their gifts, they were restless and ready to leave.

"Steph, will you be OK if we go now?" Christian asked. "Is that all right with you?"

I didn't mind. Seeing the children was emotionally exhausting—so many expectations that never quite measured up. When they left I looked at the pile of books I'd hoped to read and the movies I wanted to watch with them and wondered if we'd ever have those kinds of moments together again.

The visit left me emotionally depleted, and I asked the nurse to put in *A Christmas Story*. I watched Ralphie try to get his precious BB gun for the next hour and a half, hoping that if I stared at the screen long enough, I could forget all about my own life.

Toward the end of the movie my parents arrived, and hearing my dad laugh at Ralphie brightened my spirits, and then Christian came back to the hospital to spend the evening with me. He was wearing jeans. It was the first time I'd seen him in jeans since the accident. He looked so much like the person he'd been before, like my strong and attractive husband and not a hospital patient. It felt like a glimpse of our old life, the one where we were healthy and wore regular clothes.

We finished the day with *White Christmas*. It was a far cry from perfect, and I'd never have imagined I'd spend a Christmas like that in my life, but I saw my children and spent the day with my family, and when it was over, I realized it wasn't such a bad day after all.

A couple of days after Christmas, I noticed an unusual number of people walking past my room to Anna's. Christian had just left me for the night, so I called a nurse in.

"What's going on? What's wrong with Anna tonight?"

"She's not going to make it through the night," she explained. "They're here to say good-bye."

It was chilling news. I'd just been in therapy with her the day before. And tonight she was dying? I thought about how fragile our lives were, how easily everything we cared about could slip away. Knowing that Anna was in the next room about to leave this world, I couldn't help but think how close I had been to death. I wondered if her nana was with her, or coming.

In the middle of the night I heard someone cry out. It was a desperate, mournful wail that sent my heart racing. I pushed my call button and my nurse came in and explained that Anna had just passed away. It was her mother I'd heard.

When I asked what had happened, the nurse explained that Anna had given up. She was so depressed, and life after her accident was so hard. She'd stopped trying, and death had come.

I thought again of seeing her in therapy the day before. It was surreal to think that she was gone, that I lived in a place where death could come so quickly. I wanted to get out of the hospital as soon as I could, and I desperately wanted Christian's comfort.

"Can you please help me call Christian?" I asked the nurse. "I want to talk to him."

"It's two-thirty in the morning. You think he'll be up?"

"He won't mind," I promised.

Christian answered sleepily, and I told him that Anna had died. "I'm so afraid, Christian. Just like that, she's gone. I don't want that to happen to me. I want to live."

"You're going to live, darling. You've come such a long way. And you can't leave me now. We're going to grow old together and die at the same time, remember?"

I smiled. "I remember."

"Should I come up?" he asked.

Just the offer was enough to comfort me. "No, you should go back to sleep. I was just scared."

"I'll be there first thing in the morning, OK?"

"OK. Good night. Thank you, I love you."

"I love you, too—more than anything in this world."

After our phone call I lay in bed thinking about being alive. Tonight I was, and Anna wasn't. I thought about a story my father-in-law, Russ, had shared with me as he sat by my bedside in Arizona. It had never resonated so much with me as it did that night. Russ had told me how just days after the accident when I was in critical condition, at risk of losing my limbs if I survived at all, he had given me a priesthood blessing in which he felt strongly impressed that I would not only survive but would also live a full, beautiful life. Nothing about my medical condition indicated that would be possible, and the doctors had made it clear that death was a strong possibility, and even if I somehow beat the odds and lived, they didn't think I would ever have a normal, independent life.

The doctors' grim outlook didn't deter Russ at all. He had answered them definitively. "You're going to see a miracle. You're going to see something you have never seen before."

I believed that. I believed that my living was miraculous. It was hard—there was no denying that. My life would never be the same as it had been before the accident, and that thought regularly broke my heart. But being alive was such a gift, one that I vowed never to take for granted.

I said a prayer for Anna that night, and I thanked God, more fervently than I had ever before, for the gift of my life. I promised to cherish it no matter what it looked like. Warmth washed over me, and a feeling that new life was being breathed into every one of my cells tingled through my body. I knew it was God affirming my choice to feel grateful, helping me know He was near. In that moment, I felt hope again for things I'd barely dared to hope for—a healthy life, a happy family, more children, real joy. It was a powerful confirmation, more than just my thoughts at work, but the power of God speaking to my heart.

T wo days later, on December 31, the last day of 2008, the medical team gave the go-ahead: I could go home.

The nurses packed my room for what seemed like hours. They filled what seemed to be a zillion blue "hospital property" bags with everything I would need to continue my recovery at home—physical therapy bands and extra gauze (and more and more gauze), bandages, cream, scissors, tweezers, and plenty of instructions for me, Page, and Christian. They packed my movies and the Christmas village house my mom had given me.

I watched them working busily with mixed feelings. On the one hand, I couldn't wait to hear that door shut behind me and was nervous someone would come in and shut the whole thing down. "We thought you were ready," I imagined Dr. Saffle saying, "but you're not. You can't go home today."

But in a way, I kind of hoped he might. The nurses removed my central line IV, and I felt naked. If I were in pain, I would no longer have the quick relief of medication straight into my IV. I'd have to wait for pills to take effect. And what if I fell? Or I bled too much? Or couldn't get enough calories? All those thoughts suddenly made the burn unit more attractive than it had ever been. It was a safe place. Outside its walls, I would be so different, so embarrassed and ashamed about how I looked. The world was dangerous, and I was defenseless against it. But there was no turning back.

After my dressing change, Christian brought in clothes for me to change into. Actual clothes. He and Page helped me out of my hospital gown and into pajama bottoms and a tee shirt. I wore a pink I (HEART) MR. NIELSON hoodie that I'd received as a gift from the carnival fund-raiser. It had Christian's silhouette in red in place of the heart. And Reachel had sent me a darling white felt cloche with a big black flower from Anthropologie, where she worked. If I looked bad, at least I was wearing an adorable hat.

I stood in the doorway and said good-bye to my room, then walked into the hall to say good-bye to the staff and thank them for all their help and care. I was ready to make good on my promise to walk out of the hospital, but a nurse pushed a wheelchair over to me.

"Hospital policy," she said. "You've got to leave the hospital in a wheelchair."

I loved the dramatic image of walking triumphantly out of the hospital, where I'd lain immobile for so long. To be honest, though, I wasn't completely sure I could do it, so I didn't mind too much.

"Just let me walk out of the burn unit. Then I'll get in." I took my slow, halting C-3PO steps toward the open door.

A parade might have been nice, or a fifteen-piece band, maybe just a serenade by a few members of the Mormon Tabernacle Choir, but the nurses and staff that had supported me all those weeks gathered around and clapped as I crossed the threshold, and that was the perfect send-off.

I turned around, smiling back at the medical team, who was beaming at me, and watched the door swing shut behind us. *Thud.* It closed. And I was on the other side.

PART THREE

· · · · · · · · ·

*If you look after goodness and truth,
beauty will take care of itself.*

—Eric Gill

Twenty-seven

I *walked out of the hospital into the bitter cold. I took a deep* breath of the fresh frigid air—absent the sharp scent of antiseptic that hung in the hospital air. I lifted my face to the blue and purple sky, heavy with dusk. I was outside. Christian, Page, and my mother were by my side as I hobbled to the car, where I got settled in the front seat. It felt surreal to be outside, to be in a car, to be going home.

I looked at the hospital through the window of the car and noticed my own reflection in the glass. As we pulled away, the hospital disappeared from view, and I stared at my face for a moment. When I had dreamed of going home, I hadn't expected to look this way. *I'm going home with this face,* I told myself. *Surgery won't fix this.*

I drew in my breath as we pulled out of the parking lot into the city traffic. I had forgotten how busy traffic could be. The cars whizzed by, and their speed terrified me. It had become a morbid habit—my mind couldn't help imagining the worst. I pictured myself lying helpless in the wreckage of a car crash, trapped because I was too weak to save myself. The image startled me, and I shook my head, hoping to get rid of it. *I'm going home. Christian's here. Page and Mom are here. I'm going to be fine.*

At the first stoplight we pulled alongside another car, and I made eye contact with a woman inside. She drew back, understandably surprised. Before either of us could look away, I saw the shock and horror on her face.

"Did you see that?" I asked under my breath, not expecting an answer. *This is how people are going to look at me for the rest of my life.* Just a mile from the hospital, I found myself longing for the security of the burn unit.

The light turned green and we pulled forward. Cars lined the road ahead in both directions. As car headlights turned on, so did the Christmas lights on homes and businesses. For me, Christmas had come and gone, just like that. I'd almost completely forgotten it had been just a week earlier. We drove past grocery stores and restaurants and gas stations. Everywhere, people were going about their normal, busy lives.

I had no schedule or obligations. I had none of the usual responsibilities of a wife and mother. I didn't have a life. My only job was to heal. But all of these cars were filled with people who did, who were off to countless destinations—moms taking kids to New Year's Eve parties, teenagers planning their night out, families getting takeout. Maybe some people were going downtown to celebrate, and some were probably planning a cozy night in. Maybe that guy in the blue Honda was off to the airport to pick up someone he loved.

I watched a man open the car door for a woman outside a restaurant as we passed. I craned my head to watch her take his hand and climb out of the car. Someday, I hoped, that would be me taking Christian's hand.

But then I caught my reflection in the glass again, the ugly strain of my skin as I turned my head to look at the beautiful couple, my repulsive mouth open. We wouldn't be going to restaurants. Ever.

On the freeway, I was struck by the speed of it all. We drove fast, and the cars around us seemed to fly by. In my quiet hospital bed, I had forgotten how hectic and rushed regular life was. I used to be busy, too, I remembered. My days had been packed—grocery shopping, blogging, teaching yoga, visiting with friends; there was always something. It was hard to imagine I ever lived at that hectic pace, or that I ever would again. Seeing all those active, healthy people only confirmed that I wasn't ready for a real life yet and that the happy and healthy life I had hoped would await me in Provo wasn't going to be as easily won as I had thought. I was one step closer to being in my own home, but still so many steps away from being healthy. If I thought about the challenges ahead—managing my ever-present pain without an IV, depending on my family for all my care, and eventually caring for my children again—I was completely overwhelmed. For now, I knew I could only manage if I kept my sights set on the next ten minutes. I knew I could make it until then. And I hoped the next dose of my pain medication was within those next ten minutes, because I really needed it. Christian had set the alarm on his phone, and I was listening intently for the shrill beep that would announce I could take my next pill.

It was dark when we got to Provo, and Page asked if I wanted to drive past our new house. I was too overwhelmed. Another time, I promised. At Page's, the familiar large and colorful Christmas lights dangled from her fence. Courtney had helped the children make a sign for the door that read WELCOME HOME, MOMMY! in big bright letters. We arrived just in time to get settled before the annual family New Year's Eve party began. Page offered to set up a bed for me out in the family room so I could enjoy the party with everyone else, but I didn't want to. Not all of my nieces and nephews had seen me yet, and on my first night out of the hospital, I couldn't bear to see their reactions to me. I just wanted to stay tucked away in my own room.

"You made it, Steph! We're so happy you're here," Page said as she helped me into the bedroom next to hers. She had moved her two-year-old, Vivian, into another room so that I could be close to Page. As though she wasn't busy enough with eight children, I would be her ninth. They'd bought a new dresser for the room and brought in a bed with a crisp white bedspread. My fridge from the hospital was in one corner, full of snacks, and my mom had set up my little Christmas house as a night-light.

Thankfully, the alarm on Christian's phone went off just as he carried in the first load of my things.

"Does that mean I can have something for pain?" I asked urgently, the pain close to intolerable. I swallowed the pill Christian handed me and closed my eyes. I missed my IV.

There were cards from the children on the bedspread that cheered me—happy Christmas drawings and bright summer suns with hearts and stars. In just a few minutes I would see the children again. My heart beat faster, nervous and excited. I hoped it would be less scary for them, now that I was at Page's house and not at the hospital. Maybe our time together would be better now. I couldn't wait to thank the children for the cards. I hoped Jane would come in my room.

I got into bed just as my siblings and their families began to arrive. Christian rushed in the bedroom, delighted to tell me that Courtney and Christopher had just arrived with Ollie and the girls, and Lucy and Andrew would bring Nicholas soon.

"Stephanie, we'll all be here!" He was nearly giddy with excitement and called our children in.

Claire came in with a big smile. "Hi, Mommy! Welcome home!" I reached out for a hug, and Claire timidly came close enough for me to wrap my arms around her.

"Hi, Mom," Oliver said. "I'm glad you're here."

"Thanks, Ollie. Me, too. Can I have a hug? Is Jane out there?"

"I'm here, Mom. I'm going to stay in the hall."

"Hi, Jane," I called. "I love you. You know, I'm wearing my own clothes now. Does that help? I'm wearing a really cute hat that Reachel sent me."

Jane giggled. "OK. But I'm going to stay out here."

"I'm so happy to be home. We're going to have a wonderful year together." I was looking at Claire and Ollie but said it loud enough for Jane to hear, too. I could see the children felt the pull of the laughter from the living room as more and more cousins arrived. "Are you ready to go play?"

Claire nodded.

"Thanks for coming in. I love you so much." I squeezed Claire and Ollie again. "I love you, Jane," I called to the hall as the children ran to join the party.

Christian stayed with me, grinning. "That went great! You did so good, Steph!" He smiled all night and stayed with me as long as I would let him. I liked having him near, but I also wanted him to enjoy the party and celebrate with our children.

Lucy brought Nicholas in, and he clung to her tightly. He seemed so confused when I said, "Hi, Nicholas, it's Mommy." I had hoped he would remember me from the Christmas visit, but he leaned toward the door and pointed.

"Go," he said to Lucy. "Go."

Lucy was encouraging as she walked out of the room. "There's lots of time, Steph. He'll remember you, I know it."

My own son didn't know who I was. The jolt of it left my chest feeling empty and hollow as I remembered how inseparable Nicholas and I had been before the accident. I wondered when he would know me again.

My dad passed Lucy on her way out. "Cubby!" he boomed. "You're home!" He came to my bedside and gave me a kiss. "There's going to be another big snowstorm tonight, and we can just hunker down together. You can watch the snow out the window and enjoy being home."

I smiled. "Thanks, Dad. I'm glad you're here."

"Oh, darlin', I'm so glad *you're* here. This is just the beginning, OK? It's going to be a great year."

My brothers and sisters came in throughout the night. They were as loving and supportive as they'd always been, and genuinely happy that I'd made it home. But I noticed how they spoke to me, with such deliberate, exaggerated kindness, like I was as mentally deficient as I was physically incapable. They spoke a little louder than normal, with extra enthusiasm. I knew they were only trying to be kind, but it was a thick layer of kindness—the sort you reserve for young children or the mentally disabled—which hurt me. *That's how they see me now*, I thought. I felt like I knew a secret that no one else did: my mind was in perfect shape.

Muffled bits of conversations and jokes—real life—filtered down the hall to my room. I felt sorry for Christian that he didn't have a wife who could celebrate with him. Even surrounded by my accepting and loving family, I felt self-conscious about that. Just before midnight Christian came in with a glass of "bubbly," our family's favorite nonalcoholic sparkling juice, and sat next to me on the bed. We listened to the family count down to the New Year.

"Five-four-three-two-one," their collective voices sang out.

"Happy New Year, darling!" Christian said.

"Happy New Year," I replied, and we clinked glasses and kissed awkwardly. Glasses clinked in the living room, too, and we heard a chorus of celebration. I imagined all the kisses at the stroke of midnight and the hugs that followed.

It was a miracle I'd made it 'til midnight. "I'm tired," I said. "I think I need to go to bed now."

Christian tucked me in and knelt by my bed for a prayer. He took my hand in his, just as he always had when we prayed, and we bowed our heads to thank God that I was, after five long months, finally home. Home! Christian wept with gratitude as he asked God to help me see how far I had come with heaven's help. "Please bless Stephanie to see the changes she's already made," he said, "and please continue to bless her with strength and progress. Please help her to be comfortable here tonight, and to sleep well."

After our prayer, I sent Christian back to the party while I lay there, listening to laughter from the other room and thinking about the year ahead. Christian, my dad, and Page had often encouraged me to think ahead. "Think what a difference a year will make," they'd said. As 2008 faded away, I hoped for the strength Christian had just prayed for. *If a year will make such a difference, please let this be the year.*

I woke up the next morning at eight o'clock. I had slept through the night! It was the first night I'd done so since I'd been conscious. No interruptions to check my pulse or fluids, no nighttime shots. It was snowing outside, and I watched the big flakes float gently from the sky. The view outside the window was perfect—I could see the sky, snow-covered trees, and a bit of lawn, but no one could see in. I heard the sounds of the neighborhood outside my window— people calling to one another and car doors slamming. *Early risers off to the ski hill,* I thought as I heard engines start and cars drive away. *What I wouldn't give to be going skiing today.* Lying in bed, staring out the window at the trees and snow, I wasn't even really part of that world anymore, just an observer.

The snowdrifts out my window were so deep, they seemed permanent. It seemed impossible that there would ever be green grass under that layer of white. But I knew the miracle of spring would come to Provo, as it always did, and I could only hope that the bleak and depressing landscape of my life would blossom again along with it. Would my winter thaw by spring?

I tried to move and remembered I couldn't get out of bed on my own. I called for Page, my voice still not strong enough to be sure I could get her attention.

"Page!" I called weakly. "Page!"

Her two young girls ran past my room, little Vivian and three-and-a-half-year-old Meri. Page's teenage boys were laughing in the living room and listening to loud music. Even though I was stuck in bed, it was so pleasant to hear the shouts and laughter of a home instead of the formalities and beeping machines of the hospital.

I heard Page in the other room change the boys' music to the Mormon Tabernacle Choir, and then turn up the stereo. She hurried into my bedroom to the strains of "O, Holy Night."

"Good morning! Happy New Year!" She smiled and asked about my night as she helped me out of my burn mask and other nighttime contraptions.

"I really need a pain pill," I explained, and Page hurried to the dresser to find the right prescription among the many bottles lined up there—medication for depression and anxiety, a variety of pain meds including something for constant pain and something for quick relief, a few different antibiotics, and medication for my skin grafts, plus vitamins and blood thinners.

By this time I was desperate to get to the bathroom, and after that our next stop was breakfast. I hobbled laps around the kitchen and living room while she made eggs. I still didn't have much of an appetite, but Page's eggs were one of the first things I enjoyed eating. I soaked in the sounds of the music and the children playing together.

I sat between Meri and thirteen-year-old Emma at breakfast.

I pretended they were my own girls, except they didn't seem to be nearly as concerned about my appearance as my own children were. To Page's children, I was the Arizona Aunt Stephanie whom they only saw four or five times a year. For my own children, the stakes were so much higher, as they tried to understand how their mother had changed so dramatically.

"Why is that skin around your eyes so white?" Meri asked.

I saw it as a chance to practice what I would say to my own children. "The doctors took skin from another part of my body and put it around my eyes to help them blink better than they were. So for a little while, that skin will be a different color." I smiled at Meri and leaned in. "Kind of weird, huh?"

She giggled. "Yeah, it is."

My heart swelled with love for little Meri. She gave me hope that Jane would come around, but in the meantime I could give Meri the love my little Jane was still too hesitant to receive.

After breakfast Page helped me undress and took off my bandages so she could shower and scrub me before the home health nurses arrived. She gave me another pain pill just before the shower so that the medication would be in effect in time for the dressing change. I swallowed the pill and hoped it would cover the pain when I needed it. I feared what awaited me if it didn't.

In the bathroom, I found I couldn't lift my legs high enough to step into the tub. I tried, but when I bent my legs the skin on my knees ripped right open and bled. After a few attempts, Page finally called Vance in, and my brother-in-law lifted my naked body into the shower. That was motivation enough to get better quickly. At first, Page tried to scrub me while I was in the shower and she was out of it. But she and the bathroom floor were quickly soaked.

"Oh, forget it," she said and just took her clothes off and got in the shower with me.

We laughed at how ridiculous it was as she washed my hair and then her own, and for just a minute I thought it was very funny. But then I caught a glimpse in the bathroom mirror of the two of us in the shower. *What are we doing? What has happened to my life?*

I left a bloody trail on the tile as I climbed out of the shower. I stared at myself in the mirror and thought about how I looked like a tattoo that had gone terribly wrong, with my dark swirls and streaks. I was still exploring my new face—the terrible scars, the big lips, the strange little nose.

Page saw me looking at myself in the mirror and was enthusiastic. "Stephanie, you look so good. So much better! Already, these few months have made such a difference."

I hadn't been looking at myself for as long as Page had been looking at me, but I couldn't see any progress as far as my appearance was concerned. Her enthusiasm bothered me. Couldn't she see what I looked like? There was nothing "better" about it.

The doorbell rang, and Becca, the home health nurse, arrived to dress my wounds again. I knew it was impossible, but I had hoped that I could skip a dressing change on New Year's Day. I just wanted one day off, but holidays don't exist when you have wounds to care for, and I took yet another painkiller right before she began and hoped it would kick in. The IV had been managing my pain effectively for months now. The pain was always there, but if needed, I could have relief almost immediately through the IV. But switching over to the pills in the last twenty-four hours had come as a shock to my system, and I was feeling more pain than I had in months. I prayed that we had timed the pills and dosage right this morning, but something was off, and as Becca worked I felt incredible pain and needed frequent breaks. I was annoyed to think that we'd have to tweak my pain management routine—it seemed there was always something in the way of a comfortable life, and I was desperate to get it right.

My healing skin was dry and itchy but so thin that if I scratched it I would bleed. To help moisturize my skin, my mother-in-law had suggested olive oil as a natural alternative to all the chemical-laden moisturizers we could have used. Becca heated it a little before it was applied, and the warmth was perfect. The smell reminded me of going to dinner with Christian at our favorite Italian restaurant. I imagined myself all dressed up for dinner and walking in the door on his arm. It was romantic to think of sitting together at our own table in a busy restaurant, and it was delicious to think about that warm rosemary bread dipped in olive oil.

Christian and my mom came for lunch, and when Christian kissed me he noticed the smell. I told him how I'd dreamed of the warm bread and olive oil while Becca worked on me. Of course as soon as I mentioned that something sounded good to eat, Christian was off to pick up some takeout. But it wasn't really bread I wanted. What I craved when I smelled that olive oil was a happy, normal life. When Christian returned with the bread, I couldn't eat it.

My mom stayed after lunch to help me work out with the resistance bands the hospital had sent home for me. Beginning the next week I would go back to the hospital for physical therapy three times a week, but on the other days we worked out at Page's. After our therapy session, I was ready for a nap. I knew our children and their cousins would be coming to Page's to sled down her big hill, and I looked forward to being woken up by the sounds of their voices again.

Claire came into my room just as I was waking up. "Hi, Mom! Here." She handed me another drawing. In this one, Claire was picking apples at our new house.

"There's an apple tree at our new house, Mom. I miss our tree house, but having an apple tree is really cool." She told me how much she loved the snow, and how happy she was to be in Utah so she could play in it. "We're going sledding today, Mom."

I hung on Claire's every word and tried to absorb her energy and enthusiasm. Just before she left she said, "Mom, things are going to be OK with Jane. She misses you a lot. She takes a picture of you to bed and cries at night. I'm trying to help her. She told me she'll come in soon."

I took Claire's hand. "Thank you, sweetie." Claire was trying to help Jane and was looking out for me, too. What an incredible girl.

I asked Page to help me to the living room while the children sledded out back, and I watched Claire, Jane, and Oliver laugh and play with their cousins. The girls looked adorable in their new Christmas berets. I watched Jane especially carefully, her cheeks bright red with the cold. She seemed to laugh easily, and she squealed all the way down the hill. As she climbed up again, I noticed a maturity I hadn't seen before. Had I made them all grow up too soon?

By the time the children were ready to come inside for dinner, I was exhausted and back in bed. I ate dinner in bed and listened to their conversation from my bedroom. Being under the same roof was nice, but being at the same table was a goal for another day. Claire and Ollie came to hug and kiss me good night before they went back to Courtney's and I longed to hold Jane's little body, too, but she stayed in the hall.

"Good night, Mom."

"Good night, sweet Jane. Remember to say your prayers, sweetie. Heavenly Father is eager to hear all about your day. And will you pray for us, too? That soon we can look at each other? I miss your blue eyes."

"Good idea, Mom! I will."

After the door shut, I strained to hear their voices out in the driveway, trying to soak up every last sound the children made. But the car drove away, and there was silence in place of their laughter.

Christian stayed to help me through my nighttime routine, which started with going to the bathroom, brushing my teeth, and taking a handful of pills before I got ready for bed. Then he helped me into my many nighttime contraptions, which felt like going to sleep in a torture chamber. First there were braces that stretched my legs and arms all night long and then a special pair of mechanical gloves to help my stiff fingers bend. Once the gloves were on, my fingers were flexed and straightened while I slept. The final touch was my clear plastic face mask.

We said a prayer together, thanking God that I'd made it through another day and praying for another good day tomorrow. Christian read the scriptures to me, and though I tried to focus, my mind wandered to thoughts of being home—my first full day out of the hospital.

It had been a good day. And a hard day. And tomorrow would be exactly the same. Painful and dependent. Would my new hospital staff—Christian, Page, and the rest of my family—feel as enthusiastic in the days to come as they had today? I hoped they had more resolve than I did at the moment.

My last thoughts that night were of Nicholas and Jane. I didn't have any idea how I'd win them over, but I prayed for help that somehow my children would love me again. *Patience.* The thought was quiet as a whisper. *Just be patient. It won't be long.*

Twenty-eight

A fter two days at Page's we had a predictable routine down, and two weeks later it had little variation. Most evenings our children would eat dinner at Page's house, but we also had dinner at Courtney's sometimes. Once winter break ended and school started again, the girls would often ride the bus up to Page's after school with Page's school-age children and do homework in the living room while I listened from bed. And three times a week, Christian drove me back to the University of Utah hospital for physical therapy.

I dreaded going back to the hospital—I had an irrational fear that they would decide to keep me there. And being in therapy reminded me of the long, lonely, painful days I had spent at the burn unit. As I worked alongside the other patients, I thought about how they would be wheeled back to their lonely beds, and I was depressed on their behalf. I worked a little harder, thinking how fortunate I was that I would be walking out of the hospital on my husband's arm after a few hours of PT. The hospital patients would sit in bed all night and watch TV and I would be going home to a loving family.

This evening as usual I noted the *thud* of the burn unit door as it closed behind us and welcomed the sting on my cheeks as we walked out of the hospital into the cold January air. I cried tears of gratitude almost every time we drove away. It took us an hour to get there, then three hours in therapy, and another hour to get home. By the time we got back to Provo, I was usually ready to call it a day, but for the first time in a long time, I was actually hungry and craving my favorite Café Rio.

We had left my handicapped parking pass in our other car, but Christian pulled into a handicapped parking place anyway. I stayed in the car, and he ran in to get our food. Almost as soon as he left, a middle-aged, overweight woman came tapping on my window, pointing at the rearview mirror and the missing permit.

She screamed at me through the glass, "You are NOT allowed to park here! You don't have a permit! What's wrong with you?"

She shook her finger at me, and I looked at her helplessly. I held up my hands and tried to explain. "I can't open the door. I can't roll down the window. I can't move my fingers."

Either the woman didn't see me clearly, or didn't care. "You need to move your car now or I'm calling the police." She pulled out her cell phone. "Watch me dial."

Astounded, I burst into tears. Was this how people would treat me? I hated how much I stood out, but in that moment, I would have given anything for this woman to see what an invalid I was. I had no way to protect myself.

A few minutes later I saw the flashing lights as the police car pulled up, and an officer approached. The woman launched into her tirade again, and I shrunk lower in the front seat of the car, wanting to disappear. She waved her arms and I could hear her shrill voice through the door. "She doesn't have a permit. She can't park there!"

I was sobbing by the time the officer approached. Again, I held up my hands and tried to explain that they didn't work. I couldn't open the door or unroll the window. Finally the officer opened the door and I told him that I had a permit, but I didn't have it with me. My husband, I said, had just run in to pick up our food.

"I'm so sorry," I apologized over and over. "I am so sorry."

"Are you OK?" he asked.

I nodded.

"I'm sorry to have bothered you, ma'am." He glanced back at the woman. "This is ridiculous."

Just as the officer closed my door, Christian stepped outside, and he looked from our car to the police officer, sensing something was wrong. He walked up to the officer, who I couldn't hear, but his gesture suggested he was explaining to the woman how hurt I was. As Christian approached, she started in on him, but he cut her off and was loud enough for me to hear him. "How dare you? You have no right to talk to my wife like that. Are you kidding me?" I could see his breath in the cold air against the flashing light of the police car.

The officer stepped in front of Christian and held up his hands. I couldn't hear what he said, but Christian backed away and came to the car, seething.

I continued to sob as Christian backed out of the parking space and glared at the woman for as long as he could see her. In any other circumstance, I would have seen this situation as a baffling over-reaction, and I realized that this woman was completely irrational and unstable, but still, this felt like such a personal attack. I had barely been in public, and now my worst fears about it were coming true. I was desperately afraid of having someone jeer at me, and that's exactly what had happened. And I hadn't even gotten out of the car. This is what life would be like now: wherever I went, people would look at me, be horrified by me, see me as someone who didn't fit in, someone who was breaking the rules. I couldn't even eat the Café Rio I'd been craving.

All that week and into the next I would burst into tears when I remembered the woman's angry face. I heard her shrill voice in my head through the glass of the window over and over again. *"What's wrong with you?"*

Christian was especially gentle that night as he helped me get ready for bed at Page's. I think he was hurt, too, that he hadn't been able to protect me from her, that he had been so oblivious to what was happening just outside the restaurant. After outfitting me in my night-time contraptions, he sat next to my bed. I knew he wouldn't head back to Courtney's until I fell asleep, and it was always easier when he was there. But I also knew how tired he was. He was still healing, too, still doing physical therapy, having dressing changes and working hard to take care of me and our children. He needed rest as much as I did. So as I'd done with my brother Matt in the hospital, I closed my eyes and lay still, pretending to be asleep so he could go back to Courtney's and go to bed.

"Steph?" he whispered, and I lay there trying to breathe deeply and sleepily. "Are you asleep, babe?" He waited, and I was so still. "I love you," he said. "Good night."

I listened for the front door to close behind him, and then for his car to start and drive away. I missed him as soon as he was gone. It reminded me of when we'd dated, and how much we hated to be apart. Page's house had always been planned as an interim between the hospital and home, and I felt safe and comfortable there, but I began to think of going home with Christian. Maybe sooner would be better than later.

When Christian came the next afternoon, he brightened my room just by walking in the door. He'd spent the morning moving some clothes and medical supplies from Courtney's into our new house. He was hopeful that soon I would be ready to move in as well.

"What do you think, Steph?" he asked. "Do you think it's time to move into our own home?"

I was looking forward to it—and Christian had been ready to reunite our family for weeks—but I still felt timid about making such a big decision. I was comfortable and safe at Page's but couldn't deny the feeling that moving into our own home was the next necessary step.

"I want to. But I don't. I'm just so nervous." I wondered whether Christian could do all the things that I needed him to. We had decided Christian shouldn't return to work until I was stronger so he could take care of me full-time, and we'd live off our savings. I knew I'd have Christian's full attention, but Page was a nurse, and Christian didn't have that training. Would he really be able to help with my wounds, my therapy, and my medication? Would he be able to make me breakfast and get me to the bathroom whenever I needed? I was even a little afraid he would roll over on me in the night.

Christian had an answer, of course, for every concern. "If you have a bad dream, I'll be right there, right next to you. I can help you get up to go to the bathroom anytime. If you need medicine, I'll get up at any hour."

"What if you're still asleep when I wake up in the morning? What if I'm hungry or I hurt?"

"Hey, remember I'm doing this with you," he reminded me. "I'm going to take such good care of you. I know how you feel, Stephanie. I've been through it, too."

I had never been good at making decisions, and the accident amplified my ability to second-guess myself. Christian and I prayed about it though, and I had a strong confirmation that it was right. I should move to the new house, with Christian. It was time. Within minutes, however, I was worrying about the next step—bringing our children home. Could Christian take care of our children's needs *and* mine, especially since I was essentially a fifth child to bathe, clothe, feed, and comfort? Could he manage having Nicholas and Oliver home all day, get Claire off to school, and Jane off to half-day kindergarten? Could he make dinner and do the laundry and run the household all while managing his helpless wife? Could he do it all? And would I trust him enough to let him do it?

We had driven by our new house before, but later that day, Christian took me inside our new home for the first time. We walked up the sandstone walkway that led to the front porch—the carefully laid stone path was the work of ward members. Inside, every room had a story of people who had helped—family, friends, Church members, and contractors who'd donated their work—and that made me love the house even more. Everything in it was darling—new light fixtures and stainless steel appliances and lovely paint colors. As I walked through I felt so thankful we'd been provided a place to live, but I couldn't shake the surreal feeling that this place I'd never seen before, this home that had been chosen for me, was where our family would live now.

In the connected living room and dining room, there was a wall of windows to the east and big front windows to the south. The windows were bare, and I shrank away from them, feeling exposed and vulnerable. In the hallway that led to the bedrooms, there was a stairwell to the basement, but the railing hadn't been put on yet. I felt a sudden irrational pull, like if I got too close, I'd get sucked down that dark hole. I stayed as far away from the stairs as I could. Looking out the window in our new bedroom I saw the bare branches of the apple tree and the view of Y Mountain.

We returned to the kitchen and lingered there for a minute. I sat away from the window, on a plastic lawn chair that had been left by construction workers. Christian pointed out the tree in the backyard where he planned to build our next tree house and another tree in the side yard where he'd put a swing.

"I think I'll go to Mesa in a couple of weeks, Steph, and arrange for moving our stuff here," Christian said. "Then you can move in when you're ready, and a few weeks later, we'll bring the kids home. How does that sound?"

I thought of our home in Mesa, of the curtains I'd made for the kitchen and the huge glass door that went from the living room to the backyard. I'd never go back there again. This would be our home now. Christian would bring our things back, and we'd live here. I didn't wonder where we'd put the couch or how we'd arrange the living room. None of that really mattered to me. The one thing I did care about was having a big dining room table, big enough for a large family.

In fact, I had already ordered the table, without even seeing the kitchen. Now I pictured it against the east-facing windows. In Mesa, we'd been squeezing around the small kitchen table Christian had built for me when we got married, and we had outgrown it before the accident. I pictured the children and Christian and me all gathered around the large dining room table, laughing and happy in our new kitchen. But a big table meant more to me than extra elbow room. It became a symbol of hope for the large family I hoped we'd still have.

The image of the table was the one thing I kept coming back to as we walked through the house that day: a happy, healthy body in every chair at our table for eight.

Twenty-nine

T he next afternoon I was sitting on the chair in my bed-room at Page's, enjoying the smell of her freshly baked bread, when Courtney walked into my room with my laptop. She told me there were so many people who wanted to know how I was doing. "They want to hear it from you now," she said, "not from me."

I rejected the thought without even really considering it. My feelings hadn't changed much since the previous month, when my dad had suggested I start blogging again. I didn't want to open up about how I was doing, and besides, I only had depressing things to share. And I still felt the sting of losing that perfect life that I'd shared on my blog.

But Courtney left the computer. "I think you should do it, Steph," she encouraged.

Then Christian came in the room and talked about all the people who had reached out to me. He reminded me of everyone who had worked on our house, of the many fund-raisers and the balloon launches, and the online donations. "Just check your e-mail," he suggested.

I was hesitant, but what could it hurt? I logged in to my e-mail account for the first time since the previous August and was shocked to see thousands of e-mails. I couldn't believe it. They were the same kind of encouraging and loving words my mother had read to me in the hospital in Phoenix. I opened another and another. They all offered love and encouragement. They thanked me for the difference I'd made in their lives. I felt like I hadn't done anything for anyone in months. As I read these words from strangers who loved me, I thought back to my commitment to return to Earth and share hope. It's what I had promised to do.

I still didn't feel up to the task, but was determined to keep my commitment. If God had a plan that involved me sharing hope, I would do it.

I missed blogging, but I was still uncertain about what to say. No one would want to hear about my miserable days—readers knew the old Nie Nie, the happy, carefree version of myself. I worried about the time as well. Some days it was all I could do just to get out of bed. I knew I couldn't blog every day. And people would want pictures, but I was not ready to share what I looked like. Yet my worries didn't diminish the feeling I had that it was the right thing to do, so I pushed them aside. Maybe I wouldn't do it perfectly, but I would start . . . today. I asked Christian to take a picture of our hands clasped together in our compression garments, and he downloaded it for me.

Typing was a slow and painful process. I pushed one . . . key . . . at . . . a . . . time, with my clumsy, bandaged fingers.

It's true.
I am alive.
I look different.
I walk slow . . . and type slower.
But it's good to be back!!

I wrote about my gratitude for all that people had done for us—the prayers and letters and e-mails and gifts for the children and donations and love—and I felt a little of the weight of my grief lift. It was such a relief to begin to thank all the people who had given to me. I knew I would not be able to reach each and every person who had blessed my life and my family, but starting felt so good.

I finished the post reflecting on the fact that, despite all the changes in my life, maybe I wasn't so different after all. If I typed it, maybe I could believe it, too. At the end of the day, I realized, Christian still took me by the hand to go to bed. They were different hands now, and wrapped in compression garments, but it was something we'd done before the accident. Writing about it gave me hope.

Here's to a new Nie!
. . . but not so different.

As I continued to blog those first few weeks, it became easier. I felt the same flush I did when I had first started my blog in New Jersey, an eagerness to share my experiences that had made me run up and down those dark basement stairs whenever I could to get to the computer. Of course, I now had a very different life, but the satisfaction I took in sharing came back full force.

For my second post, I asked Christian to take pictures of the details of my new life—the row of prescription bottles, the raised toilet seat, and the supplies for my dressing changes.

I had been so completely cut off from the world for so long, venturing back in—on my own terms—felt better than I had expected. I found the therapy I think my dad had hoped for when he'd brought my laptop up the month earlier. It was in the love and support of those reading my blog, their willingness to share my sorrow and also laugh with me. And to my surprise, I found I had more to share than just depressing stories. There were moments to laugh at, like when I wrote about falling asleep in the middle of a *conversation* with my physical therapist. As I typed, I realized maybe things weren't as bad as they seemed.

The posts were short and simple, but each one was a labor of love for my slow, stiff fingers. As I watched my fingers pick out each letter I realized I was also keeping a valuable record of my recovery. When I thought of what this record would mean to my children one day, I became even more motivated to write. More and more each day, I felt that what I had written in that very first entry after the accident was true: It was good to be back.

C hristian flew to Arizona at the end of January to move our belongings to Utah. He hired a moving company to pack everything but was there to supervise. I could never have walked through the house that had once been bursting with our contentment. It took its toll on Christian, too. When he came back to Utah with an Allied moving truck full of our boxes, he came to Page's house and lay on the bed beside me.

He buried his head in the pillow and cried. "Stephanie, it was so hard." He told me how sad he'd been to say good-bye to our back porch, where we'd sat in our swing in those mild Arizona evenings and laughed at our beautiful children. Utah's gray skies seemed to hang especially heavy around us.

"I hope they don't tear down the tree house," Christian said, and like he must have, I heard the echoes of the children laughing as they climbed into Mulberry Bungalow.

I knew that for Christian, moving meant more than leaving the house we loved. He didn't say it, but I knew he was mourning for the job he had loved and the life he had built where he was the successful provider for our family, so capable and in control. He was trading it for a life of painful new beginnings and an uncertain future.

Finally, he was sharing his tears for the life we had lost.

That night I wrote on my blog.

Mr. Nielson lay next to me in tears. He smelled like the cologne I had offered him for Christmas last year—in the house.

"I sprayed it on before they boxed it up . . . reminds me of Arizona . . . reminds me of you."

He softly said, "The kitchen was lifeless without you."

The children and I had always danced in that kitchen while we waited for Christian to come home for dinner. If I'd been writing for myself, I might have just given in to tears right then. But something about sharing it on my blog helped me turn my heart to hope. I finished the post thinking about our new life, and how I couldn't wait to dance with my children again, this time in our new kitchen in Utah. Someday that would happen. I hoped Christian would read the post, and that he would feel it, too.

For the time being I was still at Page's, but now that our belongings were in Utah, Christian was living at the new house, and soon enough I would join him. The hard part was knowing when we would be ready—there was no box to check that would tell us if it was time. We had to move forward trusting that we'd know. And all we had to trust was our instincts.

The following week Christian drove me to my therapy session in a wild winter snowstorm. Wind whipped around our car and snow blew across the road our whole drive back to Provo. In my head, I knew Christian was in control behind the wheel, but my body tensed in anxious dread. I breathed an actual sigh of relief when we finally got off the freeway safely and made our way to Page's neighborhood.

But when we got to the hill that leads to Page's house, our wheels spun on the icy road. Without any traction, the car slid backward down the hill, and we were helpless. We came to a stop safely, but cold panic rippled through my body and my heart raced. Something inside me snapped. "I have to go home," I said. "I have to go home now."

"We'll get there," Christian answered, gunning the car up Page's hill again.

"No, not to Page's. I need to go home to our home. I'm not going to heal until we're all together again."

Something about sliding down that hill in our car, out of control, galvanized my resolve. I needed to be in my own home, with my husband and my children. Any doubts were erased, and I was ready to go home. I moved in with my husband the following day.

The celebration was minimal that first night together in the same bed, but it was certainly nice to sleep next to Christian. As he had done many times the last few weeks, he helped me through my nightly routine—everything but the plastic burn mask, so we could talk for a bit—but this time, he got in bed beside me. For the first time in six months I was going to sleep next to my husband.

He put his hand on the back of my neck. "What are you going to do tomorrow?" he asked. It was a little game we had played at bedtime before the accident.

"I am hoping to wake up tomorrow. And maybe eat breakfast. How about that?"

"It's a start." Christian smiled at me tenderly and kissed my forehead. "Now, what are you going to dream about tonight?"

I just didn't have the heart for much. "I don't really care," I said. "How about that I'm going to get better?"

"You are, definitely, going to get better. Good night, my beautiful wife." Christian strapped my burn mask on. "I am so thankful you're home."

Christian strapped on his own mask, too, and we fell asleep. In the middle of the night, a nightmare started brewing—bright flames and fearful screams. I reached for Christian and felt his leg against mine. The rising panic receded; my choked breath grew steady again. Christian was there. I went back to sleep until morning.

In my first half-conscious awareness the next morning, I felt Christian's warmth next to me, so comforting in its familiarity, but by the time I was fully awake, my pain was completely out of control. Christian rushed to get my medication, and I lay in bed, trying to stay as still as possible, willing the medicine to work quickly.

"Hey, we've got someone important coming over today," Christian announced as he brought in my tray of eggs a little while later.

"What? No." My intense pain had put me in a terrible mood, and I didn't want to see anyone.

"I think you'll be happy with this visitor," Christian said with a mysterious smile as he set down my tray. He returned a minute later. "Look who's here."

It was our sweet Jimmy, with terrible breath and a few extra pounds, but our dear dog just the same. He felt like home. He had caught a ride from Arizona with Christian's sister Diane and her husband, David, who had come to Provo to drop their son off for his mission.

Christian rubbed Jimmy's ears and I told Jimmy how good it was to see him. He seemed happy to see us, too, and followed Christian wherever he went for the rest of the day.

A *few days later, I sat at our newly delivered dining room* table in the kitchen of our new home while my sisters and sisters-in-law unpacked the boxes from Mesa. I couldn't do anything to help, just sit and watch as they unwrapped our old life and put everything in place for our new one to begin. It all seemed so surreal. Without lifting a finger, my life had been transported from one home to another, and my sweet sisters-in-law were doing all the work. In my other life, it was the kind of work I had loved—arranging, straightening, nesting. But now I was happy to have them do it. They chatted as they worked and occasionally asked my opinion.

"Where do you want this?" they'd ask of kitchen appliances and mixing bowls and cake plates. "How about this?" It was our orange juice press. In Mesa we'd gone out to the yard to pick oranges and were drinking the juice minutes later. I looked out the window at the snow. The juicer wouldn't be getting a lot of use here.

"I don't care where you put it. Wherever you think is fine." It didn't matter to me where any of it went, because I wouldn't be using any of it anytime soon. I had moved into this house with everything I needed: pajamas, a load of prescription drugs, a raised toilet seat, and a bunch of straps and braces for my body. The possessions that arrived in the moving truck meant almost nothing to me. After about twenty minutes of watching my sisters and sisters-in-law so kindly putting away my things, I was too tired to stay in the kitchen and had to go lie down.

I was still lying in bed when my friend Mindy Gledhill called Christian to say that she had something she wanted to give me. I think she sensed that I was hesitant to have her come over—I hadn't seen anyone but family and hospital staff since the accident—but she assured Christian that she wouldn't stay long, and I didn't even have to come out if I didn't want to see her. She just had something to give me, she said. By this time she'd done two benefit concerts for me and blessed me with music that always inspired me. I was incredibly grateful for all her support; I could hardly turn her away.

Even though it was Mindy—she loved me and I loved her—I still felt embarrassed about my appearance. Stupid, in fact, is the perfect word to describe how I felt about the way I looked and the fact that there was nothing I could do about it. But Mindy didn't seem the least bit shocked by my appearance, or if she was she did a good job hiding it. She gave me a loving note and some flowers and handed me a CD. She told me how she'd been writing a song before our accident, but it just hadn't come together, so she'd put it aside for a while. Then, when she heard about what had happened to Christian and me and thought about how much our lives had changed, the words had come together.

As soon as she left, I played the song, and then I listened to it over and over the rest of the day and all night long, and then all through the next days, weeks, and months—thousands of times. She had captured perfectly how I felt and just what I was going through, especially with these lines:

> *You're a butterfly held captive*
> *Small and safe in your cocoon*
> *Go on, you can take your time,*
> *Time is said to heal all wounds.*

I felt exactly as if I were in a cocoon, constantly wondering if I would I ever emerge. During long, lonely hours, it didn't feel like time was anything but torture. And yet, when I looked back over the three months that I had been conscious, I knew I had come so far. I could only hope that the next three months, and the three after that, would bring the same kind of progress. And hopefully some sort of acceptance, too. In the meantime, I would listen to Mindy's song over and over again, reassured by the message and hope of the lyrics:

> *Believe me when I say*
> *It's not about your scars*
> *It's all about your heart.*

Thirty

M y stomach was tight, buzzing with nerves, as we pulled into the hospital parking lot for my first surgery since being released from the hospital. Even though I'd come for therapy regularly, it had been five weeks since I'd spent the night there. I was scheduled for a skin release surgery with Dr. Morris, another of the surgeons who had worked on me during my hospital stay, and though I was only expected to stay for two or three days, the thought of being back in a hospital bed set my heart racing.

The plan was to release the tight skin under my arms. So much scar tissue had built up that my skin had to be sliced to allow for a normal range of motion. As far as surgeries go, it was a pretty routine procedure, but I knew any number of things could happen, which would mean I'd have to stay longer, and I'd lose those exhilarating feelings of freedom I'd celebrated in the past month when I had walked out of the hospital on Christian's arm and driven away.

But my real fear was that I might not come back from this trip to the operating room. I was afraid Nana would come for me, and maybe this time, I wasn't supposed to come back. By the time the nurses helped me into my hospital gown and prepped me for surgery, my heart felt tight, like a rock in my chest.

"This is only temporary, darling," Christian reminded me. "You'll be right back at home in no time. Remember, you are a beautiful work in progress."

"I love you so much," I said to Christian, holding his hand just before I was wheeled into surgery. "I might not come back this time, Christian. If I die, please remember how much I love you and our children."

"Stephanie, you're not going to die. This is a simple surgery. Everything's going to be fine. I'll be right here when you wake up, OK?"

Tears filled my eyes. "OK. I hope so." I nodded to reassure myself. "Just so you know, if you get remarried, I'll haunt your second wife."

The surgery went just as planned, and I was awake again within a few hours and on my way home within two days. I didn't remember it right away, but Nana had been there again. Once I was home, I had that familiar impression in my memory, the warm and comfortable feeling of her presence, but still it scared me. I wondered again if she had come to take me with her. But she hadn't taken me, I realized, because here I was, awake and lying in bed at home.

Later that day Page came to see me and I told her about our nana's visit. "She was back, Page, and I'm so afraid she'll come to take me away."

"What if she comes to help you?" Page suggested. "What if she's there to comfort you, Steph?"

I hadn't considered that possibility, even though the memory of Nana was always enveloped in a beautiful feeling. My own thoughts, I realized, had made her visits seem sinister and morbid.

"What if, before you go into surgery next time, you asked for her to come? So she's with you before you go in? Maybe she can help you feel less worried," Page suggested.

Page had always been full of good ideas, but this was one of her best. I couldn't believe it hadn't occurred to me that Nana was there to help, but all of a sudden, I knew it was true. That's why she had come during surgery—she was there when I was most vulnerable, when I was most at risk. I wondered if she'd been there during other times, too, but I just hadn't noticed.

After Page left, I reflected on what a tremendous honor it was to have my grandmother visit and comfort me. I saw the pattern more clearly, that she had been there to help and bless me all along. It changed the way I thought about life, knowing that my grandmother, who had passed away so many years earlier, was still very much with me. I was overcome with gratitude to realize how connected we were—not just Nana and me, but that everyone has loved ones who are watching over them. They are closer than we think. Having Nana help me was another confirmation that life does continue beyond this Earth. It renewed my hope in another life to come, when I wouldn't be hurt so badly, when my body and my spirit would be healed completely. Until then, I was so grateful to be alive, so thankful to have my body on Earth.

The night after I returned from the hospital our children came over for dinner, our first as a family at the new house. The children hadn't been inside the house yet and they explored every room and ran up and down the stairs before we gathered around our new table. Christian was both mom and dad before, during, and after the meal. I felt guilty that I couldn't do more to help, but I enjoyed the life and laughter our children brought with them.

Christian called on Ollie to say the prayer that night, and as he thanked God for the food and asked Him to bless it for us, he also prayed for me. "Please bless Mom to get better," he said.

I'd heard others pray for me for months now, but hearing the words in Ollie's own sweet voice was especially touching and motivating. I knew God heard the words of my sweet boy.

Christian asked the children to tell us about their favorite parts of the day, just like we'd always done, and it was both familiar and precious to hear their perspective.

"Snow!" Claire's favorite thing hadn't changed for weeks.

"Today we got out Valentine's decorations at Courtney's," Jane said, deliberately looking toward Christian and away from me. "I'm excited for Valentine's Day."

"I made a Lego ship!" Ollie cried.

"And then you cried when it got ruined," Claire said.

"What happened?" I asked.

Jane looked up to answer, then abruptly turned her head. "Nicholas sat on it," she explained. We all looked at Nicholas, who tossed a handful of pasta to Jimmy.

It was our first dinner in our new home, and I desperately wanted to laugh with them and hear more about every detail of their days, but my pain was getting the better of me. I smiled as the conversation went on, but my stamina was fading. I knew I wouldn't make it all the way through dinner. Christian must have noticed the look on my face, and he got up to help me back to bed. I reluctantly took his arm.

"Good night, sweethearts. I love you each so much." I ruffled Ollie's hair, and he looked up at me and smiled. I wanted to hold each of them, cradle them in my arms in their sweet childhood perfection. But now I was breathing through clenched teeth, fighting the pain.

"Eat your dinner, guys, I'll be right back," Christian said. He helped me get in bed, and I rested until dinner was finished.

Christian helped me up again when it was time for the children to go back to their respective homes at Aunt Courtney's and Aunt Lucy's. We felt the weight of our fractured family when the door closed behind them. I was still worried about how Christian would be able to handle all the work of having the children home and continue to care for me, too, but I ached to have our family under the same roof. And with our first dinner such a success, Christian had proven what he could do. I had other concerns about bringing our children home, and our conversations about it were thoughtful and serious.

I didn't want the children to see a despondent mother day in and day out, but I wasn't sure I was ready to move beyond that yet. I worried that after a few days at our house, the girls might want to go back to Courtney's. After all, Jane still couldn't bear to look at me. And if Nicholas didn't know I was his mother, how would he cope without Lucy? The next few nights we prayed together for guidance. We both felt that it was time to bring our children home. In a way, we realized it was trading the pain of being separate for the hard work of being together, but it was a sacrifice we were ready to make.

My sisters had expected that the children would transition home gradually, perhaps toward the beginning of March, but Christian and I now felt differently and knew the change in plans would surprise them. That night, Christian sent an e-mail to my sisters explaining our decision. It was the abrupt and unexpected news we had feared it would be, and Courtney and Lucy both wrote back, texted, and called, hurt and confused. They had done their best to keep our children safe and happy throughout the worst time in their little lives, and they wanted to be sure that the transition back home went smoothly. Would the home the children found themselves in with their parents be as happy as it could be? they wondered. It was a valid question, considering my physical and emotional state, but Christian and I would never have wanted anything less than the best thing for our children. We found it was difficult to express our gratitude for all my sisters had done for us and still assert ourselves as parents. In the end, we insisted that our children come home, even though my sisters thought it was too early. It was time to be a family again.

Thirty-one

·····························

The front door opened and the children walked in. It had been six months to the day since our accident, and the first night our family would sleep together under the same roof.

"Welcome home!" I called from the couch. "We're going to be all together again. I'm so happy." I held out my arms for a hug and Ollie came running and Claire came willingly, but Nicholas and Jane went to Christian instead.

"Hey, guys!" Christian picked them up and twirled them around, which caused Claire and Ollie to run over for their turn.

"I know the house doesn't look great yet," I told the children, "but we'll get all our old things out and it will be just like home again in no time."

Christian had discovered the wonders of Costco since he'd started doing all of the grocery shopping, and he'd come home that day with fresh green beans, a giant two-pack of spaghetti sauce, and a bundle of pasta. I had expected to feel so guilty that I couldn't prepare dinner for our family on such a momentous occasion, but Christian was so happy to be doing it, I didn't mind at all.

I lay in bed while he made dinner, and he helped me to the table when it was time to eat. I said our dinner prayer that night and couldn't help crying as I expressed my gratitude to Heavenly Father for the blessing of being together again. I prayed for help that our family would be strong and blessed and that we could find our way to our normal lives again.

We talked about Jane's upcoming birthday, and I asked her what kind of cake she wanted, hoping her enthusiasm for her birthday would overcome her unwillingness to look at me. She looked at the table but told me she was hoping for a chocolate cake with pink frosting.

"I'm not going to look this way forever, guys," I reminded the children. "I look like this now, but I won't always."

"We know," Claire answered, for the rest of them, because I'd been saying it for weeks now. "But how will you look different?"

"The scars won't be so red after a few months, and they'll do more surgery on my face. We'll get back to where I was before." I knew that last part wasn't true, but it was so easy to say. I wanted so badly to give them hope.

In our usual dinner ritual, Christian asked each of them about the favorite part of their day, and by the time we got around the table, I was exhausted. Dinner wasn't over, no one was finished eating, but I was too tired to stay at the table any longer. Christian helped me back to bed, then finished dinner with the children, cleaned up while they played, and then rounded them up for homework, pajamas, teeth brushing, and prayers. It bothered me that I was too frail to be any help on the kids' very first night with us, but Claire ran into my room with a book from school. She read it to me, and I checked off her homework sheet. One small step forward.

At bedtime, Claire, Jane, and Oliver were rowdy but obedient, but poor little Nicholas was confused and inconsolable. He ran to the front door screaming and pounded on it. "Mommy!" he yelled, "Mommy!" while his little fists beat against the door.

I knew he was calling for Lucy. She looked so much like me and she had cared for him as a mother for six months. That was nearly a quarter of his little life, and now we were telling him that I was his mother. I lay in bed, listening to my baby boy crying for another mother.

This was the first night of many that he went to the door after dinner and pounded on it, crying for his mommy. I would watch him from the hall, or listen from the bedroom, crying my own bitter tears. He'd only cry harder if I went near him, so I couldn't offer him any comfort. As I watched my baby sob, I felt a lot like he did. I would have given anything to escape from all the pain and disappointment that seemed to hover around me like a dark cloud. *Oh, Nicholas, I want to get out, too.*

After the children were asleep I asked Christian to help me downstairs so I could watch them. It seemed like a lifetime ago since I had seen my babies sleep. I had always loved watching their peaceful, sleeping bodies, but now there was something even more precious about how safe they seemed. Ollie and Nicholas shared a bed, and I had to move a large truck Ollie had been playing with the moment before he fell asleep so I could sit down on their bed. I whispered to Nicholas, hoping I could reach him in his sleep, since he didn't want anything to do with me during the day.

"Nicholas, I am your mother. Remember me? I pushed you out on GrandMary's bed in Arizona, and you were such a big baby. You went to sleep right away, and I didn't even see your eyes until the next day. I used to read *Goodnight Moon* to you every night before you went to bed. We took naps together in my bed, and you loved to ride on the back of my beach cruiser. Remember I used to bathe you? And hold you on my hip every second of the day? Remember, son? Please? Please remember me," I pleaded. I sat on their bed crying until Christian came to get me, which was just as well, because the pain had started pressing in on me.

Often just before bed, there was a lull between my doses of pain medications. While my daytime medication wore off and before my nighttime medication kicked it, my pain flared and settled threateningly in my body and my mind. When my pain was under control, I felt stable, but when it raged unchecked, my hope clouded over. I did my best to ignore it, but it was persistent, crowding out optimism and even faith. My joints ached, and my wounds stung. No matter how I moved or shifted, I just couldn't find relief from the pressure of having skin that was too small to cover my body. But that night, even as the medication finally quieted the physical pain, there was no pill that could soothe the pain of knowing my baby boy didn't love me anymore.

In the morning I woke up in a fog, still groggy from the meds. The girls had already gone to school. The boys were busy with their toys in the other room. No one seemed to need me much, and I wondered why I was here at all. Now that the children were home, it was clear how much Christian had to do just taking care of them. I felt like more of a burden than ever. I was just giving myself up to these hopeless thoughts when he appeared in the doorway, grinning.

"Good morning, darling!" He came over to take off my face mask and give me a kiss. "How did you sleep?" He unfastened the gloves on my hands and took my arms and legs out of the braces. He pulled open the blinds, and sun streamed in through the branches of the apple tree. He was as industrious and cheerful as a male version of Mary Poppins. "Come on, let me help you get up and we'll get you to the bathroom."

I wondered how long he could keep this up. Because Christian didn't have a job, he saw this as full-time work. I knew he was frustrated he couldn't just make everything all better, but taking excellent care of me was one way he tried. But still, I knew it was exhausting work, and I feared the day it would catch up with him. For now, though, it was hard to stay discouraged with Christian's sunny optimism shining so brightly. I knew he'd listen if I wanted to tell him how sad I felt about Nicholas, and how depressed I was that I couldn't do anything. He had always listened before. But seeing him work so hard for us made me want to try harder myself. There would be time to complain later, if I needed it, but for now, I decided to do my best to match Christian's attitude. If he could be this happy as the care-giver of a needy patient, I could try to be a bit happier, too.

That mission lasted nearly all morning, all through breakfast and my dressing change. But when the nurses left and Christian came to see if I needed anything, I broke down.

"I hate this," I cried. "This is the worst. I hate it. I'm so tired of being in pain. I'm so tired of everything hurting so much. I just want to feel better. When will I ever feel better?"

Christian held me and listened for as long as I needed him to, until I'd spoken every last frustration and cried every last tear. He gave yet another version of his confident, hopeful, faith-filled pep talk—that we could do this, that things would get better, that I was still beautiful. He reminded me to trust in God and believe in His watchful care. It was the same old speech, with the same old conviction. I needed it each time.

Before he went off to pick up the girls from school, he left me with the laptop opened to a talk by Elder Holland that I could listen to online. It was a talk that my mom had told me Elder Holland had written with Christian and me in mind. I spent that afternoon and many others listening to his familiar voice.

> *When lonely, cold, hard times come, we have to endure, we have to continue, we have to persist . . . Keep knocking on that door. Keep pleading. In the meantime, know that God hears your cries and knows your distress. He is your Father, and you are His child.*

Patience, I had been reminded. Elder Holland helped me practice it by reminding me that God knew me. In another talk he says:

> *But when we speak of those who are instruments in the hand of God, we are reminded that not all angels are from the other side of the*

*veil. Some of them we walk with and talk with—here, now, every
day . . . Indeed heaven never seems closer than when we see the love
of God manifested in the kindness and devotion of people so good
and so pure that angelic is the only word that comes to mind.*

But this was my favorite:

*I testify that bad days come to an end, that faith always triumphs,
and that heavenly promises are always kept.*

I couldn't listen to this phrase often enough. It was like getting a
new infusion of hope and reassurance, and I knew I could make it, at
least another fifteen minutes. And after a week or two, I knew I could
make it another couple of hours, and within a couple of months, I
knew I'd be okay for the next several days. Little by little, the leaks
were fixed, and I didn't run out of hope as often.

T*he children had been home for a week. Claire continued to*
astound me with her maturity and compassion, and Jane was
loving, but distant. I sensed she didn't want to hurt my feelings, but
that she'd rather be at Courtney's. Nicholas was still struggling, and
he tolerated me on two conditions: as long as Christian was around
and Lucy wasn't. We'd had to ask Lucy to stop coming over because
it upset and confused Nicholas, not to mention me. But Ollie was as
happy as could be, surrounded by the haul of new toys he'd brought
from Courtney's. He spread out in the living room with his toys
every morning and played happily all day. Physically, I couldn't
mother the children as much as I wanted to, but I looked for any and
every way to reestablish our connection.

"Claire, let's read *Stuart Little*," I suggested. She had just brought it home from school. "If you'll bring it to me, I'd love to read it with you."

Claire ran to her backpack and pulled out the book.

"You're going to read, Mom?" Ollie asked as he climbed onto the couch and settled in next to me.

Jane wandered in, too. "What are you reading?" she asked Claire.

"*Stuart Little*," I answered. "It's about a cute little mouse, Jane. I think you'd like it."

She shrugged her shoulders and sat down on the floor by Nicholas, who was playing with Ollie's army guys.

"Gigs, you want to read with us?" I held out my arms but was prepared for the answer I got. Nicholas shook his head and looked back at his toys.

"*When Mrs. Frederick C. Little's second son arrived, everyone noticed he was not much bigger than a mouse,*" I began, and Jane looked up. "*The truth of the matter was, the baby looked very much like a mouse in every way.*"

Claire giggled. "Look how cute he is with a little hat and shoes." It was more than Jane could resist, and she climbed on the couch next to Claire to see the dapper little mouse.

The children snuggled close to me as I read so they could see the illustrations. When Jane said something about the doctor examining Stuart Little, even Nicholas climbed on the couch next to Oliver so he could see, too.

I was sharing the couch with all four of my children. I wanted this moment to last forever. They hung on every word, captivated by the story of the little mouse. Hoping nothing would break this spell, I read one chapter after another. I had no intention of quitting, so when we finished chapter four, and Jane said, looking at the book, "Oh, Mom, one more chapter. *Pleeeease,*" I was thrilled.

"Another chapter?" I asked. "I'd like nothing better."

Thirty-two

I *swam effortlessly in cool, clear water, my legs extending and* bending easily as they pushed through the pool. I turned from my stomach to my back and felt the weightlessness of my body, the refreshing water lapping against me. I turned again and dove underwater, then exploded out into the bright sun again. Life pumped through my entire body. I felt completely joyful.

And then I woke up.

I was stiff and sore, just like every morning, and hazy from the medication. My joints ached from being in the same position all night, and I was faced with the double-edged sword of lying still in cramped discomfort or the pain of bending and stretching my joints. Either choice was miserable, and especially when I'd been dreaming, as I often did once Christian and I slept in the same bed again, of life before the accident. I dreamed often of the beautiful freedom of swimming. I also dreamed of going out with Christian in my little black dress and favorite red shoes. In that dream, we danced next to a beautiful bonfire. In other dreams, I ran in the Arizona heat, clocking five miles, feeling so powerful. More than anything, in those dreams I felt alive. Waking up was a bitter disappointment.

I lay there in the early morning dark, remembering the freedom of moving, the anticipation of a long run, and the feeling of independence of driving Christian's motorcycle to my yoga class. In the dark, those thoughts were heavy, and I waited for the new day to begin, watching eagerly for the sun to rise over the mountain. Everything was easier to manage in the light. I relied on that moment of light each morning. Just as the sun's first rays peeked over the mountain, it lit the apple tree outside our window. The new leaves and first tiny blossoms glowed in the bright sun, and the golden tree reminded me to thank God for all that I had now. It was a tiny bit of inspiration to start the day.

I longed to feel strong again, to feel fully in control of my body. I had always thrived on accomplishments and to-do lists, and now I had a list long enough to last a lifetime. For starters, I wanted to squeeze my own toothpaste, remove the cap of a pen, seal the Ziploc bag of carrots for Claire's lunch.

After two weeks at home with the children, I was making great progress. I had gone to Target with my parents and gotten the girls adorable matching bedspreads; I had managed to help with a load of laundry; and I was staying at the dinner table a few more minutes each night. And yet sometimes there were still heartbreaking frustrations. I was sitting on the sofa one afternoon when Claire asked me for help buttoning her jacket. I was so thrilled she'd come to me and wanted desperately to be able to prove to her that I could still be her mother. My fingers fumbled with her buttons—small things were the hardest because I couldn't bend my fingers. The skin on my hands had been so severely burned that it was too tight to allow for any movement. No amount of therapy was going to change that.

Claire watched me struggle. "It's OK. I'll just go ask Dad."

"No, wait just a minute. I think I can get it." I got the button near the hole but couldn't slide it through. I tried taking the hole to the button, but that didn't work either. I took a deep breath. "I can do this, Claire. Just another minute, OK? I can do this."

The longer I tried, the more Claire wiggled until I finally relented and she ran off to find Christian. I sank back against the sofa. I wanted to stomp my feet and scream in frustration at my inadequacy.

I needed help. *Dear God, please help me to button Claire's coat to-morrow. I couldn't do it today, but I want to so much. And please bless me to feel well enough to make it all through dinner tonight. Please bless our family that we can get through one normal meal together.*

D*ay after day I waited for the sun to rise, and then stared* at the mountain, watching the snow line get higher and higher and the green of spring creep slowly up its slopes. By early March I could see the Y trail zigzagging up the mountain. I remembered the promise I'd made to myself as we flew over the mountain in the jet on our way to the University of Utah that I would climb the trail again. And there it was, a constant reminder of my promise. My resolve to hike the Y grew stronger each morning as I stared up at the mountain.

One afternoon in early March we'd gone out with my parents to the nursery to look at flowers for my mother's yard. The hardiest spring flowers, pansies and primroses, were ready to brave the cold temperatures of March, and I was inspired by their fortitude and delicate beauty. My mom picked out her flowers, and I bought a flat for our house, too. After the nursery, we gathered Christian and our children and our dogs, and went to the Y trailhead.

After I'd shared my goal to hike the Y with Christian, he had printed out a map of the Y trail and written dates to reach each switchback so I could stay on track to reach the top by August. The map hung on the fridge, and the children loved each attempt we made at progress.

My goal today was to make it to the first switchback, two-tenths of a mile, a distance it would have taken me just five minutes to walk when I was healthy. But between scar tissue, shriveled muscles, and too-tight skin, my steps were now slow and halting. My parents and the children got there before I did, but Christian stayed at my side, cheering me on. It was hard and took forty-five long minutes. I used to go all the way up the trail and back in fewer than twenty minutes, but I tried not to think about that. My last steps to the first turn were celebrated with hugs and clapping and laughter and shouts of joy. I basked in the feeling of accomplishment.

We went home that night and picked up the house, bathed the children, laid our clothes out for church, then read bedtime stories and said good night. It felt just like old times, except for being exhausted to my very core.

The familiar feeling of being a family again meant so much, but an innocent glance at my reflection could still send me into shock. Later that night I was in the bathroom, staring at myself in the mirror, pondering unanswerable questions. *Who is that person in the mirror? Will I ever like the way I look again? Can I love myself if I look this way?*

I wondered if makeup would help. I hadn't opened my makeup bag for months, but I knew it had been unpacked and put in our bathroom. I found a tube of mascara and brushed it on my eyelashes.

I had been taught—and thoroughly believed in—my infinite worth as a daughter of God. I knew my value as a person transcended my looks, but that belief was being tested as I looked at my disfigured reflection in the mirror. Mascara didn't help.

I stood in front of the mirror crying, dark mascara streaming down my face, and Christian came in and wrapped his arms around me. I closed my eyes and tried to absorb another of his loving speeches.

There was a cry from downstairs. Nicholas. We both knew he wanted Christian, and not me. If I went down, he'd probably end up crying even louder and wake up Ollie and the girls. But I wanted to be the one to comfort him. Nicholas cried out again, and Christian started toward the stairs.

"No, let me try," I said. Maybe tonight would be different. Maybe tonight he would let me soothe his troubled sleep, like I'd always been able to before.

Christian helped me down the stairs, and when I got to the boys' room, Nicholas was crying and Ollie was zonked out in his Zorro mask. "Gigs, Mommy's here," I said softly and lay beside him on the edge of the bed. "Gigsie, I'm here," I crooned, in much the same voice Christian had used to comfort me just a few minutes earlier. Nicholas settled down a little, and I proceeded cautiously, shocked that he was letting me touch him at all. I tried something I hadn't done since the accident, our favorite bedtime game of "Chickie." Over and over, I took gentle little pinches of Nicholas's cheeks and brought my fingers to my mouth to nibble. Nicholas's big brown eyes got heavy, and he snuggled in a little closer. I watched in awe as his eyelids fluttered, then shut so peacefully. He lay beside me, breathing deep, relaxed breaths. I looked at every detail of his face and his long brown lashes resting against his round cheeks. His chubby hands nestled their way under his cheeks. Even his white-blond hair seemed to be peacefully resting on his smooth, soft forehead. His perfect beauty struck me, and I was filled with love for this little boy, and gratitude that he would let me lie down near him. I had almost missed these precious moments with my children.

As Christian and I lay in bed that night, I still basked in the joy of my moment with Nicholas. Christian turned to me. "So, what are you going to do tomorrow?"

I smiled. "Well, I think I'll play tag with Gigs and Ollie. And then find an indoor swimming pool because I'm dying to go swimming. And then I'll go grocery shopping and pick up the girls from school. After that, I think I'll hike the Y."

"Impressive," Christian said. "I like it. And how about your dreams? What are you going to dream about tonight?"

"Babies," I answered. "Lots and lots of chubby babies."

I *didn't know how Nicholas would respond to me the next* morning, but after breakfast, he asked for "Mommy" and instead of running to the door, he held his arms up to me. I sat on the couch, and he crawled into my lap. I thought my heart might explode with joy. My pain all but disappeared. He looked up at me and touched the scars on my face. "Mommy," he said, "ouch."

Nothing was more motivating than winning back the affection of our children. In the next few days, while Christian was putting up the wallpaper I'd picked out for our entryway, Nicholas kept tugging on Christian's pant leg and whining something unintelligible. Christian's hands were covered in wallpaper goop and I coaxed Nicholas over to the couch. He climbed onto my lap again and let me comfort him. Then I picked him up—picked him up!—and walked around the house with him—one entire lap with his little head on my bony shoulder.

Christian watched me in awe. "You don't have to walk around with him. He weighs a ton."

Our chubby boy was heavy, but I thought of it as weight training, and the best kind I could imagine. Nicholas settled in against me just like he'd always done before the accident. I felt all the exhilaration of a champion mother.

The children began to notice that I was stronger. Our boys had always woken up early, and since we'd all come home, they had run over to Christian's side of the bed in the morning, even though they had to pass me to get there. I'd been eager for them to start asking me for help with whatever they needed, trusting me to take care of them, believing that I could help them.

One morning Oliver came to me instead of Christian, and Nicholas just followed him. I held back tears of joy so I wouldn't scare them off. My boys needed me, and they'd asked me for help while I was wearing my scary plastic burn mask. Nothing could have made me feel more accepted as a mother. I loved being able to give them what they needed, even if it was just getting a toy down from a shelf or turning on the TV. I loved being the person who could help them with something they couldn't do for themselves. Seeing the boys first thing in the morning became a motivation for me. I had to continue to get stronger, I realized. It wasn't optional. If my boys needed me in the morning, I was going to be the kind of mother who could get out of bed, and one day soon I would be able to do so on my own.

One morning Oliver called from the bathroom that he wanted me to help him wipe himself. That's the sort of chore that I would previously have been happy to hand over to Christian, but I wanted to do absolutely anything that my children asked, and I gladly hobbled down the hall to help him. It was serving Ollie and meant that Christian could stay in bed just a little longer.

I needed to go to the bathroom next and I usually had help, but this time I did it by myself. I realized that the only way I was going to learn to do things again was to actually do them. I needed to have the courage to try and to work hard. I had to be willing to fail and then try again. And keep trying and failing until I got strong enough to succeed.

J ane still hadn't looked me in the face since her first visit in the hospital. I think she looked at me from across the room, or when she thought I wasn't looking. I figured she needed time to process on her own. I recognized that need for personal privacy as something she probably inherited from me, so I understood it very well. She needed to take it all in before she would show her reaction to the world. I think she was sorting it all out, trying to understand this drastic change in her mother, and she wasn't ready yet to look the change in the face. I couldn't really blame her.

One night in March, Jane was in the bathtub. From the hall, I could hear her singing and talking to herself. I felt a strong urge to walk in, almost like I was being pushed toward the door.

I opened the door and Jane looked up at me. Our eyes met.

"Jane, you're doing it!" I cried. "You're looking at me, Jane!"

She didn't look away. "I know," she said.

I leaned down and took her face in my hands, looking right into her beautiful blue eyes. "Janie, we can do this."

"I know, Mom. You always say that."

"I mean it, Jane. You are strong, and you can do this."

I left Jane to finish her bath and went to my bedroom in tears, to offer my thanks to God for this moment I'd been waiting for.

A few nights later I called my girls to my bed just before they settled into their own beds for the night. I'd been there since just after dinner, listening to the chaos in the house as Christian rounded them up for tubs and pajamas. The girls were happy to climb onto my bed, and their beauty struck me full force—Jane's orange hair and freckles, her blue-as-the-sky eyes and wide grin, and Claire's dark hair, dark eyes, and freckles that reminded me so much of my own. It was not just their physical beauty that took my breath away but also their beautiful, resilient spirits. So much had been asked of these little girls in the past nine months, and they were still so bright and full of life.

"Girls, I'm so sorry for all of this. I'm so sorry the airplane crashed."

The girls weren't terribly surprised when I started to cry—tears had become quite common. I was either crying with gratitude or crying in frustration, and sometimes both, at some point in every day. Claire gently patted my head and Jane wrapped her arms around me.

I wished so badly I could spare my babies all of the pain they had suffered, and the hard times I knew would come as a result of my injuries. "I won't let anything like this ever disrupt our family again. I promise," I sniffled, then held out my pinkies and the girls linked theirs with mine to bind my words with the very powerful pinkie promise. I knew I couldn't protect them from every heartache—but my commitment was to do the best I could.

As the girls jumped off my bed, I told them how much I loved them and that I believed that Heavenly Father had big plans for our family. "We don't need to worry," I said. "We just have to trust Him."

Jane stopped in the doorway and asked a question that must have been on her mind for months. "Is that why the airplane fell out of the sky? Did He do that?"

"Yes—well, no." I was a little confused myself. "No, he didn't make it happen, but He saved our lives, and that was the beginning of our big plan. We're in the middle of it right now, and it's going to get easier."

I sensed the accident had set into motion eternal lessons for each of us, and we would learn things that ultimately we'd be grateful for. At least I hoped we would. I had to believe there was a plan for our lives, and a purpose behind our struggles. It was at times a thin hope, more an idea than a driving force, but my challenges seemed manageable if I believed there was a purpose behind them. On the other side of this mountain, I hoped, a bright sun was just waiting to rise.

Thirty-three

....

At the end of April, Lucy was just weeks from having her baby. My brothers and sisters and their families were all gathered at my parents' house for Sunday dinner—easily my favorite thing about being back in Provo. Lucy was so uncomfortable she had to get up from the table to walk around. She wrinkled her nose and put her hand on her lower back. I remembered that feeling, wondering how much longer you and that little baby could share the same body.

I watched her wistfully, wishing that I, too, were nine months pregnant. For all the discomfort she was going through now, she'd soon have a brand-new baby, her first child, as her reward. Lucy had so much to look forward to. She would meet her beautiful little daughter in just a few weeks, and she would discover how motherhood deepened life's joys.

I remembered driving past the hospital earlier in the week just as a happy father was pushing his wife out in a wheelchair. She carried a little bundle in her arms, and I'd ached to feel the warmth of a new baby against my chest.

I sat down on the couch next to my dad with tears in my eyes. Before I could say a word, he was gently patting my leg, as if he could read my mind.

"Everything is under control," he said. "Don't you worry. It is all under control."

I leaned against his shoulder and felt just a little better. *OK*, I thought. *Everything's under control. I can wait.*

He rubbed my back. "Just think, in three months it will be the Fourth of July and you'll be so much better by then. And before you know it, it'll be a year since your accident. And, sooner than you think, you'll have a baby of your own."

My dad offered his famous bathtub analogy. At first when you drain a bathtub full of water, it goes so slowly, but then it gets some momentum, and at the very end it goes so fast it's practically getting sucked down the drain. "It seems slow now, Cubby, but this will go by fast. Everything's under control, darlin'."

I wanted to believe my dad—in that moment, and for as long as I could hold on to how hopeful his words made me feel. I wrote about it on my blog that night to reinforce what I had felt.

> Someday I will be pregnant again, someday I will love the way I look, someday I will be able to use my legs and play on the floor with my kids, someday I will wear my old clothes, sleep, dance, hold a baby, snuggle Mr. Nielson until he can't stand it, make my bed, pray on my knees because:
>
> Everything is under control.
> Thanks, Dad.

I wanted so many things in the wake of my recovery—to be able to sit up, and to walk, and to button Claire's jacket, and to hold the vacuum. The more I accomplished, the more I wanted to do. And the better I felt about the present, the more I thought about the future. It was a marker of progress, I thought, that I dreamed about what lay ahead. Not so long ago, I couldn't imagine being a mother to the children I had, and now I longed for more. There was still a wide gap, though, between those distant dreams and the punishing reality, particularly when my pain raged, which was often.

Despite our best efforts with my pill routine, the pain still remained relentless and unpredictable and entirely consuming at times. The most casual movement could send me reeling with agony, and in those moments it was really hard to remember everything was under control. One night I lay in bed praying that my painkiller would take effect soon. It had been a particularly hard night.

I heard a car pull into my driveway. I looked at the clock. Eleven. Who would be coming over now?

A minute later there was a faint knock, and the front door opened. "Stephy?" It was a quiet voice. "Stephy, are you awake?"

I heard Christian walk to the door. "What's up, Jesse?" he boomed, a loud contrast to Jesse's careful whisper. A few minutes later Jesse came to my room and tapped me on my shoulder. I had been upgraded from my plastic burn mask to a fabric mask that made me look like Nacho Libre, which embarrassed me, but I rolled over and waved.

"Hey, let's go for a ride. The Russian olive trees smell so good down by my office. I've wanted to take you down there, and you've been on my mind. I just felt like I needed to stop by tonight."

How did Jesse know that was exactly what I needed—to get out of the house, to smell the smells I used to love, to feel the calm night air on my tortured skin? He and Christian helped me into Jesse's truck, and Jesse rolled down my window and put my seat belt on for me. I waved good-bye to Christian as we drove away. Jesse circled the neighborhood, remembering all the places we had hung out as kids— Old Willow and our grandma Marion's, our old elementary school and our favorite cousins' house.

"I'm trying so hard to be brave, Jess," I said. "But I'm in pain all the time. I feel like it never goes away. My body just hurts. Always."

"I know it's so hard, Steph, but things will get better. You still have the things that matter most. Even though you hurt right now, this pain is temporary."

The pain wouldn't last—it was everyone's favorite message, but I needed to hear it every single time someone said it, and tonight was no different. I repeated it to myself like a mantra. *The pain won't last. The pain won't last.* Jesse was right, I had what I needed to be happy—my wonderful husband, our beautiful children, and siblings like Jesse who would be there for me when I needed them.

He drove me back and forth past the Russian olives down by his office. I did my best to put my head out the window so I could breathe in the sweet, rich smell.

When we got home around midnight, Christian was waiting for us on the porch. He came down the driveway and helped me back to the house. Christian and Jesse helped me into bed again, and I lay there, feeling so grateful. There were things the accident hadn't taken—couldn't take—and I still had those.

I didn't know if my body would ever be healthy enough to carry a baby—I still hadn't mustered the courage to ask the doctors—but a more pressing question was whether or not I could even conceive one. I was so emaciated after the accident and so traumatized that my menstrual cycle had stopped completely. I was surprised how much I missed it—without it, and because of my burns, I felt sexless. We had no way to know if it would return, but I woke up to the most pleasant surprise a couple of weeks later. My biological clock was ticking again, and it was Mother's Day, no less.

We were headed to Arizona for a consultation with Dr. Lettieri in just two weeks, and I resolved to ask him them. It would be my first trip back to Phoenix since the accident, and Dr. Lettieri would outline his plan for the next several surgeries to repair the tight skin around my neck, so strained that it pulled my eyes and lips downward. I felt the strain when I ate, smiled, yawned, or turned my head, and Dr. Lettieri had a plan to fix it.

Dr. Lettieri wasn't naturally warm, but something about his dry, no-nonsense approach endeared him to me. Behind his gentle sarcasm, I knew he genuinely cared about me, and I adored him for it. The children came to the consultation with Christian and me, so that Dr. Lettieri could meet them. I never doubted that he would provide the best care for me, but I wanted to be sure that he understood who exactly was riding on his decisions. I also wanted my children to meet Dr. Lettieri, this man who would be such a part of our lives in the years to come.

Nicholas made his own introduction by handing Dr. Lettieri a toy truck as soon as he walked through the door. Then he turned to his colleague and gave him a plastic horse.

"Well, that's Nicholas," I said, "and these are our other children, Claire, Jane, and Oliver."

Ollie looked up at the two men and smiled, and the girls waved timidly.

"Very nice to meet you, Nielsons. I'd like you to meet Dr. Jensen. He's a Plastic Surgery Fellow from the Mayo Clinic."

Dr. Jensen smiled and knelt down by the children to say hello. In a moment, a nurse kindly took them back to the waiting room for treats. Dr. Lettieri and his team outlined a plan for my neck that would take several surgeries and over a year to complete. First, they would surgically implant balloons under the healthy skin on my back, then slowly fill the balloons with saline to stretch the skin. The saline doses would increase until eventually I would have two large saline-filled humps on my back. When the skin had stretched all it could, they would remove the balloons and harvest the stretched skin from my back to use on my neck. That procedure would give me the extra skin I needed to relieve the strain on my neck and face, but it would require another surgery months later to trim and shape the skin into a normal-looking neck.

Asking Dr. Lettieri about having a baby was still on my mind, but I was caught up in thoughts of the lengthy procedure he described. As amazed as I was at the innovation that could make the process possible, I still cringed to think of the pain and lengthy recoveries involved.

Unlike with many of my previous procedures, this time I had many questions. The doctors patiently explained everything until I was satisfied. I felt like I had a voice in my care again.

Putting our lives in Dr. Lettieri's hands had elevated us past a handshake, and we thanked the doctors and hugged good-bye as we all got up to leave. Just before Dr. Lettieri walked out of the room, I mustered my courage, but tried to act nonchalant. "Do you think I can have more children?" I asked, staring at the wall.

He stopped in the doorway. "Yeah, I don't see why not," he answered easily. "Let's have another look at the skin on your abdomen."

He examined my skin to evaluate its flexibility and then reviewed my chart—no internal damage. "It's possible," he said, "but wait until this procedure is done. We'll have to keep a close eye on your tummy to be sure it's stretching enough for a baby to grow. But wait until we're finished with your neck, OK?"

I was beaming when Dr. Lettieri left the room, and as soon as the door closed behind him I squealed, "We can have a baby!"

Christian grabbed me by the waist and lifted me gently so my eyes were level with his. "Darling, a baby!" he said, and we kissed through our smiles.

While we were in Arizona, Christian drove the children past our Mesa house for old times' sake, but I didn't go with them. I felt the pull of our home, of course, but refused to think about it. I stayed at Russ and Mary's, distracting myself with thoughts of the upcoming surgery and the beautiful news that we could have another child.

When we returned to Provo, it felt like home. This was where we belonged now, in our cozy house nestled against the mountain. And we arrived back just in time to meet Lucy's brand-new baby—a little girl named Betsy. That night Christian and I lay in bed with our windows open. Our apple tree was full of blossoms, and the scent wafted in on the night breeze. I'd spent the afternoon holding Betsy and taking in her new-baby smell, and I'd listened to every detail of Lucy's labor and delivery story. And then I'd spent the evening pitying myself and feeling downright jealous. I was happy, too—so happy for Lucy, and so sorry for myself.

Suddenly, the sound of a siren in the distance interrupted my thoughts and sent my heart racing. Christian and I instinctively turned to look at each other. I felt immediate comfort in Christian's gaze, in knowing that he understood what happened to me when I heard sirens. It didn't take much to get us thinking and talking about the accident. One way or another it came up every night in our bedtime conversations.

"Remember when the sirens were for us?" I asked.

Christian closed his eyes. "I do." He was quiet, then asked, "Did you hear me scream?"

I shook my head.

"I thought you might be dead," he said.

We lay facing each other, but silent, each of us engrossed in our own memories.

"Thinking about Lettieri's plan made me remember all those weeks you spent in the hospital. I've been thinking about that a lot today."

I felt the weight of his words, the grief he had almost never shared.

"I tried so hard to be strong for you."

"Christian, you were. I could never have done it without you."

"At Courtney's I wanted to be strong for the children, and at the hospital I wanted to be strong for you. On the way up to the hospital, though, I would just bawl. I figured I could cry until I got about twenty minutes away, and then I had to pull myself together, or you'd know I'd been crying."

Christian buried his head in the pillow, then looked at me again. "I thought I might lose you, Stephanie." His voice broke. "I'm so sorry for what happened. I'm so sorry you're hurt. I want to take away your pain. I want to make everything all right for you, and I can't. I'm so sorry." Heavy sobs suddenly shook his body. "I can't take it away. I'm so sorry."

I put my hand on Christian's chest and felt his heartbeat. "Oh, Christian, I know you want to take it away. Christian, it's OK. None of this is your fault."

I pressed my hand against his chest as he cried, grateful he would finally tell me what he'd been through. He'd been so optimistic, so stoic, for so long. For once, he needed *me* to comfort *him*. It felt good to be able to give like that. I reached for his face. "Christian, it's OK. We're doing great. *You're* doing great. We're going to be OK."

I forgot about feeling sorry for myself, I just wanted to help Christian understand how grateful I was for all he had done for me and that I didn't blame him for any of it. For now, even if for just five minutes, I would be the strong one. I could carry some of the burden he had carried for so long.

"Christian, I could never have made it through this without you. You *have* made things better, so much better for me and for the children. Where would we be without you?"

Christian looked at me gratefully.

I continued in just the same way that Christian would have for me. "We have each other. We were both hurt in this accident, you know what I've been through and I know what you've been through. We can do this as long as we are one. Christian, if you're next to me, I can do anything."

"That's how I feel, too," Christian said. "As long as you're close,

I can do anything." He took my hand and held it against his chest. "I prayed so hard for you to come back. I'd lie there in my hospital bed pleading with God every day to bring you back. I'm so thankful you're here."

It was a miracle that either of us had lived through the accident, and our conversation turned toward other miracles of our recovery. Soon we were talking about our families and all they had done for us, and then our children and how blessed we felt to be able to take care of them.

"There's a plan for us, Christian. I know God is taking care of us," I said.

Christian squeezed my hand. "I do, too."

I nestled my head against Christian's shoulder, and he reached his arm around me and held me close, then leaned in for a sweet kiss.

I sat on the couch after dinner the next evening while the children played around me. Outside, Christian was happily watering the flowers on the front porch. I was relieved to see that he was back to his cheerful self. After all the encouragement Christian had given me over the last eight months, I felt proud I was there for him last night, even if I would never balance the scales. I remembered when I was at the hospital and heard the nurses talking about failed marriages, how one in five marriages didn't make it through an experience like ours. I felt so lucky that our relationship was getting stronger, not weaker. Christian was patient and tirelessly caring, flashing that genuine gap-toothed grin that had stopped my heart all those years earlier in my father's office. It still did, every morning when he brought me breakfast. It was strange to think now how there was a moment when I hadn't wanted to see Christian when I first woke up. I was in such a different place then, it was hard to even imagine feeling like that. Or that I hadn't even considered being intimate with Christian again. I had hated my body then and didn't believe Christian could ever want me. And if somehow he did want me, I felt too unattractive to even dream of being physical with him again. We'd come a long way since then. Christian knew just how to touch me so that my poor body didn't flinch in pain. And I loved his touch because I loved him. The way he tenderly helped me into my compression garments each day was as romantic as any passionate kiss we'd shared before the accident. Like my other after-crash milestones, being intimate with him started with just a hint of belief that maybe, just maybe, I could do that again.

Jane climbed up on the couch next to me and interrupted my thoughts. She started in on an elaborate plan for the art project of the century.

"It will be painting. No, coloring. No, wait, Mom, do you have glitter? We have to have glitter—all different colors. Oh, and Popsicle sticks and those fuzzy things that make those cool things on the butterfly heads . . ."

She continued, and I didn't mean to tune her out, but Christian caught my eye out the window. He was standing on the front porch in his white shirt and jeans, watering the flowers. Dark thunderclouds were gathering behind him, and his hair blew ever so slightly in the wind. I thought about how much I needed him. A slow smile spread across my face as I watched him care for the flowers that delighted me. I knew he took such good care of them because I loved them, and I thought of all the things he'd taken such good care of, including me, as we had patched our lives back together. He was the glue, without a doubt.

And then, as though he could feel me thinking about him, he turned around and flashed that trademark smile.

"I want to make a picture of the day and one of the night. What are you going to color, Mom?" asked Jane.

I didn't take my eyes off Christian. "Daddy."

That night Christian and I lay in bed and the night breeze ruffled the curtains. The air outside smelled sweet and fresh. I leaned into Christian and ran my hand across his chest and arm. I put my head on his shoulder and closed my eyes, remembering passionate moments we had shared before the accident.

Christian reached for me as though he knew what I'd been thinking about. He put his hand on my hair and traced his fingers down my face and neck. His touch was exactly what I had hoped for, but then I remembered how ugly I was and wanted to pull away. Christian drew me closer, and I tried to trust that my looks didn't matter to him. He wanted me because I was *me*. A rush of desire swelled through me as Christian kissed me. With every touch, I forgot about being burned. I forgot that I was hurt, that I felt ugly. Christian wanted me, and I wanted him—like we always had. I felt completely worthy of his desire and closed my eyes. Not so unlike our wedding night all those years ago, I savored the thrill of being Mrs. Christian Nielson.

Thirty-four

I can do this. I can do this. *I gave myself a pep talk as I* looked toward Old Willow Lane, my old childhood stomping ground. Today, a perfect, bright June morning, I would attempt to run, or something resembling that. I had Christian lace up my running shoes, and then I sought out the secluded path, where I could be sure no one would see me. This would not be pretty. Just yards from my house, Old Willow had the slope of the mountain on one side and thick trees and brush on the other. I took a deep breath and managed to take a few shuffling steps with flailing elbows. I tripped more than once, and the slightest bend of my knees pulled my skin painfully tight, but that familiar satisfaction of my lungs filling with fresh air, my heart pounding purposefully—that was exhilarating. After a few yards, I walked the rest of the little path. But I planned my next run, and the next run after that, where I would go farther and farther each time. Little by little, my strength was returning. I could finally see the progress my doctors and family had promised. I heard my dad's voice in my head. *Think about the difference a year will make.*

I was determined to make good on my promise to hike the Y, and running on Old Willow was excellent training. Slowly, I walked home, very tired but satisfied, and headed straight to the kitchen for a drink of water. I stared at the map of the Y trail on the fridge. Earlier in the week I'd crossed off the third switchback. I stood in the kitchen with a glass of water in one hand, and flipped through the pages of the calendar on the wall with the other. I looked for the day of the anniversary, Sunday, August 16, 2009. I put my glass down and wrote a big *Y* on Saturday the fifteenth. That would be the perfect day to go all the way up. I'd climb all one thousand feet and all twelve turns one year after the accident. I pictured myself on the trail, hiking alongside Christian and our children. I hoped my brothers and sisters and their families would join me, too.

I looked forward to putting this first year behind us. We'd made it through one harrowing year. For the actual anniversary, I planned to invite my parents and brothers and sisters to gather with us that evening and celebrate the miracles that had kept our family together. I pictured everyone in our backyard, where we'd sit on the Adirondack chairs Christian had made for me, with music, cupcakes, and stories of how we'd all made it through. It would be the perfect chance to tell my family how incredibly grateful I was for each of them—especially my sisters—and all they had done.

I stood in my kitchen, picturing a perfect late-summer evening, and looked at the calendar again. By Sunday, August 16, I would have hiked the Y. I smiled at the thought. If I could hike the Y on the first anniversary, who knows what I could be doing by the second, and what about the third? Life felt full of possibilities.

Later that day my mom took me to a consultation where the doctors and physical therapists noted my progress and improvement. I loved consultations when the news was good. On the way home my mom asked when I was going to post a picture of myself on my blog, and I immediately answered, "Never." That was my gut response, but the truth was that I had been thinking earlier in the day that it was time to post a picture.

Before the accident, my blog had been full of pictures of me. I liked how I looked and was happy to share those pictures. I knew blog readers would be wondering what I looked like now. I'd come a long way since that evening I had first put on mascara, but I certainly wasn't completely reconciled to how I looked. Little by little, seeing myself had become easier, and I felt I'd reached a turning point in my recovery. I wasn't as beautiful as I had been, but I was coming to accept that I was still Stephanie. I did fear that the negative reactions of others would destroy my hard-won progress, but the burden of worrying about what people would think when they saw my new face was becoming too heavy to carry. I couldn't keep up with the emotional weight of fearing the reactions of others every time I left the house. I couldn't escape the fact that this was how I looked—no amount of worrying would change that—and I couldn't hide forever.

In a moment of bravery that night, I decided I would post a picture of myself. I would prove—to myself more than anyone else—that even though this was hard, I had the courage to confront it. I took a picture with the webcam on my laptop. I stared at the image for several minutes, examining the web of red lines across my new face, the uneven texture of my skin, and my lack of eyebrows. But there were my green eyes, still recognizable. I cropped the photo in a rectangle around my eyes. *It's just my eyes, but it's a start,* I told myself. A glimpse of my old self was there in my eyes. Maybe my readers would see it, too.

I put the picture in the blog post and wrote a little more about how unsettling it was to see an unfamiliar face in the mirror every day.

> Now I look in the mirror and see someone else, but it's still me. It's . . . well . . . weird. I have to learn to be me again. I have to accept and hope. And I should stop saying "should" and replace that with "get." I GET to have a second chance at life.

I took a deep breath, hit "publish," and the post was up.

Almost immediately the courage I'd mustered was lost in second guesses. I stared at the picture, trying to see it as other people would. There were obviously scars, but maybe they didn't look too bad. There was that slant at the top of my nose, though. And the longer I looked at my eyes, the sadder they seemed. Finally, I gave up wondering what people were going to think. I had a life to live, and I was so much more than just my body. A weight lifted as I closed my laptop.

It required another leap of confidence to log in to my computer a few hours later and see what the reactions were. *What would people say? Would they tell me I still looked beautiful? Would I believe that lie?* I scanned through e-mails quickly. I didn't see the word *ugly*—a start. In fact, e-mail after e-mail was loving and generous, such a gentle reentry into the world. Some people sent well-intentioned e-mails that pitied me, and I wished I didn't inspire that sort of response. It was one thing if I wanted to feel sorry for myself, but I didn't like having other people feel sorry for me. But there were also notes that celebrated my courage, and those were the ones I kept close to my heart.

I n the middle of June Courtney called me. "*Oprah's looking* for you," she said. A producer had tracked down Courtney's number and told her they wanted to do a segment on me. "If they call, you have to answer," she told me.

Sure enough, a few days later they did. When the producer said Oprah was especially interested in how I loved being a mother after what I'd overcome, I agreed to be on the show. The yes came so naturally, and not just because I was flattered, although I certainly was. I wanted to share my miracle with the world, and saw this as a rare honor to share my challenges and many blessings of the past several months. But later that night I wondered what I had been thinking. If I was on *Oprah*, I'd have to *be on Oprah*. They would film me, and millions of people would see me. I'd just shared a picture of my *eyes* on my blog, and that had given me anxiety for days. I wasn't ready to share my face, my neck, my body. My doubts were gaining speed when that quiet feeling I recognized so well settled around me. *It's the right thing to do.* I felt like I had my answer—*Oprah* it was, and I tried to let go of my fears about being seen by millions of people. It was another catalyst toward accepting how I looked, forcing me to face the fact that I couldn't hide all my life. I looked the same, whether I was on TV or not. Someday, after countless surgeries, maybe I'd look different. But for now, this was me.

Over the next several days I thought a lot about being on TV. I pictured myself on the famous couch, sitting next to Oprah. *Oprah Winfrey and me on the same couch.* I joked with Christian about him jumping up and down on that couch, professing his love for me, like Tom Cruise had done for Katie Holmes.

For months now, I had lived in the cocoon of my own home, buttoned up tight with the blinds in my kitchen and living room vigilantly kept closed. But there was a beautiful world happening just on the other side of those windows. Was I really the kind of person who would close out the world just because of my appearance? No, I was the kind of person who would hold her head high and talk to Oprah Winfrey. I was the kind of person who would finally open her blinds.

T*he next night Claire bounded in as I was folding laundry,* one of those everyday tasks that I had dreamed of doing while I lay in my hospital bed. Before the accident, laundry had just been another chore. Now each little tee shirt and pair of pants represented something more, and I was so grateful to be matching socks and making neatly folded piles.

"Mom, I want to go to a restaurant," Claire said. "Courtney and Christopher took us to this sushi place, and I think we should go there for dinner tonight."

"Sushi?" Courtney had really raised the bar on our dining experiences.

"How about Café Rio?" I suggested.

"But we never go inside," Claire complained.

It was true. We'd frequented Café Rio for months now but always got our food to go. We'd drive down by the lake to eat or go up the canyon because it was easier for me than going inside. But I remembered how special it had been for me as a little girl to sit down in a restaurant with my family.

"OK, let's go inside this time," I offered, hoping it would get me out of sushi.

Claire clapped her hands together and ran off to tell Jane. "We're going to Café Rio and this time we're going *inside*!"

I was anxious, but Claire's excitement overshadowed my worries. First step: get dressed. I spent most of my days lounging in yoga pants and tee shirts. I pulled on a loose skirt over my compression garments and a zip-up hoodie, which was the only kind of shirt I could put on myself. I still wasn't flexible enough to pull a shirt over my own head or brush my own hair, so Christian did my hair for me, yet another skill he picked up after the accident.

"Can you put a barrette in, too? How about that one?" I pointed to a silver barrette with small flowers, and Christian clipped it in.

I put on a little mascara and called the children. "Time to go to dinner, guys! Let's go!" Jane and Claire ran up. "Mom, are we really going inside?" Jane put her hands on her hips and tipped her head to one side.

"Yes." I laughed. "We're really going inside."

Jane stood openmouthed for just a few seconds and then threw her arms around me. "Yay! We're going inside!"

The girls and Oliver climbed in the back of our SUV, and Christian buckled Nicholas in, then helped me with my seat belt, and we were off to dinner at Café Rio, just like any other family on a Friday night. Except for a few major differences, which I tried to ignore. I'd been to Target and the grocery store with Christian and the children before. As long as they were near me, I felt protected.

The familiar smell of fresh tortillas and spices wafted toward us as soon as Christian opened the door to Café Rio. We made our way through the crowded restaurant and found a table while Christian went to the counter to order our food.

The girls were eager to go get cutlery for everyone, and Ollie and

Nicholas headed straight to a bowl of mints by the soda machine. For just a minute I was at the table alone, and I felt eyes around the restaurant turn toward me. Although I'm sure this wasn't actually the case, I felt like I caused a hush in the room. I was just beginning to regret the decision to come in when the children rushed toward me.

"Here's a fork for you, Mom," Jane said. "And I got one for Dad and the boys and a whole bunch of napkins." She held up a stack four inches high.

"Thank you, Jane." I smiled. "We just might need all of those." With my numb lips and clumsy fingers, I had become a very messy eater.

She giggled, and Claire arrived with a drink of water for me. Nicholas came over and held up his hands. "Mommy, look!" He showed me a fistful of red-and-white-striped mints.

Ollie sauntered back to the table with his own handful of mints. Just before he sat down, he leaned toward a man at the next table. "Stop staring at my mom," he said loudly.

The man, and several people around us, quickly looked away. My first instinct was to reprimand Ollie—we didn't want to hurt anyone's feelings. But thankfully I stopped myself. He was protecting me, defending my scarred face, because I was his mother. I would let him stand up for me just as much as he wanted to.

"He was looking at you. Why was he doing that?" Ollie asked as he sat down.

I patted his hand and whispered, "It's OK, Ollie. Thank you."

The embarrassment of being stared at vanished, chased away by Ollie's brave blue eyes, Jane's careful attention to our forks and knives, Claire's thoughtful water delivery, and Nicholas's eager fist of mints. As Christian arrived at our table with the food, I thought, *Let them look all they want. Let them go ahead and look at me, the luckiest mother alive.*

Thirty-five

On *the morning of the fifteenth, I stood at the window and* stared at the Y. Today I would go all the way to the top. I thought back to just six months ago when simply getting out of bed seemed impossible. All I could do then was stare at the mountain through the window, hiking the trail in my mind, every familiar turn etched in my memory. Before I could climb the Y there had been so many other mountains to climb: getting strong enough to lift Nicholas, looking Jane in the eye again, looking in the mirror without crying, bending my knees. But I'd met all those challenges and many more. Hiking the Y was the last thing to cross off my list before the anniversary of the accident.

We pulled up to the parking lot at the Y trailhead just a little before seven on the evening of the fifteenth. Lucy and Andrew were already there, and Christopher and Lisa and their children. I saw my cousin Jayne and her husband, Jed, and their children waiting in the parking lot, too.

I turned to our children in the backseat. "We're here! Are you guys ready?" I could hardly wait to get started. We all tumbled out of the car, gathering water bottles and tying shoes, and made our way to the trailhead.

"Mommy, who are all those people?" asked Jane, pointing at a crowd gathered a few yards in front of us. It did seem strange; the trail usually wasn't this crowded.

Then I noticed that people in the crowd were holding balloons in their hands and wearing the I (HEART) NIENIE tee shirts with Christian's silhouette. *Could they all be here for me?* On a whim, I had posted plans for my anniversary hike on my blog the day before, thinking that some of my friends from high school who'd helped with our home or organized fund-raisers might come. I had never dreamed that anyone else would come to join me and was astonished to see the faces of some two hundred smiling strangers. People who had prayed for me and sent my children gifts, whose support had meant so much during my dark days in the hospital and beyond, were here in the flesh. They had come to hike the mountain with me. My dad shouted out a booming welcome to the group, and I stood at the start of the trail and hugged and thanked every person who had come. They pressed notes and cards into my hands. One girl had tears in her eyes and said, "You help me do hard things."

"Thank you for coming," I repeated with each hug, with tears in my eyes, hoping the recipient would know just how much I meant it.

Forty-five minutes later, the evening sun was fading, and I set out on the trail surrounded by my family, holding Christian's hand. Lucy's husband, Andrew, carried Nicholas, and Oliver rode on the shoulders of one nephew and then another. The girls walked with Christian and me, taking turns holding our hands or walking with my parents. My brothers and sisters and their children were ahead of me on the trail.

"Here we go!" I cried, squeezing Jane's hand in mine.

The smell of dirt and sagebrush was subtle and earthy, and the scent carried the memories of a lifetime of climbing it. During my practice runs, I'd only been to the fifth of the twelve switchbacks, but each new turn was like greeting an old friend. Every rock and scrub oak seemed familiar and welcoming, as though they were as glad to have me back as I was to be there.

Hiking the trail wasn't as difficult as I had expected. I was relieved that my training had paid off, and I was terribly proud. At turn six, someone had spelled out NIE in rocks in the dirt.

"Look, Mom!" Claire and Jane were delighted.

I looked out at Utah Lake across the valley, the early evening light shimmering on its surface. From here it was just a partial view of the entire valley, and I smiled, remembering the expansive view that waited for us at the end of the trail.

"Mom, you're doing great!" Claire encouraged as we rounded turn ten.

"Claire, I am! And so are you!"

I put one foot in front of the other, and before I knew it we had rounded the last turn. I surprised myself by not being out of breath at all. I was finishing even stronger than I had hoped. I was strong and healthy, and had just climbed a quick one thousand feet to prove it. Like I'd regained a personal treasure, the Y was mine again, and I was liberated to realize I could come back anytime I wanted.

The mountain curves outward just before the trail opens up at the base of the giant cement *Y*. When I rounded that final curve, family, friends, and strangers shouted and cheered for me.

I held my arms out wide. "Thank you!" I shouted. "I made it!" My sisters rushed forward to hug me, and the people who had come to hike with us released balloons into the sky. I hugged Christian and my mom and dad and Claire and Jane and anyone who was near enough to be hugged. *I made it!*

Just then the *Y* lit up, and we were awash in a warm glow. The *Y* is outlined in lights that are turned on for special occasions like graduation and homecoming. When it's lit, you can see it across the valley. A maintenance crew happened to be on the mountain when I arrived, and it was such a surprise for me when they turned on the lights to celebrate my arrival.

I turned to look at the view, and Christian stood next to me and wrapped his arm around me. The entire valley stretched out wide below us, bordered on the opposite side by Utah Lake and the mountains that sit behind it. In the city, windows sparkled gold in the early evening light. Out of habit, I scanned the view for the landmarks I'd looked for all my life. First, my parents' house—easy to spot with its red roof and the huge pine tree in their yard. Then I scanned the neighborhoods for the spire of the Provo temple, which since our wedding day had become a symbol of the commitment Christian and I shared. Then up to the crisp, rugged line of Mount Timpanogos off to the north. And finally, out over the lake again. As the sun made its way toward the western mountains behind the lake, the water shone brilliantly.

But now, I had a new landmark to find. I gathered the children around.

"Can you find our house?" I asked.

They pointed toward our neighborhood, and we picked out our home, with its sandstone walkway and apple tree.

"Look how small it looks!" Claire shouted.

"I see Dad's car!" said Ollie.

I soaked in the magnificent views. I was just where I had hoped I would be, and with just the people I had hoped to share the day.

We watched our support team of family and brand-new friends leave the mountain, and Christian and I were the last ones down. Boosted by a great combination of adrenaline and triumph, my joints didn't ache at all. I walked down the mountain basking in what I had accomplished. I hadn't done it alone, though. I'd hardly taken a single step over the last year without someone by my side. Yes, I was very proud of *me*, but I was even more grateful for *us*—the people close to me and far away who had created a community that helped me heal. Christian and my parents, my brothers and sisters and their families, my beautiful children, and the strangers and friends who had reached out to us when we needed them. I couldn't have done it without them.

August 16, 2009. *I woke up in the early morning dark,* waiting for the sun to come over the mountain. I pictured myself a year ago, rushing around trying to get the children ready to go to Russ and Mary's and still make it to the airport by 7:00 A.M. I had tied Ollie's shoes and cleared Jane's oatmeal bowl from the kitchen table. I had just left the pizza dough on the counter to rise before I hustled everyone out to the car.

I looked out the window, this morning, just as the sun tipped over the mountain and lit the leaves on our apple tree in the backyard. Nicholas and Oliver ran into our bedroom wearing superhero capes. Christian stirred next to me. Time to get up and get ready for church. There were shoes to tie this morning, too, but Christian would have to do that now. I could clear the oatmeal bowls, though, and hustle everyone out to the car.

All day I watched the clock, thinking back to the day of our accident. At 11:00 A.M., we had arrived in Grants. By noon, we were on four-wheelers out on the ranch. At 2:00, I had put on my moccasins. At 3:40, my world had fallen apart. A year later it still wasn't back together and probably never would be, not completely. But that morning, instead of longing for my old life, I felt grateful we'd been given the chance to create a new one.

I thought over the milestones of the last year—standing on my own feet again, and taking my first faltering steps. I remembered the first time Nicholas ran to me in tears, seeking comfort. I thought of Nana, and how she'd comforted me when I needed her. As I sat in church that morning, I thought about a particularly sacred moment a few weeks before, when I got to meet Elder Holland, who I'd always revered and who had been such an important spiritual guide for me and my family. He was in Provo to speak on BYU campus, and we were invited to meet with him the hour before the speech.

Of the millions of people in the Church, and with the busy schedule that I knew he had, this was a privilege.

He greeted us warmly. "It's so good to see you, Stephanie. I'm thrilled to see you're up and walking."

As we talked he told me to be proud of my scars. "We look for Christ's scars because they are evidence of what He did for us. They'll be the first things He shows us when we see Him again. Your scars tell a story, too. Although they may not make you feel attractive, they are a witness of a miracle, that God blessed you to live, and that you have accomplished very difficult things."

I was on a slow but steady path to accepting my scars, but it had never occurred to me to honor them for what they represented.

I asked Elder Holland for a blessing, and he readily agreed. He invited Christian, Russ, and my father to join him, and they all laid their hands on my head. As soon as Elder Holland began, I felt a power rush through my body, like I was being filled with light. As he blessed me with many things—a long and healthy life, a happy family, a strong marriage—I felt majestic, like my spirit was ready to answer the truth of his words. I was absolutely certain, as Elder Holland testified, that God knew me and my trials. He blessed me to know that my Heavenly Father was proud of me and that He was pleased with how I was handling the challenges I faced. He wept as he spoke, and Christian told me later that the Apostle's tears fell on Christian's hands.

When I got home, I wrote down every word I could remember, but the thing that mattered the most to me was the absolute certainty I felt that God knew me personally, that He understood my heart. I thought about that now, and on this day, the day when my life changed forever. I sat in church between Christian and Jane, with Nicholas on my lap and Claire and Ollie close. I remembered Elder Holland's words and repeated them over and over. *My scars are a witness of a miracle.*

That evening my parents and brothers and sisters and their families gathered in our backyard. We spread out blankets and lawn chairs, and Christian built a little fire in the fire pit. Page's son Layton played a hymn on his trumpet, and then Christian stood. He read from a passage in the Book of Mormon about our faith in the resurrection.

"'*The soul shall be restored to the body, and the body to the soul; yea, and every limb and joint shall be restored to its body; yea, even a hair of the head shall not be lost; but all things shall be restored to their proper and perfect frame.*' I look forward to that restoration, when Stephanie and I can enjoy healthy bodies again and be free from pain. I know that resurrection is possible because of Jesus Christ, and we look forward to that day. But I also know the Savior has, and will continue to heal her now—her body and her heart. And I'm so thankful for that."

My brother Andrew stood next. He had been the first of my siblings to see me after the accident. He'd flown straight to Phoenix from a business trip when he heard. My body was covered in bandages—practically mummified—and I wasn't breathing on my own. My face was unrecognizable. The doctors were talking about amputation and severe lifelong complications.

"Nothing could have prepared me to see you like that," Andrew said. "It broke my heart." He paused and cleared his throat, trying to control his emotions. "When I saw you lying in that hospital bed, Stephanie, in such bad shape, I thought you were already gone. In fact, I hoped you were. I didn't want you to suffer for the rest of your life. I prayed that you would be able to die." He put his hand over his eyes and shook his head. "I just didn't see how you could survive, but you were so determined. One miracle at a time you got better. And my prayers changed and I hoped you could live and be happy. We all did."

He gestured to my family, spread out on blankets and chairs. Children were nestled against their parents. The younger cousins sat on teenage cousins' laps. This was the net that had saved me—their prayers and sacrifices and confidence and faith.

"Almost losing you changed me—I think we're all different now, and I'm thankful we went through this together. I'm a better husband and better father. This year I learned what's really important in life—your accident taught me that more than anything ever has. And now here you are, Babbs, a year later, and look at how far you've come. I'm proud of you for working so hard. You're the same Baboon, determined and courageous as ever."

Andrew also shared his faith that God's hand had been in my recovery, and so did my other brothers and sisters. One by one they stood, and talked about how going through this with me had taught them so much about life and faith. They all said how much they loved me and how proud they were of my progress. By the time they were finished, my heart was bursting with love and gratitude for my brothers and sisters. I stood up to thank them for all that they had done for me and Christian and our children—for their prayers and visits and sleepovers and parenting and never-ending care. Even in that moment, their smiling faces encouraged me. I could never have made it through the past year without them.

As I stood before my brothers and sisters, I talked about how my faith had grown. I had testified of my faith in God and Jesus Christ in the past, but now I spoke of things that I *knew*, because I had lived them over the past year. I felt a power like I'd never felt before.

"Heavenly Father loves us so much. I know He knows us, each one of us." My voice trembled as I looked at the little flames in our fire pit. "And above all, I know that He wants us to be happy."

After the accident, there were moments when I was convinced I would never be happy again, that, in an instant, the life I'd built and longed for had been destroyed. Even just six months earlier, I hadn't really believed life would get better for me. I'd been lost, and in pain, trying to balance hope for the future with a dismal present. Confused and depressed, I had often despaired, but my faith and my family had nudged me forward when nothing else could. And now, here I was in my new backyard, surrounded by the people I loved, testifying, of all things, about happiness. I hoped again for what I'd always dreamed of—a happy marriage, a home full of children, and a life of faith and joy. That's what I had always wanted.

And that's exactly what I had.

Epilogue

Writing this book has often been painful and challenging. I have re-lived some of the darkest times in my life, moments that still carry a painful sting, moments that would have been more easily left in the past. But the motivation to share my story always outweighed the difficulty of the process. That motivation has come, first and fore-most, from thinking of my children and their children. I want them to understand how I got through this time in my life, and how God blessed me through it all. He had help, of course, from many people on Earth, and my appreciation for them also inspired me to write. It's that gratitude that has pushed me forward. I am grateful for what I've overcome, but I am most grateful for all that I've learned—about myself, about life, and about faith over the past three years. I don't have all the answers, of course, but almost dying has taught me valu-able lessons about living, lessons I wouldn't trade for anything, les-sons I'm honored to share.

I made it through the weeks and months after the crash, and through every day since, because I have faith in something larger than myself—faith that God has a plan for me. That belief is a source of inner strength that leads me to peace, comfort, and the courage to cope, even when I don't really feel like coping.

I was also surrounded by loving people who supported me and cared for me at great personal sacrifice and with pure love. It would be impossible to overstate what a difference that care, compassion, kindness, generosity, and endless support from my family and others has meant. Christian's commitment to our marriage and to my recovery has been boundless, and his love has meant the world to me. My parents and my brothers and sisters consistently believed in me, and they continue to support me in all aspects of my life. Loving blog readers and friends have also reached out to me in countless generous ways, offering me encouragement and compassion that has strengthened me and nourished my spirit. And my children continue to be the light of my life, guiding my way forward.

These cornerstones of faith, family, and community were the framework of my life before the accident, and I thank God that they were strong enough to support me afterward, too. When the worst happened, that foundation withstood tremendous pressure but didn't collapse. Quite the opposite: it carried me, and in doing so confirmed my belief that the single most important thing in life is to hold your family and your friends close. Beautiful possessions and material comforts are wonderful, and looking and feeling great are blessings, too. But the connections I had with my Heavenly Father and other people—my husband, children, parents, siblings, and friends—had always been the priorities in my life. I hope I appreciated how lucky I was to have those things before the accident. I know I have been thankful every day since.

But even with all that others were willing to offer me, I realized along the way that ultimately nothing *they* did could make me happy. I felt comforted by family and my faith, but peace was different from happiness. At first I thought stubbornly that the only thing that would make me happy was for life to look like it did before the accident. But no one could give that to me, and no one else could *make* me happy. Happiness was my choice, and though it is hard won, I am the only person who can stand in the way of it. As I gradually accepted my responsibility to choose happiness every day, I rediscovered the beautiful life I had always wanted. I still have to remind myself to choose happiness almost every morning when I wake up in pain, and I expect I will need reminding throughout my life, but the amazing thing is the more I make the choice to see and feel joy, the more joy there is to see and to feel.

I *was very happy to put the first year of the accident behind us* and settle into regular life again. I had surprised myself with my progress and just how hard my broken body could work. I carried daily hope that I would continue to get stronger, and that made everything that first autumn after the accident a little more beautiful. Autumn is my favorite season, and it was my first autumn in Utah in years, but most importantly, unlike the previous year, I was *awake* to celebrate Nicholas's third birthday and Claire's eighth. We harvested apples from our tree and ate apple pie as the leaves turned bright orange, yellow, and red outside.

In October 2009, Christian and I spent a few lovely days in Chicago, where we filmed *The Oprah Winfrey Show*. It was our first time leaving the children since the accident, and I worried about being apart from them. I was also nervous about appearing on television, but I wanted to share what I had learned, and show the world that even though I felt vulnerable, I worked hard to overcome my challenges, and would continue to work hard to have a full and happy life. I wasn't giving up because I looked different and had limitations. I still had so much to look forward to. (And of course Christian didn't jump up and down on the couch, but Oprah did call me Steph during a commercial break, like we were old friends.)

Just because I was rediscovering my worth, though, didn't mean others automatically saw my inner beauty, and it certainly didn't make me immune to gawking stares and insensitive comments. But I had learned to hold my head high anywhere I went, even if my confidence was fragile. In November, a frazzled woman turned to me in the grocery store checkout line and said, "Oh, I feel just the way you look." Her words felt like a slap and shattered the confidence I had gained. The next day, I lay on my couch, staring at our vibrant yellow weeping willow, its leaves moving so gently against the deep blue autumn sky. The hurt of her insult lingered, but in that quiet moment the inspiration that I'd come to rely on returned to me like a peaceful whisper. God was speaking to me. I felt again how much He loved me and that He was proud of my progress. I was reminded that He sees so much more than I do. In a moment, I felt beautiful again, restored. That peace is always waiting for me after I despair. In the quiet moments, inspiration and comfort always come again. Every time, without fail. Piece by piece, God puts me back together and I keep moving forward.

As autumn 2009 turned to winter, we were just settling into a fairly normal routine when we began the process for repairing the skin on my neck that Dr. Lettieri had outlined for us earlier that summer. In January, we were back in Mesa, staying with Russ and Mary while I had surgery to implant the balloons in my back that would gradually stretch my skin so that it could be harvested and grafted onto my neck—truly an amazing concept and process. Our children joined us, and we enrolled Claire and Jane in the same school Christian attended as a child for what we thought would be about a month. But because of complications during the very first surgery, we were still there two months later. The balloons had been expanded over the course of several weeks, and I had two very uncomfortable saline-filled hunches on my back. In March, I developed a serious infection at the inflation site, and the balloons had to be removed. We returned to Utah with a plan to start over when I was healthy enough. I was devastated to think I'd have to endure the entire painful process again, but in May I returned to Arizona so the balloons could again be surgically implanted and flew back and forth once a week so they could be expanded. By early June, there was enough skin to harvest for my new neck, so I was back in Arizona for about a month for two follow-up surgeries.

The long process of repairing my neck was one of the many times along the way that I've had to exercise patience. Right after the accident, I had this idea that at some point, after enough hard work and treatments, a switch would flip and I'd suddenly be healthy. But nothing in my recovery was achieved *now,* as I so hoped it would be, and my patience has been continually tested. Gaining the strength to stand required patience, then learning how to walk required even more patience. I needed patience as I learned to eat, patience to manage my pain, patience to endure having my eyes sewn shut (twice after that first time in Arizona) while trusting that all those steps would eventually lead to the outcomes I hoped for—especially feeling like a woman and mother again, the most precious parts of me that felt most at risk. In certain moments, I felt I had used up all the patience I could possibly muster, but more was required and I had to develop patience with my lack of patience and patiently wait to develop additional patience. Oh, patience.

My new neck gave me such relief from the constant strain I had been feeling across my face. I was thrilled—until I looked in the mirror. I had traded my hunchback for a swollen, bloated neck that I'd have to live with for a year until the follow-up surgery to tighten the skin again and create a chin. Until then, I had to remind myself— yet again—of all I'd learned about vanity, self-worth, and self-acceptance. I know, now, without a doubt that the true source of happiness, self-worth, and authentic beauty doesn't come from the outside. Women are constantly being persuaded to want something

unachievable, to look younger or thinner and above all to fit in because being different is too painful and embarrassing. I have accepted
myself in a world that does not accept me, because I have learned—
and more than any of the lessons of my accident, this is the one I wish
I could teach everybody—that our hearts matter most. *Your* heart
matters most, so be gentler and more patient with yourself, and
their hearts matter most, too, so be kinder and more compassionate to
others. It's a beautiful heart, not a perfect body, that leads to a beautiful life.

My body, of course, is far from perfect, but it truly amazes me. As
I move from one goal to another, it has met every challenge. It may
take longer to get there—but it's infinitely more meaningful when I
do. By winter 2010, I set my sights on skiing again, and in early 2011
I went to the same resort (Sundance) where I had first learned to ski as
a nervous three-year-old. I had those same unsure feelings on my first
run as a twenty-nine-year-old. Christian and my brother Andrew
were there with me, ready to pick me up if I fell. But I think I surprised them, and I may have even surprised myself a little. The memory of skiing was embedded deep in my muscles, and after my first
cautious run, I remembered how to gently lean in for a turn and bend
my knees going over a bump. I gained speed and confidence, and the
wind rushing against my face was exhilarating. I was thrilled to think
that I'd be able to teach my children to ski, something I'd always
looked forward to. Skiing was yet another accomplishment I'd reclaimed from life Before the Crash.

That's how I had come to think of things. There was BC, life
Before the Crash, and AC, life After the Crash. I often compared the
two and was committed to meeting all of BC's physical accomplishments with my AC body. For a time, BC and AC were vital distinc-
tions, and I celebrated every step I took to reclaim my BC life, but
gradually the importance faded away and then it didn't matter so

much what I could or couldn't do before. This was now, and I didn't want to continue monitoring the differences between the two. Life AC simply became *life,* something I enjoy very much.

Every day I live with how close I came to losing this precious life. And not a day goes by where I don't ache thinking that our dear friend Doug did. As Christian and I have pondered why we lived and Doug died, we've never come up with an answer that satisfies us. We miss him. Sometimes Christian will use a phrase or expression that Doug would have used, and we both smile as we remember our friend. We admired his cheerfulness, dignity, and energy. We speak with his wife, Roslyn, occasionally and admire her strength and courage, too. The fact that Doug died and Christian and I lived is all the more motivation to cherish each moment.

O ne of my greatest fears as I lay in the hospital for all those months, and even after I came home, was what effect this all would have on our beautiful children. I marvel at how resilient they have been, considering the upheaval of their little lives. I was especially worried about Nicholas's adjustment and, of course, concerned and heartbroken when Jane had such a struggle looking at me. Time, and lots of prayer, healed those wounds. My children now see me as their mother. Though much has changed, much is the same in our lives. It's amazing what a pair of jeans and earrings can do—sometimes that's all it takes to make them feel like I'm the same mom I've always been. I am so grateful they can see me through my scars, and love me even though I'm not as strong as I used to be.

Just a few months ago, Claire brought me an ornate silver hair clip with little red and blue jewels. "I took this from our house when everyone was packing us up to move to Utah," she told me. "Everyone was so busy, and I ran into your bathroom and grabbed this. I just wanted something to remind me of you."

Hearing this broke my heart all over again for my strong little six-year-old who'd had to grow up very quickly. And it made me feel even more grateful that I could hold her in my arms now. I told her I thought the clip should belong to her now, to keep as a reminder of how far we've come. I was thankful for Claire's wisdom and maturity as she approached our new life, but my heart understands Jane's, too, and I am thankful for her bravery. Oliver and Nicholas continue to be bright and vibrant boys, and I am a lucky mother, that I will get to watch them grow up and become men.

Just as I am certain that God has a plan for me, I know He has a plan for these children, and that they were meant to be mine. I wish my children had not had to go through this, but I hope this experience has taught them how strong they are and that God is always there for us, especially in our darkest moments. They will also grow up with a special understanding of people who look different, and I hope that blesses them with compassion and kindness. My brother Stevie tells me they are learning grace and confidence from me as I hold my head high in the grocery store while people stare. I hope so. I will never know all that my children went through or all the ways they have been changed, but what I do know is, today, their future is just as bright as it was before the accident.

I *am a big believer in happy endings, like those classic movies* I used to watch as a little girl. This story has a special one. In April 2012 we expect to welcome a new baby into our family. I could hardly believe my eyes when I looked at the pregnancy test, but after I took four more, I believed it—my dream of having another baby would come true.

Dr. Lettieri still has a long list of work to do to help my body heal, but I wanted a baby more than I want a lovely neck or flexible fingers. There will be time for more surgeries later, and other milestones to reach for, but for now, being pregnant is the most significant one of them all.

The accident took so much, in just an instant, but over these last three years I feel like I have, slowly but surely, reclaimed everything that truly matters from the wreckage. Being a mother is at the top of my list.

I undergo regular checkups to make sure my tummy is stretching properly, and so far so good. It's been challenging to wean myself off the chronic pain medications that make life normal for me, and, just like my pregnancies before the accident, I am severely nauseated. But all the discomfort is worth it. I cannot wait to welcome our child into this beautiful world.

It has been a long journey, but I see this time in my life as the best part of my story. Not because I've overcome so much, but because I've learned so much and I wouldn't have been taught these valuable lessons any other way. So I don't feel bitter at all, I feel grateful. Now I face trials with a better understanding of who I am, and the strength that comes from knowing I've survived worse. My body was scarred and disfigured, but just the opposite happened to my heart. Today, my heart is triumphant, my body is strong, and my life is full of everyday blessings.

As I wrote this book, I wasn't sure what the title should be, and even when my editor suggested *Heaven Is Here*, I wasn't convinced. I know there is a heaven awaiting me that is infinitely more beautiful than our life on Earth, and I look forward to it with my whole soul. Hope for heaven, when my body will be restored to "its perfect frame," motivates everything I do so I can find eternal happiness there, with Nana and the rest of my family. That belief comforts and blesses me every day. But I hope that is a long time from now, after my children are grown and married, after Christian and I have grown old and gray.

As I write this, I am looking out at the mountains, watching the children play in our new tree house and feeling the baby kick, and I do think that insofar as heaven is a joyful place filled with people you love, and where you feel peaceful and genuinely happy, then it's true. Heaven is right here.

Acknowledgments

So many people have blessed my life in countless ways, and I still haven't gotten over the fact that I'll never be able to write enough thank-you notes. I am so touched by and deeply grateful for all the people who have contributed to my recovery—from the amazing medical staff who worked so hard to save my life and repair my body to the complete strangers who read my blog and prayed for me.

I'm so grateful to those in the city of St. Johns, Arizona, who rushed to our aid when we crashed and for the medics who attended us there.

Thank you to the Arizona Burn Center doctors, staff, and nurses. I never expected to laugh in the Burn Center, but when I return there now, they feel like family. I am also very grateful to the doctors, staff, and nurses at the University of Utah Burn Center. I also want to acknowledge my amazing physical therapists—you know who you are—and my home health nurses. I could not have survived without the dedication and training of these amazing people. I am indebted to anyone whose hands touched and healed me. To all of you, thank you.

I'm grateful for all those who organized fund-raisers on our behalf—so many incredible events. Thank you for your love, time, and sacrifice. We're humbled by the many donations that were made to cover our medical bills. Your generosity amazes us still, and we are so grateful.

I want to acknowledge the Kinneard family and their strength and confidence.

My deepest heartfelt gratitude goes to Amy Hackworth, who patiently wrote this book with me. Actually, words can't express how thankful I am for her help.

Thank you to Christine Pride and everyone at Hyperion who has worked so hard to make this book happen. I'm so thankful for all you've done.

Of course, I am deeply grateful to the entire Clark and Nielson families—our grandparents, parents, siblings, nieces and nephews, cousins, aunts, and uncles—for their support and love throughout our entire lives and especially in the past three years. Our families mean the world to us.

And finally, to my husband, Christian, let's grow old together, and die at the same time. I love you so much!